D1503295

A Crowd of One

A Crowd of One

THE FUTURE OF INDIVIDUAL IDENTITY

John Henry
CLIPPINGER

PublicAffairs
New York

Book design by Trish Wilkinson
Set in 11-point Goudy by the Perseus Books Group

Library of Congress Cataloging-in-Publication Data

Clippinger, John Henry, 1943–
    A crowd of one : the future of individual identity / John Henry Clippinger.
        p.   cm.
    Includes index.
    ISBN-13: 978-1-58648-367-8 (hardcover)
    ISBN-10: 1-58648-367-6 (hardcover)
    1. Identity (Psychology)—Social aspects. I. Title.
BF697.5.S65C58 2007
302.5—dc22

                                                                        2006038500

First Edition

10 9 8 7 6 5 4 3 2 1

To Alma for Her Patient Love,
And for Emma to Invent a Kinder Future

Contents

Acknowledgments

THIS BOOK HAS BEEN A LONG TIME IN THE MAKING. IT COVERS themes that first engaged me as an undergraduate in college, where I did my senior thesis on a cybernetic analysis of myth. It is a journey that took me down many paths, which from any perspective but my own may appear to lack any semblance of direction and coherence. But to me the dots connected across diverse disciplines and I followed the dots as I saw them. Throughout my career, I have been engaged in issues of social and technological change. I have long been of the opinion that technologies are the handles by which substantive social and institutional change is possible—not a position popular with some of my colleagues. So, special gratitude to those many friends and colleagues who have helped and supported me. I am especially indebted to those odd-ball organizations that span diverse disciplines, are suspicious of orthodoxy, and have a high tolerance for ambiguity. Such organizations have been my havens.

One of the real ballasts in my intellectual life over the last twenty years has been the Aspen Institute. For this I am wholly indebted to my good friend Charlie Firestone, and his gracious wife, Pattie. Charlie's seminars and workshops, his good humor and rare capacity to bring together people of diverse backgrounds to make sense of complex topics introduced me to a wonderful community of engaged people.

Another such bulwark has been Ester Dyson. She is an institution in and of herself. Her personal commitment to important new ideas and her efforts to find and connect people, especially the outlier, has made her one of the valuable shapers of the Net. She has a thoughtfulness and quiet generosity that is rare in so highly visible an individual. She lent a helping hand at a critical moment in making the open-identity Higgins project and digital institutions a reality. Paul Saffo is another such old friend with whom I have had many debates and discussions over the years and who has generously introduced me to many wonderful people, including Dick O'Neill and Della van Heyst.

Della van Heyst is a quintessential people-idea connector. I first met her when she headed the Stanford Publishing Course many years ago. She cross-pollinates people. She has organized many successful conferences for *Fortune Magazine,* thought leaders, tech leaders, and the Aspen Institute. Della has a nose for the next thing and is a fun and good friend.

For many years the Santa Fe Institute has been a regular stop for me. My involvement began during its earliest days, when I was with Coopers & Lybrand, then a corporate sponsor. Through the help of Ellen Goldberg and Susan Ballati, I became a regular at the Santa Fe Business Networks and came to know David Stark, John Padgett, Michael Mauboussin, Andy Clark, Chris Langdon, John Holland, Stuart Kauffman, and Brian Arthur.

More recently, I have become active in another interdisciplinary institute, the Gruter Institute, which sparkles with the vigor of the multiple disciplines of evolutionary biology, economics, neuroscience, evolutionary game theory, law, and technology. Founded by Margaret Gruter twenty-five years ago and continued by her granddaughter, Monica Gruter Cheney, the Gruter Institute has succeeded in bringing together many of the best minds in their fields to introduce fresh evolutionary perspectives into the law and economics. It is through the Gruter Institute that I met Carl Bergstrom, Kevin McCabe, Vernon Smith, Paul Zak, Elizabeth Phelps, and Sarah Bronsan. But I am especially indebted to Oliver Goodenough, with whom I have had the pleasure to have many clarifying conversations and the opportunity to co-chair successful workshops and conferences.

I am currently a senior fellow at the Berkman Center for Internet & Society at the Harvard Law School. Without that appointment this book would not have been written. I owe special gratitude to its very talented executive director, John Palfrey, who brought me into the Center and was willing to support my Social Physics Project. He took a flier on a project few people understood at the time. The Berkman Center is an extraordinary place with great people, and an energy and openness that is unique in my experience. An environment of openness and experimentation was first created by its founder, Charlie Nesson, and the founding faculty members, Terry Fisher and Jonathan Zittrain, There have been many great exchanges with my colleagues—Chris Lydon, Jake Shapiro, Colin McKay, Lewis Hyde, Doc Searls, Mary Rundle, Drummond Reed, Kaliya Hamlin, Ethan Zuckerman, Rebecca McKinnon, Urs Gasser, and David Weinberger. It was at the Berkman Center that I was given the latitude and the resources to pursue my research on open identity and digital institutions and to host seminars and workshops with Oliver Goodenough, David Johnson, Beth Noveck, and Susan Crawford. It was at the Berkman Center that the "identity gang" was first launched through the Social Physics Project and the Higgins Project got its start. It was also through the support of the Berkman staff, especially Catherine Bracy and Erica George, that we were able to have a successful international conference, the Identity Mashup, on open and independent identity. As the architect and driving force behind Higgins, Paul Trevithick has been an incomparable friend and colleague in sounding out and refining my ideas about identity, digital institutions, and social networks.

I will not reiterate the ways in which the Highlands Forum and its founder, Dick O'Neill, educated me about national security and network warfare issues. That should be apparent from the Prologue in the book. Dick introduced me to Dr. David Alberts of the Command and Control Research Program of the Pentagon, which provided significant support and commentary for this book.

One of the underlying topics of this book has been the commons and the open source movement. I have had many conversations with a wide variety of people on these topics, especially David Bollier, with whom I co-authored an article covering many themes similar to this book. I have also had important conversations with Elinor Ostrum, Jon Ramer, Paul McLean, Greg Steltenphol, Mary Ruddy, Benn Konsynsky, Allison Koch, Jamie Lewis, John Wells, Cory Ondrejka, Reed Hunt, John Sviokla, George Goldmsith, Nathaniel Foot, Judith Donath, Jeff Sonnenfeld, Jim Goodale, Jonathan Hare, Michael Kleeman, George Lakoff, Philip Evans, Larry Weber, Julia Jitkoff, John Rendon, and Kim Cameron. Also thanks to those friends who provided me places to work on my book—Tim and Becky More, Tim and Merle Thompson, Randy and Cricket Lewis, and Bruce and Geline Edmands.

I very much appreciate the advice of my agent, James Levine, and a special thanks to Clive Priddle, my editor at PublicAffairs. Clive worked patiently with me to transform a jargon-laden and often impenetrable manuscript into what I hope is an accessible and worthwhile read for many.

Prologue:
On Being Open

IT WAS AN IDEAL PERCH. A WRAPAROUND BALCONY PROJECTED OVER a small private cove. The waves below swirled and smacked against the Carmel coast and a cluster of pines stood out in a perfect silhouette against the Pacific's horizon. Underneath, a Japanese rock garden unfolded, a fan of radiating pebbles and bonsai trees.

The Highlands Forum is an invitation-only meeting funded by the Department of Defense (DOD) and chaired by the assistant secretary for networks and information integration. As one who has long been involved in advanced technology, especially self-organizing networks, computational linguistics, and artificial intelligence, I have received a number of invitations to participate in a variety of Highlands Forums. This was my first invitation from Dick O'Neill, a retired navy captain and the forum's founder, whom I had met through a mutual friend at the Institute for the Future in California. In my youth I had wanted to join the Marine Corps; they struck me as the very best, and I wanted to be one of them. But with the onset of the Vietnam War and my active resistance to it in college, I became wary of most things military. I respected the discipline, the sense of service, and the valor, though I was suspicious of the apparent closed-mindedness and blind obedience to authority. But Dick exhibited no such negative traits: He was open-minded, straightforward, informal, and curious. The others at this year's gathering—captains, rear admirals, generals, colonels, majors, and commanders—were also candid, approachable, and open-minded. Some questioned official policy, others openly challenged their superiors. One navy Seal bioterrorist expert had two Ph.D.s. "Special Ops" officers, intelligence officers, fighter pilots, and former commanding officers of aircraft carriers and battleships—none of them seemed to tow a particular line.

Also present were members of the civilian DOD leadership. Three years earlier, they had funded the Highlands Forum to bring to the DOD leadership new ideas, new technologies, and new points of view from the outside world. Despite the prodigious achievements and accomplishments of everyone at the gathering, there was one individual to whom they all seemed to defer—not directly, but in body language, glances, and deferential seating arrangements. He sat at the back of the room, expressionless behind thick, black-rimmed glasses. I never heard him utter a word. Now eighty-five years old, Andrew (Andy) Marshall is an icon within DOD. Some call him Yoda, indicative of his mythically inscrutable status. During the 1990s, he was the impetus for the Pentagon's effort to transform itself into a more agile organization. He had served many administrations and was widely regarded as above partisan politics. He was a supporter of the Highlands Forum and a regular fixture from its beginning.

Exactly which people are invited to attend from the outside depends upon the theme of the meetings and who is in Dick O'Neill's network at the time. He is typically in constant motion, reading the latest books, articles, reviews, and blogs. He crisscrosses the globe to attend conferences and workshops and is an inveterate talent spotter—at universities, DOD, institutes, small and big companies, and nongovernmental organizations (NGOs). His penchant seems to be for "thought leaders" and out-of-the-box thinkers, those on the cutting edge of new approaches to issues with implications for DOD. Participants have included CEOs, CTOs, chief scientists, and innovative thinkers from the computer, software, biotech, entertainment, and financial services industries. There have also been science fiction writers, online game developers, hackers, inventors, entrepreneurs, management consultants, musicians, defense contractors, officials from NGOs, and ambassadors. It does not matter whether someone has dreadlocks or epaulets. In the meetings I've attended, some of the Pentagon officials and "dark" defense contractors appeared to be on "real-time" alert. During one meeting in 1999, six cell phones went off simultaneously, leading me to conclude that there had been a terrorist attack. There was no attack, nor was any explanation given. But such interruptions have not been uncommon.

Some of the Highlands Forum meetings anticipated events to come, as they dealt with issues of how to defeat terrorist networks and curb the proliferation of weapons of mass destruction. In the early 1990s, long before 9/11, the Pentagon was asking itself whether it was appropriately organized to respond to the likely threats around the world, specifically "headless" terrorists networks that did not follow the "rules of engagement," form battle lines, or acknowledge international conventions. The memory of the debacle of the U.S. and UN intervention in Somalia was fresh, and there was a general consensus among those at the Highlands Forum that the DOD needed to become more agile, flexible, and decentralized.

Part of the mission of the Highlands Forum was to keep the Pentagon leadership current with those global technological, ecological, and demographic trends over the next decade that represented security challenges that could ultimately result in profound changes to how military force would be exercised in the future. The principal drivers of these transformative trends are unprecedented technological innovations that span the information technologies, robotics, life sciences, energy, transportation, weapons, communications, and nanotechnologies. In combination, the technological changes that result will permanently redefine the global landscape. There is a very real danger that the current and seemingly unmatched military and economic advantages of today's dominant military forces could be rapidly usurped by an unanticipated combination of new players and technologies.

There will also be new actors, often operating out of new nation-states, many of which are barely functional as legitimate sovereign states, and are in essence rogue states run by some combination of drug lords, arms merchants, corrupt officials, fundamentalists, and despots. Given the widespread mobility of people, information, and communications around the world, the integrity of nation-states will continue to be challenged by networked organizations that fluidly function across national borders and jurisdictions, establishing their own authority and legitimacy through persuasion, bribery, and intimidation. With the collapse of traditional cultural and civic institutions, new "millennial movements" are likely to emerge, promising unrealistic solutions and seeking out ways to extract resources, concessions, and payments from wealthy individuals, companies, NGOs, and countries. If global environmental conditions deteriorate, as is projected by many environmental scientists, then the pressure to extract ecological reparations by disaffected countries, cultural movements, and religious groups is seen as another potential impetus for global terrorist activities.

The scope and pace of global technological, ecological, and cultural change in the coming decades will be vast. Given the tremendous momentum and rate of ongoing technological change, no military advantage, regardless of how dominant it may appear for the moment, is impervious to failure. Not only will military concepts and doctrine need to keep pace with technological and global trends, but perhaps more important, the policy, cultural, and organizational structures that shape them will need to rapidly coevolve with the times to yield the capabilities needed for the twenty-first century.

Throughout history, innovations in either military technology or doctrine often resulted in significant and often unanticipated shifts in the balance of power and influence. Each historical epoch and dominant civilization can be characterized by some military technology accompanied by a complementary organizational innovation. Military organizations have been the instigators and harbingers of major social and institutional change, from Napoleon to Bismarck. What is being investigated in the U.S. military—innovations in organization structure, command and control, a new Internet communication system, logistics, and notions of joint command—may presage another social revolution. Moreover, it has always been my belief that even the smallest changes in an institution with the largest budget and greatest concentration of raw power in the world will have far more repercussions than any large change in organizations of lesser scale and import. So, what happens at informal gatherings such as the Highlands Forum could, over time and through unforeseen curious paths of influence, have enormous impact, not just within the DOD but throughout the world. One of the most persistent themes throughout the Highlands meetings has been how to achieve force transformation. How do you trans-form an organization in which hierarchy is both the source of authority and the reward for achievement, into one that is faster, more adaptable, and open to individual initiative, in which authority is neither set by rank nor given as a reward? Instead of having four commands that act independ-ently—the army, navy, air force, and marines—how do you institute "joint commands," knowing that they will undermine the tradition, autonomy, and culture of the different services? How do you rethink the primary mis-sion of the Pentagon, which has historically used force as the primary vehi-cle for defeating a enemy, principally another nation-state, and convert it to use other means—such as economic, medical, cultural, and educational inducements to transform adversaries who increasingly are not nation-states, but networked, "asymmetric" opponents?

The Highlands Forum has been asking such questions for more than a decade, during which time it has moved from being heretical to main-stream. Ideas that were anathema in 1999 had been adopted as policy just three years later. The new policy's name was significant: It showed the de-gree to which the military had begun to think of itself not in terms of its historic structures and roles but in terms of the potential offered by new technology. The name did not commemorate newer, more lethal missile systems—more efficient killing hardware is not in itself novel—but a whole new approach to how the military might understand its role and potency. The policy was named Network Centric Warfare (NCW).[1] In embracing the idea of the network, the military welcomed a radical new synthesis of ideas and technologies that, at their most dramatic, sought no less than to redefine human nature itself. This concept also provoked new questions: Who is my enemy, and who is my friend? How do friends recognize each other? How is influence parlayed into power? Those in-quiries are too numerous and too consequential to be left to the military alone. Lethal force may be momentarily useful, but as an ongoing strategy it can act more as a provocation than a deterrent.[2] This book, motivated by the example of those wise men and women who have seen and de-ployed force, and who understood both its instant power and its limita-tion, is an investigation into the alternatives to the "vicious circle" of violence. It is a pursuit of the ultimate "virtuous circle" that might under the right conditions yield trust, reciprocity, and the will to not go to war.

Chapter One

The Good and the Bad

THE CAR COMING AROUND THE BEND ON I-93 BLINKS ITS LIGHTS repeatedly. I instantly hit my brakes. Just the other side of the bend lurks a New Hampshire state trooper, like a great northern pike crouched in the weeds, waiting to take down its prey. This day I was lucky. I heeded the warning and avoided a ticket.

Why did this stranger take the time to warn me? I will never see him again. There is nothing in it for him. Is he just simply a good guy, a saint of the interstate? Or did he have some grievance against state troopers? Whatever *his* reason, afterward I found myself blinking my lights at perfect strangers to warn *them* of the speed trap ahead. It was infectious. And apparently inexplicable.

But not entirely. I live in an isolated region of northern New England that has not quite let go of the nineteenth century and perhaps, even parts of the eighteenth century. These "North Country" Yankees leave their wares—be they farm produce, crafts, or even golf balls in baskets or cartons on the side of the road, and you, the buyer, the stranger, are trusted to deposit your money in the jar or the basket and take out the right amount of change. Likewise, when you pay for gas, you pump first and then tell them what you owe them. Not long ago, before electronic pumps, the gas station owner didn't even bother to look up the amount. Vyron Lowe at the Country Store would just thank you and ring it up.

Some years ago, back when I was doing my own haying, late in the afternoon of a very hot day, sweaty, covered in grass, without a shirt, and dressed only in coveralls, I went into my local bank. Having forgotten my wallet, I asked for a blank check, filled in my account number, and got my cash. They didn't blink, hesitate, or even ask for any ID. They just handed over the blank check, and then the cash.

In this world, when you want to do some business with someone, you don't go up to him and ask him if he would mow your field, paint your house, or repair your car. You should not appear rushed or impatient. You talk about the weather, then the moose you saw in the field, comment on his new "rig," then damn the foolishness of politicians, but never, ever, talk about what you want to have done. That simply comes up. As if by chance. You even look sideways, shuffle your feet, tug on your hat, and give the other guy a ton of room to say whatever he wants.

These habits reveal that in certain parts of the world, New Hampshire among them, what matters is relationships, not transactions. The priority is to make room for people, not to cramp them, and in so doing to let them express who they really are. An extreme example occurred when I was wiring my barn and about to connect the wires to the junction box. I could see on the face of my neighbor, Robert, a certain discomfiture. Then as I was within an inch of connecting the wires and pulling the handle, Robert, quite out of character, flatly stated, "John, I wouldn't do that if I were you." I asked him why not. "You will electrocute yourself." And he was right. It required a death threat for him to break the habits of a lifetime and speak out.

The whiff of a transaction can ruin a relationship, because it obscures the issue of personal honor and what is fair. My neighbor, Alden, is my carpenter, plumber, painter, and general Mr. Fixit. We built my barn together, along with his brother, Austin, and father, Clyde. When he finished putting a new hardwood floor in my house, rather than bill me, he said, "What do you think it's worth?" Alden is not a wealthy man by any means, having been severely incapacitated by lead-paint poisoning, and yet he has raised over thirteen foster children and adopted two. The foster children he and his wife take in have been rejected by other foster families and are no walk in the woods. You can't put a price on some things.

This most northern county in New Hampshire is the poorest in the state and has many of the same demographic and social statistics as the poorest states in the Deep South. And yet there is relatively little crime—though everyone has a hunting rifle—and there is a high degree of local trust and acceptance. A gay male couple with an adopted son moved in without a flicker of resentment or protest. The family was accepted into what is a "blue-collar" community. There is little judgment and a high degree of tolerance all around—and this from loggers, millworkers, truckers, farmers, and what locals themselves call "the working man."

This society, by no means perfect, is starting to erode. It is a very different experience than Boston, New York City, San Francisco, Washington, D.C., or other places I frequent. Is it because there is a genetic strain that distinguishes people in this community from others? Hardly. Change the conditions, and the same people would act very differently. Bring in new people and lo and behold, many—but by no means all—start to imitate the old-timers and perpetuate the social code. There is civil discourse. There is a sense of the other person: the sense that "our" people can be picky but at the same time inclusive. People who are willing to work and contribute are accepted. There is a relationship, a bond of implicit trust. People are known to one another. People here by circumstance are dependent upon one another. The winters are long and arduous. Once when I was away, a winter northeaster blew open my door and filled my home with snow; my neighbors, Robert and Pauly, came in and cleaned up the snow and fixed the door and didn't even tell me about it.

These experiences are not unique to northern New Hampshire. They are repeated around the country, around the world. This seems to provide evidence of "good" people and "good" communities. But what makes them good? Can these same good people do "bad," indeed, "evil" things in different contexts? There is the temptation to say that these people— my crowd, with whom I have all these rich, warm, and rewarding relationships—are "good" and that anyone who threatens these relationships is "bad." But as we know all too well, the modest bookkeeper, the army reserve private, the schoolteacher can, under other circumstances, become something quite different: the "butcher of Buchenwald," the murderer, the torturer of Abu Ghraib. Goodness too often is equated with likeness.

So what distinguishes "good" people from "bad" people? Or more accurately, what distinguishes our assessments when we try to make such a judgment? For most people, it is very difficult to answer such questions without moralizing. Were one an economist or a social scientist, one might try to distinguish between "rational and irrational" actions. Almost always, the introduction of rationality into the equation means that the judgment is underpinned by the idea that the individual has made a choice before acting and has been able to discern various options and outcomes, and that the outcome is not predetermined. A lot depends on those assumptions. Sweep them away and what basis do you have to hold people accountable for their actions, for fairness, justice, retribution, punishment, and differential reward? Pull that peg out of these supports of the social order, and the whole artifice of civil society, rule by law, and the legitimate authority of the state as sovereign would collapse. The reflex of most people is not to go there.

Yet throughout history this is what "political and social realists" have done. Because these thinkers have removed the "ought to" of human conduct and have simply looked at the history of the how and why, their perspective has been condemned by moralists and labeled "amoral" and reductive. Though such realism has long been a part of Western culture, going at least as far back as Homer, it was during the Renaissance that the foundations were laid for such realism to underscore a succession of arguments, writing, debates, and conflicts that have built contemporary, secular, humanistic institutions and framed the debate over what components characterize a free and just society. It's tempting to think that Renaissance thinkers became interested in the ideas of freedom and justice precisely because they had peered deep into the institutions that were supposed to represent goodness—not least of them the Catholic Church—and found that human goodness did not seem to be reliably represented there. Realizing that if it wasn't innate to the church, it might not exist at all, they set about crafting some rules for society before anarchy ripped it to shreds.

Realism and Humanism

During the Renaissance, Europeans began to break with the prescriptive perspectives of the church and started to document and describe life and nature as it really is, rather than as it should be. From da Vinci's lifelike drawings of the anatomy of dissected cadavers to the highly psychological portraits of Michelangelo's statues and frescos, a new humanism and secularism was born. In the political sphere this was exemplified by Niccolo Machiavelli's treatise *The Prince*, an unflinching account of how power actually functioned in Renaissance Italy. It wasn't idealistic or romantic, but objective and descriptive: This was power in the raw, a kind of handbook on how to get results—fame, recognition, and influence. Machiavelli was one of the first to record with a dispassionate and highly accurate eye the "social physics" of the wielders of power of his time. Here are the mechanics of power. The good Prince—meaning an effective prince, a prince who survives—is one who understands these rules. The fifteenth century was a harsh and violent period of Italy's history, and not surprisingly, so were many of the recommended remedies and strategies. Though Machiavelli's Prince could be despotic and brutal, he was, nonetheless, preferable to the chaos of warring mercenaries, clerics, gentry, and dispossessed peasants. He provided order, security, and the opportunity for prosperity within his protected walls. He may not have been "good," but he was better than the alternative.

Implicit in Machiavelli's description of the power of the Prince is the need to defend against the unruliness of the unfettered mob. Here he anticipated what became a political reality 200 years later when the ruffians finally deposed and decapitated one of Europe's great kings. It was not until the English Civil War, and the unthinkable decapitation of a king, Charles the First, by a commoner, Oliver Cromwell, that the "myth" of the inherent brutality of man in a state of nature became a permanent fixture throughout Western political and economic discourse. Through the persuasive and prolific writings of Thomas Hobbes the debate about the inherent brutish nature of man in a natural state and the need for order and a single sovereign—what he called the Leviathan—was framed. Like Machiavelli, Hobbes purported to be an unsentimental realist, having experienced the chaos and brutality of a civil war firsthand, himself the target of intrigue and violence. In was in this context that the notion of the primacy and even the necessity of self-interest was in effect "invented" as a founding principle of human activity. The subtleties of Hobbes's arguments have been vastly simplified and caricatured. He did not contend that *all* men were brutish and self-interested, only a number sufficient to require the intervention, force, and protection of the sovereign. Yet Hobbes does argue that while man is in a state of nature, every individual has the duty and the right to ensure his own self-interest and self-preservation:

To this war of every man against every man, this also is consequent: that nothing can be unjust. The notions of right and wrong, justice and injustice have no place.[1]

In effect, Hobbes argues that in a state of nature, all things are possible and permissible. It is a perfect moral vacuum; there is no authority, hence, no morals, no laws. He took a materialistic and mechanistic view of human nature. In fashioning his argument for a state of nature, he imagined a human condition—a sort of anti-Eden—that is void of any proclivity to cooperate or share. It is an idealized dystopia. Like the popular caricatures of Darwinian natural selection as being wholly "tooth and claw," it was grounded in the assumption that individuals in a "natural state" have no "other-regarding" nature. All sense of cooperation and "civitas" lies outside the state of nature, only to be found within the confines of the walled city of the sovereign, the Prince, the Leviathan.

Unfortunately, Hobbes's argument was not just a seventeenth-century intellectual artifice but has come over the centuries, and especially in recent years, to represent a kind of accepted wisdom among the "realists" of the Right, whose political philosophy of international politics, and to some extent domestic politics, contains the conviction that without the firm hand of a presiding authority, the world will revert to a Hobbesian state of nature in which anything goes. This is the argument offered by some neo-conservatives, whose more adamant "public intellectuals" have suggested, as Charles Krauthammer did in his American Enterprise Institute speech of 2004,[2] that America has a moral duty to assert its imperial ambitions, and by virtue of its historical imperatives is exempted from the moral constraints of lesser nations. To Krauthammer, America is the Prince, with a moral obligation to become a global Leviathan, under the rubric of spreading democracy. The same logic was embraced by President George W. Bush and his war cabinet, who decided that once America was attacked, it could be understood as being in a continuous state of war, which conferred on it the moral legitimacy to pursue whatever means it sees fit to defend itself and to avenge any and all parties who support or harbor its shadowy enemies. You are either for us or against us. Bring it on. This same moral immunity appears to extend to the domestic arena as well, by virtue of the fact that some potential terrorists may be domestic—

hence, the invocation of Hobbes's state-of-nature argument for domestic surveillance and the weakening of the First and Fourth Amendments. Hobbes has been much in evidence so far in the twenty-first century.

Woven throughout much of Hobbes's argument is the presumption that people in a state of nature make poor judgments, that they are incapable of reconciling their differences or overcoming their fears. There is the strong presumption that better judgments, and better decisions, can only emanate from a single, central authority. From Hobbes's perspective, realism and better judgment tells us that a centralized, hierarchical form of control is the most effective means for governing civil society. Not surprisingly, contemporary Hobbesians tend to be patriarchal, authoritarian, and conservative in their social and cultural policies, wanting to grant powers to a single sovereign. However, they experience a conversion when it comes to free market economies that lack hierarchies or state or princely interference. There the marketplace is a benign state of nature, where competition and a lack of supervision result in more efficient outcomes. It's a contradiction to which we will return.

In a state of nature, whether political or economic, where competing parties do not share a common set of rules or morals, there can only be one kind of outcome: one party wins, one party loses. It is a zero-sum game in game theory terms, and under such circumstances, it becomes vital that each party not capitulate to the other. You attack me. I attack you. Tit for Tat—the name of this game—has made up the "rules of engagement" for much of human conflict for millennia. It continues today as the heart of American foreign policy toward Iran, Iraq, the Palestinians and all suspected "terrorists" and "evildoers" around the world.

Yet it also creates what the evolutionary psychologists call Hobbesian traps, cycles of violence that have no end and last for generations, even hundreds of years, until one or both parties exhaust or destroy themselves. Such cycles construct and perpetuate their own niches and norms. If there is no vehement adversary, a participant caught in this behavioral trap will create one and launch the cycles of violence anew. Such cycles only cease when one party is utterly defeated or a sovereign for both parties emerges. It is a war of attrition to the death. Unless the sovereign has inordinate powers and can uniformly impose his will—like the perfect Leviathan upon the defeated—there will be always continued resistance, insurgency, and guerrilla warfare. So, if you believe humans revert to a state of nature, you must believe in the necessity of an authority to impose order. If you believe in that, you must accept that zero-sum contests between rival authorities will turn violent, and breed cycles of violence. It's a philosophical package. The only way to avoid it is to change the rules of the game so that there can be more than one winner. That sounds absurd; in America we don't like ties. We like decisive point scoring and clear victors and vanquished: white hats and black hats but no gray hats.

Perhaps these sentiments are not just American, but they may also be more deeply ingrained than we would like to think. During the heat of combat, human beings, like most other mammals, have an intense fight-or-flight response that physiologically alters their brain and body. Adrenaline is pumped throughout the body to provide new sources of strength and stamina, testosterone surges to enhance not just strength but aggression. The brain becomes bathed in neurotransmitters that heighten awareness and select for those emotions and cognitive processes that enhance their chances of physical survival. Instead of opening the brain to new options, options are foreclosed, simplified, and narrowed. We like to think of this as a warrior impulse. That seems to be a good way to recognize it. But there is another aspect that we neglect that neuroscience is only now beginning to reveal to us. In combat, great warriors from Achilles to Horatio Nelson think not of their own survival, but of regiment or clan or nation: their cause. Contrary to Hobbes's state of nature in which every man is for himself, human beings and virtually all other social species have evolved highly sophisticated behaviors for cooperating, fighting, and dying in defense of their group. Over time, we have evolved the ability to experience and literally feel what others of our kind experience and feel. Through mirror neurons, the emotions of "empathy" are made possible. Contrary to the presumption for the need for centralized control, as in the figure of the Leviathan, mirror neurons and their accompanying emotions of empathy and trust suggest that we don't need to be told what to do in the interest of the greater good: We have the power within our individual brains to recognize and respond to a cause that is greater than ourselves, even when it threatens our individual survival. That is what made men run headlong into machine guns in World War I, land on hazardous Pacific beaches in World War II, participate in the near-suicidal Tet Offensive, and finally, most recently, strap explosives to their torsos and detonate themselves in restaurants and checkpoints, in markets and police stations.

There is mounting neuroscientific, behavioral, and experimental scientific evidence to show that people do not choose—that is, make conscious, rational decisions, as was presumed by many of the Enlightenment thinkers—whether they are going to fight, flee, trust, reciprocate, or negotiate. Rather, these responses are more often than not reactive. They are not frontal cortex reflections, but reflexes deep in the amygdala, and therefore, terribly difficult to modify, monitor, or rescind. Threat-induced emotions come to construct their own social reality. Hence, it is less a matter of "rational choice," or even moral, immoral, or amoral choice, and more the result of the social physics of the situation. Once certain social signals and behaviors are in play and reach a critical threshold, the responses of the different parties become predictable and law-like.

Under such circumstances, what is good or bad is a matter of perspective; it depends on whether one is in the "in-group," that from which one's identity and survival are derived, including such considerations as kin, clan, tribe, religion, or nation, or whether one is seen as being in a threatening "out-group"—non-kin, clan, tribe, religion, or nation. In adversarial confrontations between groups, boundary definitions become critical and are a trip wire for triggering or suppressing social emotions. As a consequence, highly visible and reliable social markers, such as distinctive forms of dress and speech, which enable members of a group to differentiate between members and nonmembers, are essential to preserving a social order. Such markers become the basis for defining the boundaries of social identity. Hence, there is the proliferation and persistence of traditional dress and body markings—burkas, yarmulkes, tribal scars, gang signs, tattoos, beards, haircuts, and more recently, luxury brands to make visible boundaries of difference.

Within the polarized rhetoric of today's debate over global terrorism, the notion of a good suicide bomber is unthinkable to Westerners. Those who willfully destroy innocent life, even when sacrificing their own, are, by prevalent Western moral standards, immoral, if not "evil." Yet this judgment requires us to accept Hobbes's argument for a state of nature in which morality is to be imposed by the strong over the weak by all necessary means. What is good and what is evil is the prerogative of the victor. That is why some have argued that the losers in warfare are the "war criminals" and the winners are the judges. By this logic the suicide bomber is inherently no different than the professional soldier or pilot—he is just less powerful. Whether one indiscriminately kills by car bombs or air bombardments does not matter. According to Hobbes, both are equally moral or immoral. By this logic the Bush administration is consistent in its attempt to sidestep the Geneva Conventions. Yet as every general and military planner knows who has fought in combat, the Geneva Conventions are important because they help protect all soldiers. Veterans of combat recognize what Hobbes did not: There are inherent, innate rules of reciprocity, even in the bitterest warfare. The need to understand reciprocity is especially acute when the goal is to change the will of a people, to get them to adopt your point of view. Both Lao Tzu and Carl von Clausewitz recognized that this was the real challenge of a military leader and that it defined the limits of military power. Coercion and humiliation do not lead to the building of the necessary relationships to build shared norms and objectives. The Germans in World War II tore through Russia at the beginning of the war not simply because of their superior military might but also because the Russian people and army were tired of Stalin and did not resist them. But when the SS started to torch villages and execute peasants, and pursued their scorched-earth policies of brutality and humiliation, the Russian people and the army quickly reversed their positions and ruthlessly destroyed the Wehrmacht and the SS. The fact that the Germans acted as if they were in a Hobbesian state of nature was instrumental to their defeat. Throughout the history of organized human warfare, warriors have shown respect for one another and in many, but not all, cases abided by a shared code of honor. Through such codes they were able to mitigate the excesses of war, and thereby made the transition to peace and the fruits of victory easier. The Geneva Conventions comprise just one recent such code. During the many conflicts and battles from the thirteenth through the sixteenth centuries, opposing armies would assemble, size up one another, conduct a few maneuvers, and often with a minimum of armed engagement, mutually determine the victor and either retreat or advance accordingly—without bloodshed.

This code of honor was not just confined to a warrior culture per se but carried over into the political realm as well. Arguably, the notion of parliamentary processes of the loyal opposition, and prior to that, even the notion of *habeas corpus*, the right to be heard before a ruling body, in the thirteenth century evolved out of warrior norms of peer respect and consensus building. Again, absolute conflict was limited by a mutuality, born of a recognition that there were shared interests in the outcome. Putting opponents into absolute categories—such as "evildoers" and "infidels" only escalates conflict in this state of nature. When values of good and evil are inserted, there can only be one winner, and all things are permitted and legitimized. Yet as will be argued throughout this book, Hobbes's state of nature is a fiction, unsupported and even contradicted by neuroscience, anthropological, and behavior research.

Therefore, the perception of what is good, bad, or evil can depend upon where one is standing in regard to the line of social identity. As the aphorism has it: One man's terrorist is another man's freedom fighter. What is considered courage within one's own group is dismissed as fanaticism by others; what is lauded as patriotic at home is labeled brutality abroad. Nancy Hart was born in North Carolina and raised in Virginia. She served as a confederate spy during the American Civil War. Captured by the Union, she gained the trust and confidence of her guard, then took his weapon and shot him dead. She was totally remorseless. She nonetheless is treated as a heroine of the American Confederacy. Yet how different is she from Wafa Idriss, the first Palestinian female suicide bomber? She defies all stereotypes of a suicide terrorist. A twenty-seven-year-old Palestinian divorcée from the West Bank city of Ramallah, she wore makeup and sleeveless dresses, worked as a schoolteacher, and volunteered as a paramedic. Yet one day she blew herself up in order to resist what she regarded as an aggressor to her homeland.

Captain Nathan Hale was hanged by the British as a spy in the Revolutionary War. General Washington recruited Hale, then only nineteen, to act as a spy because he desperately needed information on the British position in Manhattan. Without this information, Washington's army and the fate of the American Revolution were imperiled. However, Hale's Yale friend, Captain William Hull, tried to convince him not to do it: He considered spying a deceit unworthy of a officer and a gentleman. While Hale was in Manhattan, disguised as a Dutch schoolteacher, New York was set on fire by "patriots." This act was considered an act of "terrorism" by the British, and as he was attempting to escape, Hale was captured. He bluntly confessed

that he was a spy, and a day later was convicted of treason without the benefit of a trial. He requested a Bible, which was denied him, and the letters he
wrote to his mother and brother were both destroyed. His body was left
hanging for several days, and he was buried in an unmarked grave. Yet his
statue stands in the Old Campus of Yale with his famous last words:

> I ONLY REGRET THAT I HAVE BUT
> ONE LIFE TO LOSE FOR MY COUNTRY.

To the British, this hallowed American patriot was a terrorist. What is
remarkable is that even one of his peers, Captain William Hull, considered his disguising himself as a spy dishonorable. The fact that the British
treated him so brutally is indicative that they too believed he breached a
code of honor that was prevalent among officers and "gentlemen" of opposing armies. It was not uncommon for captured officers of the British
and American armies to attend one another's balls and social events during the Revolution. This tradition continued even up to World War I,
when the British, after having finally shot down and killed the "Red
Baron" von Richthofen, gave him a military burial with full military hon-
ors and twenty-one gun salute. In this case, their shared identities as military officers surpassed their national identities.

It is striking that among the officer corps, the true professional warriors, a group that one would think would act in pure Hobbesian terms, a
powerful, shared code of honor prevents the flourishing of a Hobbesian
morality. Although each was trying to kill the other on the battlefield,
rules of mutual respect were upheld. A warrior culture is an ancient tradition and probably derived from innate traits that have evolved over the
millennia to encourage both aggressive and cooperative behaviors. This
was the recurrent theme of Homer's *Iliad*. In recounting the *social physics*
of his era, Homer attributed the demise of the quintessential warrior
Achilles to the frivolous Paris, because Achilles desecrated the body of
the noble warrior Hector, whom he humiliated in personal combat in order to avenge the death of his companion Patroclus.

So is evil absolute, or are absolutes evil? The extreme moralists believe
that there is only one uniform and absolute moral order, and that to

accommodate those who do not share that morality is to condone and encourage evil. Therefore, to be good is never to accommodate, but rather to adhere to a set of fixed principles. Such is the pretext for some religious wars, total warfare, "neutralization," pogroms, genocide, and "ethnic cleansing" (a prevalent but horrible Orwellian term) where the only outcome tolerated is the total annihilation, conversion, or subjugation of the other. This degree of conviction has seldom been shared by the best professional military strategists. Instead it is the position of the zealot, who can only see and tolerate the position of his own group, who universalizes parochial beliefs, turning them into general truths and absolutes. Such is the earmark of fanaticism and fundamentalism of all stripes—Islamic, atheistic, Christian, Jewish, and Hindu. It is also the mark of political fundamentalism on the Right and the Left. When such beliefs were confined to warring tribes and nation-states with limited means of warfare, they did not threaten the entire survival of our species' life on the planet. But the world has changed. For the first time in the history of the planet, a single species not only has the capacity but perhaps even a penchant for rendering not just itself extinct, but all other major species as well. It is without precedent. It is one of those things that can go wrong only once. No second tries. No mulligans.

It is a philosophical debate of no particular consequence if we get it wrong on whether the destructive deed or the mindset that made it possible is more deserving of the term "evil." History won't be able to judge, if we have obliterated all the historians, along with everyone else. Instead, we must satisfy ourselves with assessing the intent, which cannot be evil if we are trying to protect the world from Hobbesian proclivities. We can do this in two ways: first by denying their validity, and second, by demanding a more subtle and sophisticated understanding of human nature, one that matches the reality we all, however secretly, acknowledge. The race is on.

The writings, beliefs, and final acts of Mohammed Atta, the leader of the September 11 attack, reflect an absolutist mindset. The depth of his uncompromising contempt for the West, especially the United States, and the vitriol of his orthodoxy reflected in his writings and especially his last will and testament, reveal a man of unyielding intolerances with a special contempt for women. He is a man without doubt: He unequivocally believes that not only does he possess the Truth, but that it is his mission to uphold, protect, spread, and enforce it. His truth is The Truth. It is the absoluteness of his beliefs that gives him a special stature, an unassailability in the eyes of his followers, qualifying him as a genuine martyr. To his victims, however, it is hard to imagine him as a hero, much less a martyr. But to see how this might be possible, consider an opposite and yet equivalent hero and patriot.

General Curtis LeMay is revered by many Americans as an exemplary patriot and hero of World War II and the Vietnam War. He was the architect of America's modern air force and nuclear security defense strategy, the Strategic Air Command (SAC). It is hard to challenge his many accomplishments. He is the recipient of twenty-two medals and decorations from thirteen countries: from the United States, the Distinguished Service Cross, Distinguished Service Medal, Silver Star, Distinguished Flying Cross; from France, the Legion of Honor Degree of Commander, and Croix de Guerre with Palm; from Great Britain, the Distinguished Flying Cross; from Japan, the First Class of the Order of the Rising Sun; and from the Soviet Union, the Order of Patriotic War–First Degree!

Yet General Curtis LeMay also commanded massive air strikes on sixty-four Japanese cities, including the firebombing of Tokyo that incinerated sixteen square miles of the city. Official estimates put the figure at 330,000 people killed, 476,000 injured, 8.5 million people made homeless, and 2.5 million buildings destroyed. LeMay was later quoted as saying, "There are no innocent civilians, so it doesn't bother me so much to be killing innocent bystanders." During the Vietnam War, he advocated "bombing Vietnam back to the Stone Age," and during the Cuban Missile Crisis, he did everything in his power as the head of the Joint Chiefs of Staff to launch air attacks on Cuba, even after the Russians agreed to leave. He was the vice-presidential running mate of the arch segregationist Governor George Wallace of Alabama and campaigned on his willingness to use nuclear weapons. He remarked that had the United States lost World War II, he would have been tried as a war criminal. Yet regardless of how the world would have judged him, Curtis LeMay believed it was his duty to execute any and all air attacks, whatever the consequence—military or civilian. My country right or wrong. Like Atta, he was a man void of doubt and indifferent to the consequences of his convictions and actions. He competently and resolutely pursued his beliefs and was an inspiration to the many who served under him and believed in him. Yet if he had had his way, he could well have triggered a global thermonuclear war.

Both Atta and LeMay remain heroes to their own. Both are perfect Hobbesian protagonists, from which philosophy they derive their shared moral legitimacy. But Hobbes is wrong, scientifically wrong. It is no longer just a question of theoretical philosophy or opinion, but of replicable scientific observation. Hobbes got human nature, and for that matter, "Nature" wrong. There are shared rules even in a state of nature. Tragically, however, by explaining violence as natural and inevitable, Hobbes legitimated cycles of violence as an acceptable and inevitable aspect of human conduct and policies. But since 1945, the natural cycles of competition and predator-prey conflict are no longer tolerable. Nuclear and biological weapons do not lead to increased "fitness" for survival; extinction confers no victories. That is why, in a small way, the person who flashed his or her headlights at me to warn me of the coming speed trap was making a contribution to saving the world from the madness of mutually assured destruction. The instinctive act of flashing one's lights at a stranger to help that person avoid a speeding ticket shows that people do not simply act in their own self-interest but have a genuine, natural interest in the welfare of others, that even the distinction between self-regarding and other-regarding is a misleading dichotomy. Our sense of self is not something that we solely control; furthermore, it is not something that can be divorced from how we see and are seen by others. We really are a crowd of one—and one in a crowd. We are ourselves and we are also others. Just as Descartes' claim that "I think therefore I am" falsely set thought apart from emotion, so has the Enlightenment separation of self-interest from common interest falsely bifurcated human identity. Modern identity is an open wound in need of healing.

Over the course of history, religious observances, prohibitions, and taboos have evolved to encourage health and hygiene practices. The avoidance of pork, the cleansing of one's hands, washing of feet, circumcision, and burial and incest practices have all served to limit the spread of disease. People did not know why such practices worked, or why they were even important, and so they found higher order reasons, divine mandates, to enforce these good habits. In time such repeated practices became rituals and mores that marked and differentiated groups from one another. Since such observances were likely to extend life and enhance health, they were naturally seen as evidence of the group having gained the special favor of God or the gods. The practices offered tangible advantages over those who were not observers, and hence, a social identity that could convey high status as well as evolutionary advantage.

As medical knowledge progressed and the scientific basis for disease became established, no longer was it necessary to use religious invocations and observances to encourage good health. People around the world have become educated as to the how and why of bacteria, parasites, and the spread of disease. Medical advice has replaced religious insistence in matters of health. A comparable development is unfolding in the scientific understanding of the social emotions of people—how they trust, cooperate, empathize, reciprocate, and forgive, punish, and resolve conflict. These findings resonate with the wisdom of those religious traditions that advocate empathy and reciprocity as a foundation for a just and stable social order. The discovery of mirror neurons is especially germane.

From them we now know that Hobbes's model was wrong. Our own sense of identity is taken from our interactions with others—it is given to us by others. We get into the most trouble when we sever our relationships with others and reduce them to objects, to something nonidentifiable. Nothing furthers this faster than the capacity to characterize others in absolutist moralistic terms—making ourselves good and others evil.

Whatever your view of it—whether you believe it literally, metaphorically, lyrically, or not at all—the Bible is arguably the world's most influential book. Its message speaks to more people than any other single set of narratives or scriptures. Yet in passages of the New Testament, there are repeated attempts to give priority to outsiders—the prostitutes, the poor, sick, the tax collectors—those very segments of the population that are least fit, least likely to benefit wider society. There are two fascinating aspects of this. The first is the suggestion, in evolutionary biological or "social physics" terms, that there is an advantage to society in continuously expanding the boundaries of identity to include the most egregious outlawed groups—sinners, enemies, and infidels, those very people for whom one might be most justified in making absolute judgments of good and evil. The second is that part of the appeal of the narratives contained within the books of the Bible lies in our sense of the social rightness of the stories, however much they superficially seem to contradict our modern perspective. If our social emotions and capacity for empathy evolved to offer genuine evolutionary advantages, if we need the diverse crowd to thrive as individuals, then advances in neuroscience and the evolutionary sciences, as well as the compassion of the Bible, may provide an alternative to some of the most dangerous social diseases of our time—Hobbesian traps, fundamentalism, absolutism, and warfare.

Such a suggestion will no doubt trigger cries of "utopianism" and "social engineering." To presume that human behavior can be studied scientifically and put in a larger context of evolutionary theory is to invoke the wrath of the Left and the Right. On this, the extremes of both the Left and the Right are in agreement: Human nature is absolute and irreducible—it is sacred ground. The Left argues that our scientific knowledge is incomplete, and hence, to presume to even embark on the slightest scientifically grounded prescription for human behavior is to invoke the hubris and evils of social Darwinism and social engineering. On the Right, the claim is that it is a sacrilege to apply science to human values and conduct—that human values, behaviors, and emotions are beyond the reach of science. It is a mystery to be left to nature. There is a huge resistance to seeing human nature—reason, emotions, free will, and choice— as being subject to certain law-like principles. So strong is the need to preserve a safe corner of human exceptionalism within nature that the topic is virtually off limits for many forms of debates. Yet if that same logic were applied to medicine, we would still be burning witches to stop plagues and exorcising spirits to cure migraines. Whatever the uniqueness of human beings may be apart from other creatures in nature, it is without question that we are, nonetheless, part of and derived from nature. And let's not be complacent: It is also true that we evolved in ways that are not optimally adapted to our current circumstances. In short, our inherent, innate natural proclivities, drives, and competences are in many respects, inadequate to the challenges of the twenty-first century.

Our Pleistocene bodies and brains are being overwhelmed by the scope and pace of technological change. It really is too much, too fast for our little brains and bodies to process. There may, however, be an out. The reason that biological evolution is so slow—compared to technological evolution—is because it occurs over generations through sexual selection and reproduction. Even when the selective pressure is intense and concentrated, as in breeding for new strains of dogs, it is still a physical process and takes lots of time. Social adaptations, on the other hand, can occur far more rapidly because they do not depend upon sexual selection, physical growth, and change. Social evolution is far less physically bounded than biological evolution and consequently can transpire over the course of days and years rather than generations. Digital encoded relationships, transactions, information, knowledge, images, content, even institutions, for all practical purposes are frictionless and can form, dissolve, and evolve in seconds and minutes rather than days, years, or generations. They offer a unique, wholly new opportunity for accelerated learning, speculation, and social innovation. In the digital sphere, moreover, measurement, storage, memory, and security all come virtually for free. It is possible to create online digital organizations and institutions—banks, courts, currencies, firms, schools, charities, currency exchanges, and governing bodies for a tiny fraction of what it would cost in the physical world. Furthermore, it will become possible to have governance by algorithm—that is, have computer-based rules assign reputation scores, rate the performance of members of a social network, identify and expel free riders, and maintain the requisite checks and balances between competing interests. The systems can be set up to default to good behavior. So much of contemporary life is already computer run: Computers are no longer simple clerks and bookkeepers for financial transaction, they increasingly make investments and manage the portfolios of mutual funds and hedge funds. The shift has already occurred. We're largely digital, we just haven't appreciated what it can tell us about ourselves.

The scope and scale of experiments in digital institution building can go beyond anything practical in the physical world and the results can be easily measured, compiled, and interpreted. The intent is not to relegate governance to the computer or even to have the online world displace the physical world, but rather to fix an appropriate mix of the two so that people and institutions can learn and adapt at the speed and scope required to survive in an environment of interdependence and constant change. That's the promise of the technology; it can help us learn about ourselves anew.

Chapter Two

Oops—Apocalypse

As mankind enters the first decade of the twenty-first century, we find ourselves facing challenges for which we have not prepared, in an environment of continuous, escalating change. Change is no longer the exception; it is the rule. Every corner of our world is transforming at an unprecedented rate, from how governments and businesses operate to what kind of food we eat and what clothing we wear. Many of these changes are happening without our full understanding or ability to control.

According to a noted Harvard environmental scientist, "[W]e are performing massive, blind experiments upon the planet and ourselves for which we don't have the faintest idea what the consequences might be. We are flying blind into a future at a pace unprecedented in the earth's evolutionary history!"[1] Should the current exponential rate of technological change continue into the future, each new day will have progressively less and less in common with its predecessor, until, theoretically at least, change is so rapid that no day bears any meaningful relation to its predecessor. Society will cease to be marked by known cultures, norms, and expectations due to the constant flux in technologies, proficiencies, and the limits of what is possible. At present, this sense of discontinuity is being experienced on a decade-to-decade basis. Consider a future in which the cost and performance of communications, manufacturing, transportation, life sciences, and weaponry improves by an order of magnitude every ten years: What effect will this have on the ability of social, cultural, and civil institutions to adapt? If product life cycles become measured in weeks or even days, then what happens to social and cultural institutions, such as relationships, work, marriage, church, government, and schools? How will they not be rendered anachronistic? Will biotechnology enable us to undergo "complete makeovers" on an annual basis, changing our bodies, personalities, and brains as fashion dictates?

Technology has become the pervasive driver of change as never before, a double-edged sword that is transforming everything—the planet's ecology and climate, life expectancy, agriculture, literacy, communications, transportation, and weapons of individual and mass destruction. These changes, combined with the fact that the great majority of nation-states in the world today are new, weak, and hard-pressed to provide even the most rudimentary of government services, have created a global security environment of unprecedented volatility. Given this pace of global economic, political, and technological transformation, successful governments and businesses will need to anticipate and plan for the new rules of global engagement, power, and legitimization that will frame the future of global security or they will become anachronisms. For governments, it's a case of adapt or perish. They should be smart enough to use new technologies and strategies to neutralize future adversaries and threats, but they also need to be aware of their own vulnerability if they treat the future as an extension of the past.

Three converging global trends are driving the world community toward a point of "hyper-instability" (see Figure 1).

1. Moore's Law of Weaponry,
2. Small World Effects, and
3. Global Population Growth.

Until very recently, these three trends were relatively independent, but they could potentially converge, driving competitive pressures toward weapons that are smaller, cheaper, and more lethal and evenly distributed, thereby eliminating the prospect for any sustainable security equilibrium. What propels these trends toward convergence is the rising

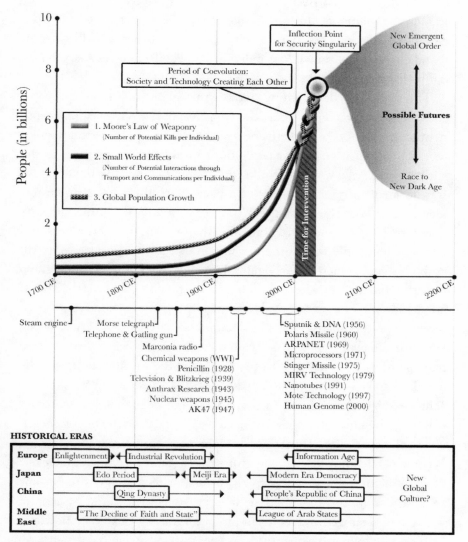

FIGURE 1   The Security Singularity: Vectors of Hyper-Instability

Special thanks to Dr. David Alberts of the Command and Control Research Program, DOD, for assistance in preparation of diagram.

population, the increasing possibility for global interaction, and the growing destructive capacity of easily obtained weaponry.

The simultaneous growth in these three areas reinforces each realm and accelerates the movement toward convergence, or hyper-instability— in ordinary language, a global catastrophe. The combined effect is unique in human evolutionary history. *Homo sapiens* is endangering itself to a degree that will sorely test our capacity to adapt and survive without profound changes, not only in our individual and collective behaviors but in our biological composition as well.

The first major destabilizing trend is that of Moore's Law, applied to the cost and effectiveness (kill power) of weaponry over time. The exponential increase of cost-effectiveness in the technology of destruction is a recent phenomenon. Earlier revolutions in military affairs, such as the stirrup, the longbow, the machine gun, the submarine, and the airplane, transformed military strategies at a pace that allowed their countermeasures to coevolve with them (armor, the tank, the mine, and the anti-aircraft gun) and were controlled by organized governments and nation-states. Only within the last fifty years has the "cost per unit kill power" begun to increase exponentially—independent of countervailing factors—to the point where an individual at modest expense (the cost of an automobile or a house) could potentially kill tens of thousands, even hundreds of thousands of people. That crossover event has yet to occur, but with the availability of "suitcase nukes" and biologically engineered pathogens, that day may not be far off. One of the striking features of the attacks of 9/11 was their relatively low cost: Al Qaeda spent $500,000 to achieve a significant loss of life and a very large economic loss to America. With the inevitable and continued development of the biological sciences, the specialized expertise of bioengineered pathogens could soon become public knowledge—something that a smart teenage "bio-hacker" of 2015 might know how to exploit. If nuclear technology is to become smaller and more tactical, then it is possible to imagine a scenario wherein nuclear warheads could fit into a car, van, or cargo container and be produced in massive quantities. What is still—though barely—the secure providence of national governments could become the equivalent of a "consumer" durable. Autonomous technologies under development now include little computers the size of a thumbnail that can sense and send information by video and self-organize themselves into "meshnetworks" that can work with one another and transmit their data to a satellite. When these technologies are placed upon micro-aerial vehicles the size of a fly, called roboflies, they represent another packaging and delivery option for which effective countermeasures would be hard to sustain.

If current trends are any indication, technological innovation and cost reduction in consumer technology are proceeding at a pace equal or even superior to military technologies, and the difference between commercially beneficial technology—especially a biologically engineered technology—and a terrorist application is often technologically insignificant. The long-term trend of weapons becoming smaller, cheaper, faster, and more deadly will continue and can only be destabilizing, especially when their development and deployment is outside the control of accountable governments or institutions.

The second trend adding to the general volatility is small world effects, the consequence of major innovations in mobility and connectivity (transportation and communications). Through increases in mobility and connectivity, not only are *people* able to move about faster and less expensively globally, but so are ideas, information, expertise, and work products. Since 1996, we have seen exponential growth in knowledge connectedness, primarily through the Internet, as well as physical connectedness through the proliferation of motorized vehicles and inexpensive air travel. From the standpoint of the spread of ideas, innovations, and viruses (both organic and electronic), the measure of connectedness is very important because the more connected populations are, the more vulnerable they are to the spread of social trends and biological diseases.

The final destabilizing trend is the growth in global population, which naturally conflicts with other social and environmental forces and constraints. Population growth increases population density, which in turn creates increased economic, social, and psychological pressures. Studies on animal and human populations suggest that increased population density can lead to increased aggressive behaviors, infanticide, criminal activities, and delusional collective actions (millennial movements) if the social and economic systems cannot adapt to the changes. This is one of the explanations given by Jared Diamond in his book *Collapse*[2] for the genocide in Rwanda. As the number of people on this planet continues to increase, societies will be forced to either compete more fiercely for our limited natural resources (including land, fishing rights, mining rights, and so on) or to find new resources to better support our rising population. With history as a guide, we can reasonably predict that this increasing competition will lead to conflicts (financial, political, and military) before it will lead to solutions (renewable energy, recycling, more efficient agricultural techniques). Competition for resources among nation-states has long been a major impetus for warfare and eventual social and political change.

The cumulative effect of these three exponential trends is the potential creation of a "hyper-unstable" environment where virtually anyone with a minimum of capital and expertise could "veto" or nullify the existing social arrangements and contracts. Given the number of potential weapons and the number and diversity of adversaries, it would be virtually impossible to devise a "six sigma" fail-safe defense to effectively eliminate destabilizing effects on the economy and political and social institutions. Unchecked, such a trajectory of technological competition would be a race to the bottom, leading the global community to a state not dissimilar to that in Somalia or Haiti. Clearly, exponential growth curves such as these cannot continue forever. There will be "corrections." In this respect a "correction" would constitute a human disaster measured in hundreds of millions of lost and ruined lives. Policies that interrupt, dampen, and redirect these trends prior to that point will be pivotal to achieving global security. Rather than generations of new hard military technologies, new forms of soft technologies will be called for to support organizations that are agile and smart enough to anticipate and avert many of the crises and issues that are portrayed in the introductory nightmare scenarios.

Just as the most effective diplomatic initiatives are those that are effective without being visible, so too will successful military actions in the future be best measured by their use of soft techniques to manage and avoid conflicts, rather than by their use of force to end (or prolong) them. Several nightmare war-game scenarios envisage a moment when global opinion equates the deterioration of the earth's climate with the "excesses of the West"—thereby legitimizing the principle of terrorist attacks and reparations payments. Should such a moment occur, it will be too late for any form of corrective action. While clearly fictitious, this scenario may be more plausible in the near future than it might seem at present. Significant shifts in global climate patterns have historically had an enormous destabilizing effect upon global populations, causing massive migrations and deadly conflicts over food and resource-producing territories. The first human migrations out of Africa were driven by drought and climate change, as were the migrations out of Central Asia into Central Europe 15,000 years later. The periodic rise and fall of civilizations throughout North Africa and the Middle East were also a consequence of changing climates and drought. In more recent history, famine was a key factor in triggering the French and the Russian revolutions. Recent studies into the effects of pollution on our global climate have produced extremely divergent predictions: Some studies support a theory of global *warming*, while others indicate that regional *cooling* will result (see Figure 2 in the Appendix). In either scenario, the effect will include highly disruptive natural disasters such as storms, wildfires, and flooding, as well as droughts and animal extinctions, all of which will have a dramatic impact on human society. The most important aspect of these studies is the recognition of the very real potential for global challenges, hardships, and even disasters over the next century.

In order to appreciate how new types of technologies are shaping the future global security environment, and hence how they might be used by individuals, terrorist organizations, and nation-states alike, we must first examine the nature of these new technologies and begin to understand their impact on society.

Until relatively recently, technology was discussed as though it was something independent of the core of human activity, something we chose to embrace or reject, something about which experts made assessments. The Office of Technology Assessment in the U.S. government was founded in 1974 on the premise that governments could assess the impact of technologies to determine which technologies to adopt or reject. A whole discipline of "technology assessment" arose during this period, to advise governments and companies on technology impacts and choices. Although there are debates as to the advisability of pursuing some of the new technologies, such as stem cell research, and indeed efforts to curtail basic scientific research are being made by cultural conservatives, it is widely recognized in the scientific and technological communities that there will always be "safe harbors" for technologies that promise power, wealth, or longevity. Under this traditional mindset, societies and individuals were believed to be able to exert conscious control over technology. In retrospect, this perspective seems naive and simplistic. Recently, the language has changed subtly but profoundly, shifting from discussion of technology as a force within our control to recognition of the coevolution of technology and social institutions and markets. The Office of Technology Assessment itself was shut down in 1995.

Among the more extreme technologists and futurists such as Raymond Kurzweil,[3] Hans Moravec,[4] and Victor Vinge,[5] there is talk of a "technological singularity" whereby human evolution and technological evolution are inextricably converging to create a new, technologically circumscribed global ecology composed of "carbon and non-carbon life forms."[6] Whether such a combination is likely—let alone when it might occur—can be debated, but what cannot be disputed is that we are in the midst of a "scientific revolution" that is fomenting a cross-disciplinary revolution. The ensuing changes should not be equated with a catalog of new physical devices, but with a revolution in the principles that inform the design of smaller, faster, self-organizing devices. In other words, there has been a fundamental shift in emphasis in scientific descriptions about the way the world works. We are moving away from mechanical models of mass, force, and volume to ones that stress the importance of the rules, grammars, and protocols that enable complex forms of control, replication, and communication. The cross-fertilization of scientific disciplines and philosophies has spawned a new technological ecology of devices that combines the properties of nanotechnologies, the biological sciences, and digital technologies. The prospect of "nanobots" cleaning our arteries and removing plaque from our brains may be exhilarating to some, but horrifying to others. The power of these technologies lies not in their size, mass, or force, but in their ability to sense and control highly complex processes. In a variety of scientific and technological circles, there has been a shift toward the notion that networks of the small and the agile that can control and direct themselves are far more effective than a few, large, non-networked, hierarchical organizations such as traditional militaries, governments, and corporations.

For any strategic planner, the importance of this shift cannot be overemphasized. Stated bluntly, the time-honored, classic doctrine of controlling an adversary's or competitor's behavior through brute force is about to be rendered obsolete. In the long term, physical bullying, either through punitive conflict or through attrition, is an attenuated, costly, and ineffective method to get people to change their behavior. It is especially clear that the outcomes of attrition strategies of lethal engagement are potentially uncontainable and counterproductive. Instead, it may be far more effective to be smart, precise, and targeted rather than powerful and blunt. Intelligence and speed will trump power and trial and error every time. Precedent is generally a poor guidepost for anticipating the magnitude of the security challenges that confront the world. The all-encompassing scope and the diversity of the forms of technological change—biological, weapons, communications, transportation, energy, and computational—are unique. They will demand an uncharacteristic form of management and response, requiring new levels of leadership, commitment, and imagination.

The nature of the future adversaries is also different. They very likely are not the nation-states, which are targets too easy for counterattacks. A new kind of adversary is on our threshold.

Chapter Three

Terrorism's
Shattered Identities

FOR THE BETTER PART OF THE LAST THOUSAND YEARS OF HUMAN history, territorial definitions of identity and affinity have been the accepted natural boundaries of community and governance. However, with the introduction of low-cost global transportation and instantaneous communications over the last twenty-five years, identity and affiliation have become less attached to a physical place. This has weakened the effectiveness and legitimacy of the nation-state, especially the newer nation-states, and this in turn has accelerated the erosion of territorial identity. Many of the newer nation-states have neither the resources nor the skills to fulfill even the most basic of governmental functions. Some are faltering, unable to manage their economies, collect taxes, or enforce their laws. Some of the newer states, especially those throughout Central Asia, Africa, Latin America, Eastern Europe, and Southeast Asia, have become kleptocracies run by alliances of drug lords, arms merchants, smugglers, corrupt officials, fundamentalists, and self-appointed despots. This failure of the newer nation-states to maintain social order, control corruption, foster commerce, or sustain meaning has spawned what anthropologists call "millennial movements,"[1] grass-roots movements that await a new millennium or golden age expected to resurrect traditional values to usher in a new and just global order. Since the people of failed governments typically cannot trust their governments, they turn to religious or communitarian organizations to provide a modicum of security, sustenance, and sense of purpose. South of the equator in Africa, for example, the fastest growing millennial movements are not Islamic, but rather Christian offshoots—the Lumpa Church in Zambia, and in Uganda, the Lord Resistance Army, the Movement for the Restoration of Ten Commandments, and the Holy Spirit Mobile Force.[2] These millennial movements may have differing religious traditions, but they share a common "literalist" mentality whose assertions for a new order are grounded in unassailable, purist traditions. Although such movements can embrace supernatural solutions and espouse profoundly dysfunctional behaviors, they are not easily uprooted or discredited. They can be powerful motivators and have successfully recruited millions of believers and followers. Millennial movements can also combine more secular movements such as Marxism with forms of indigenous animism to create strange but brutal hybrids, such as the Khmer Rouge in Cambodia and the Shining Path in Peru. Because the rewards for participating in such movements are spiritual or supernatural, these movements are difficult to influence through the more secular means of military attrition and punishment.[3] Who fears a bullet if the reward is eternity?

Religion is not the only motivation for political upheaval or violence. Under conditions of extreme uncertainty, the power vacuum is filled by the simplest forms of control: loose tribal and clanlike structures often headed by a charismatic leader. Examples abound of terrorist networks in Ossetia, Chechnya, Moldova, Indonesia, the Philippines, Yemen, Colombia, Peru, and Uganda, where power is unaccountable, despotic, and sustained through bribery and intimidation. However brutal, anarchic, and corrupt such organizations may be, they can also be quite sophisticated in their uses of technologies to thwart their adversaries, control their populaces, and generate significant cash reserves. Organized crime rings span the globe from the port of Buenaventura in Colombia to Tripoli, Western Europe, Laos, and the Caymans, and on to Cambodia, North Korea, and the Shan Province in Myanmar. According to a Russian senior diplomat,

despite significant variations in means, methods, goals, and forms of activities of terrorists and criminal organizations, there is a clear trend of merging of these structures which may become irreversible. One of the signs of this threat is direct use of terror by criminal groups. Mafia and drug dealers, through terrorist acts against the state and state officials, attempt to impede investigations and implementation of governmental policies to fight them.[4]

In the future, these tactics are likely to be imitated by terrorists, liberationists, and opportunists of varying religious, political, and religious persuasions if they perceive these to be successful methods.

Unlike conventional nation-state enemies, these global asymmetric adversary networks attempt to work within their targets as parasites to their hosts, spreading undetected to undermine vital domestic institutions and organizations. Their objective is not the annexation of territory, the installation of a new form of government, nor even the defeat of a standing army, but rather the weakening of the will of organized governments to exert control over them. They want to create a cost—either in social and economic disruption, lost lives, or sheer uncertainty—that is simply too high for a governing body and its people to bear. Like any guerrilla force, they have fluid lines of engagement, and they can "shoot and scoot," slipping out of the grasp of a conventional army to engage their adversaries on their own terms, seeking the cover neither of night nor air support, but of civilian populations, world opinion, and the safe harbor of sacred and protected places. The Baathists, criminal rings, and militant Islamists in Iraq exemplify such resistance fighter-entrepreneurs. They are masters of defining the rules of engagement and legitimacy of outcomes in their terms, as their practices are not fettered by treaty or international law. These they can breach with impunity, whereas the breach by a legally constituted entity or army can bring down a torrent of public rebuke and condemnation. The battle spaces of these kinds of wars are not the physical points of conflict, as measured by the securing of a territory, or the sum of a body count after an encounter, but the minds and sentiments of those who benefit from the status quo and give legitimacy, recruits, and resources to terrorists and criminal networks. What becomes "true" in such conflicts is what is believed to be true: The managed perception becomes the reality. Hence, proficient movements are very adept at manipulating and sustaining a "desirable reality" in the minds of their supporters and at the same time, targeting their enemies. The Somali warlord Mohammed Farah Aideed was especially talented in this regard, staging massacres to rally his own people and engage the support of the foreign press. Sunni and Shiite insurgents in Iraq murder their opponents more for "propaganda" purposes than to secure any particular territory. Such movements achieve their legitimacy and credibility by giving their followers credible, simple, and repeatable narratives of good and evil that explain and promise to transform their circumstances. They are fictions, but very artfully designed ones to appeal to the needs and sense of injustice of their adherents. As such, a fiction can quickly become in practice a self-justifying reality. Such narratives are often embedded within older local narratives, both religious and cultural, that explain how "alien" (foreign, infidel, or demonic), "unjust" forces created the current circumstances, and how these forces in turn can be eliminated through "just" action. An asymmetric adversary's effectiveness, indeed, its legitimacy, depends upon the credibility and coherence of these narratives, and anything that bolsters such narratives increases their power, longevity, and effectiveness; anything that diminishes their credibility weakens their will and viability. We have always known this, which is why such severe punishments have been handed out to those who tell the "wrong" story. Lord Haw Haw, a British propagandist for Germany in World War II was hanged for treason for his radio broadcasts—no first-amendment defense for him. Nor was there for Iva Toguri d'Aquino, known as Tokyo Rose, who was sentenced to a decade in prison for being one of several women to broadcast to America for the Axis forces during the war in the Pacific, before she was very discreetly pardoned on Gerald Ford's last day in office.

As digital, wireless, satellite, and other technologies come to play pivotal roles in warfare, the focus of much of military activity will shift from the physical domain to the information, cognitive, and social domains. Given the potential for retaliation on civilian populations, highly covert and targeted information warfare campaigns will become the preferred means for preempting operations, influencing will, and degrading the effectiveness of state and non-state actors.

For nation-states and international "peacekeeping" coalitions like the United Nations and NATO, operations other than war are frequently

conducted in impoverished regions such as Somalia, Kosovo, Afghanistan, and Yemen, countries that have regularly incubated and sustained
terrorist activities. Many of these containment operations have a strong
informational component, including operational security (OPSEC), psychological operations (PSYOPs), and electronic warfare (EW). They are
part of a command and control warfare (C2W) strategy with a mandate

> to decapitate the enemy command structure from its body of combat
> forces. Effective C2W is described as enabling the commander to seize
> the initiative by forcing the enemy into reaction mode, while main-
> taining, protecting, and/or enhancing the effectiveness of friendly C2.
> It combines the denial and influence of information, deception, dis-
> ruption, and destruction to counter adversary C2 while simultaneously
> protecting friendly C2.[5]

This capability is currently still regarded as an adjunct to the primary
military mission and therefore is not fully developed as a coherent, coordinated arena of engagement with its own resources, specializations, and
objectives. But rather than being treated as peripheral to a primary military mission, well-articulated warfare doctrine and practices for the information, cognitive, and social domains could significantly reduce the need
for more traditional military methods of influence and control. Using dis-
information and propaganda as a weapon is anathema to most democratic
societies because many believe that if their governments become engaged
in distorting information of any kind, even in the pursuit of national security, their countries would soon cease to be democratic. Most democracies categorically deny the military the enormous power to manage the
national media, to intentionally propagandize to the global media. Yet in
order for true information warfare capabilities to be developed and de-
ployed to fight in the information, cognitive, and social domains, such issues will need to be resolved. Information-related operations play an
increasingly vital role in achieving global security.

The 1993 campaign in Somalia launched by the United States and
the United Nations troops to capture warlord Mohammed Farah Aideed[6]
illustrated how a technologically inferior adversary could successfully

compete against the most sophisticated military forces on earth. Somalia exposed the relative vulnerabilities of the American military to asymmetric challenges.

Aideed's ability to mount a highly effective perception-management campaign did not depend upon advanced communications technologies but rather upon word-of-mouth and line-of-sight signaling such as burning tires to direct and coordinate his operations. Before the conflict, Aideed was not in a politically strong position. He was one of many contending warlords, some of whom had a greater popular support base than he did. But after the conflict, he was able to expel both the United States and the UN, solidify his power base, and become a hero not only to his people, but to the Fourth World—that is, Afghanistan, Yemen, Chechnya, and much of sub-Saharan Africa, in sum, the poorest of the world—by showing how an underdeveloped country could defeat a superpower.

Very early on, Aideed knew that the fractiousness of the competing kinship clans would dissolve in the face of a perceived attack by outside interests upon Somalia. By making the UN and American efforts to capture him appear as if they were attacks on the Somali people and their sovereignty, he was not only able to demonize his foreign adversaries but was also able to achieve a new legitimacy in the eyes of his people. This reduced the influence of those warlords who had sided with the foreigners who opposed him. Aideed accomplished this by carefully manipulating the media:

> For example, Aideed released false reports that Italian businessmen, with the collaboration of his factional rival ali Mahdi, had dumped toxic chemicals in Somalia. These disclosures were made in an attempt to preclude Italian involvement in the peacekeeping operation and to discredit ali Mahdi.[7]

But this was only the first of many steps that he took to influence the Somali people's perceptions of outsiders in order to build loyalty to him. The remarkable fact was that there were no successful countermeasures by the United States, the UN, or even the world media. Aideed regularly staged events for international media coverage, such as demonstrations outside the hotel where the media were staying, knowing that they did not like to venture outside. While his staged anti-UN demonstration received widespread coverage, a pro-UN demonstration, which was 100 times larger, went uncovered.[8] According to a detailed study of his information campaign, Aideed thoroughly trounced his American and UN adversaries through his carefully coordinated campaign of perception management.[9]

Aideed was not averse to slaughtering his own people to stage an event to galvanize world opinion against the UN and the Americans:

> For example, during the 12th and 14th June ambush on Pakistani peacekeepers, Aideed's gunmen surreptitiously fired into a Somali crowd in the presence of international press coverage in order to convey the impression that the Pakistanis were firing on noncombatants.[10]

Not only was Aideed dominant in his perception-management capabilities, to the detriment and eventual withdrawal of American Ranger and Delta forces, but he also succeeded in degrading and denying UN and American information-related capabilities:

> In Somalia, each side sought to achieve comparative advantage from those resources at its disposal, but in the realm of information degradation and denial, it was the relatively low-tech Somalis who were able to define the technological intensity of the battlefield to their own benefit . . . While the Somalis were not able to disrupt the U.S. C4I2 infrastructure (Command, Control, Communications, Computers, Information, Intelligence), they were able to deny the coalition intelligence concerning their movements and intentions by deciding not to utilize available electronic C4I2 assets which would have been vulnerable to interception.[11]

The United States tried to turn the conflict into its own war, run by U.S. rules, but was thoroughly unsuccessful in doing so.[12] American radio-jamming capabilities were ineffective against the sporadic radio broadcasts, and the United States had very little local knowledge, having to depend upon the last-minute recruitment of Somali translators. The Americans missed an opportunity due to their failure to understand the local rules that governed kinship relationships and how leadership and power were retained in Somalia.

The American and UN failure in the Somalia conflict illustrates the weakness of relying on technological and conventional military measures when combating a skilled information warfare campaign. Aideed was able to expropriate and exploit the resources of his adversaries against them. He staged events and exploited the international media's news cycles through their penchant for simplistic and dramatic sound bites and images to project his view of events. He denied the Americans and the UN forces situation awareness by using crowds as cover to successfully conceal his troops' moments, while at the same time having high-quality intelligence about the movements of American and UN Pakistani troops. The Americans and the UN had not understood the effects of a well-executed information campaign plan and, though militarily superior, were forced out of Somalia. So, Aideed, despite a technological disadvantage, won his battle in the information domain.

Nowhere was the power of information and kinship networks more dramatically demonstrated than in Rwanda in 1994. As in Somalia, the weapons and technologies were very limited (the primary instruments of execution being machetes). However, when coupled with a tightly knit ethnic network, the Hutus performed with an efficiency unmatched by even the Waffen-SS in 1943. In just six months, 800,000 Tutsis were exterminated in a fever of controlled savagery. People from all sectors of Rwandan society were recruited, not the least of which were many prominent Catholic and Protestant clergy. The head of Rwanda's Seventh-Day Adventist Church, Elizaphan Ntakirutimana, was subsequently indicted for genocide, as were the three Hutu heads of radio and newspaper outlets. The radio stations were transformed into a highly effective network that directed and coordinated the genocide:

Witnesses told the court that once the slaughter had begun—it lasted about 100 days—Radio Mille Collines was vital in steering the militia and calling direct hits. They said the radio station would broadcast the names and addresses of people who were targets along with their vehicle license plates and the hiding places of refugees. "There was an FM radio on every roadblock, there were thousands of roadblocks in

Rwanda," a police investigator said. He told the court in prison inter-
views that "many people told us they had killed because the radio had
told them to kill."[13]

Even songs and entertainers were used to incite the genocide. A well-
known Rwandan singer, Simon Bikindi, was indicted for genocide for com-
posing songs of hate and participating in militia gangs' murder. Pauline
Nyiramasuhuko, former mayor and minister of family and women's affairs,
was also convicted of inciting the murders of hundreds of Tutsi women and
children. Virtually all segments of Hutu society were complicit in the sys-
tematic slaughter.[14]

In Rwanda, as in Somalia, sophisticated communications technologies
were not needed to create a highly efficient and effective network that
could achieve a high degree of shared awareness among a large group of
individuals and organizations.

Sophistication in information technologies is likewise not required to
develop and employ a highly effective perception-management campaign,
which can be one of the most powerful and least appreciated instruments
for determining the outcome of political projects. Understanding how
narratives, images, and orders are created, legitimized, and transmitted
through the media and a complex network of tribal relationships can play
as important a role in securing a desired military or policy outcome as any
sophisticated military maneuver or smart munitions. When the objective
is to change the behavior and mindset of groups of individuals, and where
they are organized into kinship, tribal, criminal, religious, or military networks, a contextualized understanding of the mechanics of social networks
can be a far more effective instrument than the raw punitive power of military action. What is clear is that success depends very largely in knowing
who your adversary is. The question of identity, especially when the power
of the nation-state to confer it has largely dissolved, becomes acute.

The ability to define your own identity and that of others is becoming
the battleground of the future. So-called terrorist organizations such as
Hezbollah and Hamas are succeeding in part because they give their recruits a sense of purpose and belonging, and place their struggles within
a larger mythic, religious context. They gain the support of their civilian
populations because they provide health, educational, and welfare services

not offered by the established governments and because in many cases, they are not obviously corrupt. Blunt efforts to suppress, contain, or "neutralize" such organizations through strategic bombing and shelling only reinforce the resolve of the recruits, lending them further legitimization in the eyes of "the street." Deploring the immorality of the "terrorists" for placing their weapons within civilian neighborhoods, American and Israeli diplomats and generals try to have it both ways: They too send their smart munitions into civilian areas, boasting of their accuracy and lamenting collateral camouflage, depending on the outcome of the attack. They don't refuse to bomb, any more than Hamas and Hezbollah refuse to jeopardize neutral civilians by keeping a distance from them. So the positions of both adversaries seem morally equivalent: Each knowingly endangers noncombatants. It would appear that the Americans and the Israelis are virtually alone in the world in not realizing that the rules and weapons of warfare have changed. At a time when the positions on both sides have become more intransigent and absolutist, and the weapons have become cheaper, faster, and more mobile and lethal, it is more important than ever to contest for influence with appropriate means. Otherwise the blowback will be disastrous.

Chapter Four

Unlikely Heretics: A Prussian and an Economist

ONE OF THE FIRST MODERN CHALLENGES TO CENTRALIZED MILITARY authority began—improbably—with Carl von Clausewitz, the nineteenth-century Prussian general, whom some military scholars consider the intellectual father of modern warfare. Clausewitz wrote extensively on the unpredictable nature of warfare, emphasizing that war was essentially nonlinear: Small, unpredictable changes could result in massive, unanticipated outcomes that he attributed to the "fog and friction of war." Once the war begins, the battle plan often becomes obsolete, and the commander must count upon the resourcefulness of the troops to make their own judgments. This was the same argument that Secretary of Defense Donald Rumsfeld made in 2003 during the Iraq War when he argued that battle plans continually change and that one of the achievements of the new U.S. force structure was its ability to revise a battle plan constantly. The press misconstrued this to mean that Rumsfeld had no battle plan at all. Although that was certainly true for what has been ironically called the "post-conflict" phase of the war, the Pentagon did have a process for making and revising war plans in the midst of the conflict. The failure was in not recognizing that domination on the battlefield is one very limited means for controlling a population or enemy and is also incomplete and contingent upon the success of other factors outside the field of battle. The Pentagon's distinction between the conflict and post-conflict phases in its planning and subsequent occupation is indicative of how deeply it has misunderstood Clausewitz's insights about the nature of war.

However, the Pentagon has been a genuine pioneer in its attempt to flatten the chain of command. It has pursued new technology to enact its networked structure. It is constructing the $17-billion Global Grid,[1] a communications and sensor network that provides real-time intelligence as well as the capability for any "asset"—human or technological—to communicate and coordinate with any other asset on a global basis. The system is equivalent to a parallel, private Internet. The Afghanistan War in 2002 showed that a corporal on horseback now has the technological means *and the decision rights* to call in a B2 bomb attack through a satellite linkup, something unheard of six years earlier. The technological as well as the organizational challenges are daunting: How do you interconnect tens of thousands of "assets"—human and technological—and decide who or what is to be trusted, who has the right to decide, who has the right to intervene and override, and how these rights should be assigned or revoked? Clausewitz had acknowledged the problem of the unpredictably of battle, but it took a century of technical innovation before the Pentagon in its doctrine of Network Centric Warfare of 2002 began to address it through the creation of a global self-organizing network. There is more than a little irony here. Here is a case of what many would consider one of the most hierarchical, authoritarian, and hidebound institutions on the surface of the planet leading the way to one of the most fundamental and profound changes in how large organizations are to be networked and peer managed and governed. However, it is by no means clear, after the disasters of the Iraq War and the disaffection of many of the senior military leadership who helped construct the transformation in the 1990s, whether these reforms will survive the highly politicized and ideological tenure of the Bush administration.

Although former Defense Secretary Rumsfeld was a vocal proponent of the doctrine of Network Centric Warfare, stressing agility and deceit and the role of information in warfare, he was, nonetheless, very traditional in his understanding of the use of force to "change behaviors," a phrase he used with some frequency. Rumsfeld had a traditional view of power: If you want to change a regime's behavior, use force. Lots of it. Many, including some within the Pentagon, see the absence of a post-conflict plan as not only an enormous and altogether avoidable failing but a demonstration that Rumsfeld had only understood in a limited way the concept and opportunity presented by network-centric conflict.

Among the Bush civilian leadership of DOD, there is an unwavering conviction that force, fear, and intimidation are not only effective deterrents but are the necessary ingredients for fostering democratic behavior around certain parts of the world. Implicit in this policy are a number of unexamined assumptions about human nature. It is assumed that to shy away from the use of force is to communicate weakness, that it will only encourage further aggression. The historic example of Neville Chamberlain's attempt to placate Nazism, rather than Winston Churchill's defiant antagonism, is often offered as justification. Churchill, as a model, has lost little of his luster; Chamberlain never had any. But their examples are generalized out of time and context. Foreign policy options are framed as absolute moral imperatives, where the objective is the conquest of Evil by Good. Accordingly, victory requires the complete submission of the opponent. It is a position that fails to examine how different cultures and religions actually respond to threat, force, and humiliation. This perspective is axiomatic to the Bush civilian leadership of the Pentagon, but it is not shared by many of the most seasoned uniformed leadership, especially among the most respected senior leadership, such as retired Marine Corps Commandant General Anthony Zinni, one of the leaders in the transformation of the DOD.

At one of the Highlands Forum summits, a former commanding officer of a battleship eloquently expressed doubts about the efficacy of hard power in the fight against terrorism, reflecting that "there is nowhere to point your guns." Many military leaders are thoughtful about the appropriate and changing role of the military, not least because unlike the civilian leadership, the career military leadership has a commitment to the long-term viability of the institution. Committed to the service of their country—as citizens, not just soldiers—they are cautious in asserting a military solution to highly complex problems. This reluctance has been stigmatized as a lack of courage by some of the nonserving civilian DOD leadership, but that is far from the truth. One of the tenets of informed and reflective military thinking is the importance of the subordination of military goals to political ones. Clausewitz wrote:

> It is of course well known that the only source of war is politics—the intercourse of governments and peoples. . . . We maintain . . . that war is simply a continuation of political intercourse, with the addition of other means.[2]

But he did not intend his words to justify warfare as a legitimate extension of diplomacy. Instead, as Clausewitz repeats throughout *On War*,[3] political outcomes—that is, the "intercourse of governments and peoples"—should be the benchmark of military success. In certain circumstances, when the destruction of one adversary creates ten more, it was obvious to Clausewitz, and the much-cited Chinese strategist Sun Tzu,[4] as it is to many senior American commanders, that war is not the most effective means for achieving a political end. Both Clausewitz and Sun Tzu believed that the end goal of war was to break the will of the enemy to fight. Unless "victory" meant total annihilation—something neither advocated—it really entailed achieving a psychological state rather than a physical condition. Consider the conflicts in Kosovo, Palestine, the Congo, Afghanistan, Somalia, Lebanon, and Iraq. Was "force of arms" really the most effective means—disregarding any moral concerns over loss of life—for "changing behaviors," eliminating the will to war and promoting the building of civil society? Force may be required; but how and when it is used and by whom becomes critical, and the attainment of classic combat objectives, such as temporally "securing a city," does not necessarily translate into "political" outcomes that Clausewitz saw as the ultimate measure of military success. Although "nation building," "peacekeeping," and policy functions have been disparaged by the civilian leadership of the Pentagon, it is these components of the U.S. force structure that are most in demand.

It is vital that this be appreciated because violence itself seems to be an inescapable human component. From the time of Homeric epics to the present, cycles of violence and retaliation reflect an apparently immutable aspect of human nature. Heroes of all ages seem to be aware of the tragedy and waste of warfare, but are unable to avoid it. But perhaps they simply lacked the information and the understanding, in the same way that complex natural science was imperfectly and metaphorically understood. Now that our world contains weapons of mass destruction that in the future may become available to anyone who wants them, warfare as a means of "deterrence" seems not just questionable but collectively suicidal. In a world where an adversary can surface anywhere, anytime, and has the means to inflict enormous damage through nuclear and biological means, the classic military option increasingly seems untenable. This is especially true in asymmetric conflicts, where the "us versus them" objectification of the enemy that military engagement requires doesn't work. Where the goal is to change people's will to use violence, as the war in Iraq demonstrates, the power of military might is never so great that it can clamp down on all aspects of opposition without destroying the very "intercourse of government and peoples" that is the ultimate objective. Instead, we have to create a circumstance and an environment in which we can explore what we have in common, not what divides us.

Going to war to resolve conflicts need not be the habitual option it has been. If warfare were the single and predominant mode of human collective behavior, it is highly unlikely that we would have evolved the way we have. Fortunately, all human beings possess highly innate abilities for social exchange, and it is this ability to trade with friend and foe that offers the greatest hope for building cooperative and noncoercive situations and institutions. No one knew it better and said it better than the eighteenth-century philosopher and economist Adam Smith, writing in the book for which he is best known, *The Wealth of Nations* (1776):

> Every individual necessarily labors to render the annual revenue of the society as great as he can. He generally indeed neither intends to promote the public interest, nor knows how much he is promoting it. He intends only his own gain, and he is in this, as in many other cases, led by an invisible hand to promote an end which was no part of his intention. By pursuing his own interest he frequently promotes that of the society more effectually than when he really intends to promote it. I have never known much good done by those who affected to trade for the public good.

It is not from the benevolence of the butcher, the brewer, or the
baker, that we expect our dinner, but from their regard to their own
interest.[5]

These often-cited quotations have long been held up by free market advocates to argue that the public and individual interests are best served
by everyone acting in their own narrow self-interest. By this argument, it
is both "rational" and natural for people to maximize their own self-
interest, and in doing so they advance the public good. People can negotiate their self-interest and unleash a process where goods and resources
are efficiently sourced and allocated. The market, in this interpretation,
is not merely efficient: It is morally good.

But Adam Smith also argued for the limits of human self-interest. In
an earlier book, *The Theory of Moral Sentiments* (1759), Smith argued that
there were certain virtues and innate moral sentiments that were essential for civilized society, the rule of law, and the function of fair and free
markets. In this book, individual rights are not seen as absolute. They are
constrained by the individual's ability to have sympathy and constrain
his behavior through "virtue." Indeed, it was these moral sentiments that
mitigated people's other propensity to exploit one another. Human
sympathy—a moral capacity to feel with "exquisite sensibility"—balances
the excesses of self-interest:

How selfish soever man may be supposed, there are evidently some
principles in his nature, which interest him in the fortune of others,
and render their happiness necessary to him, though he derives nothing from it except the pleasure of seeing it. Of this kind is pity or compassion, the emotion which we feel for the misery of others, when we
either see it, or are made to conceive it in a very lively manner. That
we often derive sorrow from the sorrow of others, is a matter of fact too
obvious to require any instances to prove it; for this sentiment, like all
the other original passions of human nature, is by no means confined
to the virtuous and humane, though they perhaps may feel it with the
most exquisite sensibility. The greatest ruffian, the most hardened vio-
lator of the laws of society, is not altogether without it.[6]

Smith argued that a civilized and commercially viable society depended upon the virtues of its citizens, the ability of the individual to assume what he called "self-command":

Concerning the subject of self-command, I shall only observe further, that our admiration for the man who, under the heaviest and most unexpected misfortunes, continues to behave with fortitude and firmness, always supposes that his sensibility to those misfortunes is very great, and such as it requires a very great effort to conquer or command.[7]

Though Smith extolled the value of reason in commercial transactions and deplored the intervention of the state as overly intrusive, such as he had observed in the highly centralized economy of France, he also acknowledged the social cost and injustice of the absence of moral sentiments and attachments. In this quotation, he seems to anticipate the social costs of *too* commercial a culture:

In commercial countries, where the authority of law is always perfectly sufficient to protect the meanest man in the state, the descendants of the same family, having no such motive for keeping together, naturally separate and disperse, as interest or inclination may direct. They soon cease to be of importance to one another; and, in a few generations, not only lose all care about one another, but all remembrance of their common origin, and of the connection which took place among their ancestors. Regard for remote relations becomes, in every country, less and less, according as this state of civilization has been longer and more completely established.[8]

As a leading member of the Enlightenment, Smith separated intellect and reason from emotions and passions, regarding them as two separate spheres. In this respect he was no different than any of his contemporaries, among them David Hume, Thomas Jefferson, Edmund Burke, Adam Ferguson, and Benjamin Franklin. Crucially, he recognized that reason and narrow self-interest were not sufficient for both commerce and civilized society. Rather, Smith understood that underlying the social and commercial order was an innate sense of right and wrong. Such sentiments underpinned laws and markets; it was not the markets that underpinned morality. A noted Smith scholar makes this point in a preface to Smith's *The Theory of Moral Sentiments*:

> Smith took a completely new direction, holding that people are born with a moral sense, just as they have inborn ideas of beauty or harmony. Our conscience tells us what is right and wrong: and that is something innate, not something given us by lawmakers or by rational analysis. And to bolster it we also have a natural fellow-feeling, which Smith calls "sympathy." Between them, these natural senses of conscience and sympathy ensure that human beings can and do live together in orderly and beneficial social organizations.
>
> So our morality is the product of our nature, not our reason. And Smith would go on to argue that the same "invisible hand" created beneficial social patterns out of our economic actions too. *The Theory of Moral Sentiments* establishes a new liberalism, in which social organization is seen as the outcome of human action but not necessarily of human design. Indeed, our unplanned social order is far more complex and functional than anything we could reason out for ourselves (a point which Marxist politicians forgot, to their cost).[9]

Since the 1990s, significant advances in evolutionary biology, brain-imaging technologies, neuroscience, and cross-cultural studies have made it possible to explore with scientific insight the Enlightenment notions of human nature. For at least 300 years, emotions have been considered as irrational "passions"—something from our lower nature, something that had to be curbed and certainly not something that was intelligent. But suddenly the invisible hand of moral sentiments—to use Adam Smith's term—can be tracked and modeled. For the first time, science can help to explain what Adam Smith could only express symbolically: that rational self-interest and moral sentiments are combined in the human brain in ways that are analyzable, and predictive. Human nature, then, is not what we thought it was, any more than Clausewitz's battlefield remains befogged. We now have the technology and insight to see into both.

We can now understand how emotions and reason are interwoven in the human brain. The most recent neuroscientific research shows a strong and unequivocal conclusion that there is no such thing as "pure reason" in human activity.[10] The dichotomy between emotion (irrational) and reason (rational) is no longer scientifically valid. Neuro-economics, for example, is beginning to demonstrate how a combination of social emotions and higher cognitive processes combine to become not just the invisible hand of markets—but other forms of human social activity.

Chapter Five

Human Nature, Language, and Social Networks

THE STEADY STREAM OF RESEARCH FROM THE EVOLUTIONARY SCIENCES and neurosciences means that today's understanding of human nature is becoming a precise experimental science, drawing upon many rigorous disciplines and producing findings that are overturning many strongly held myths about human rationality and motivation. Consequently, these branches of science offer insight into how people naturally trust and govern one another, how they are able to build durable relationships, detect, and respond to cheaters and free riders, and influence the behaviors of their peers without recourse to violence.[1]

Human beings, it is now known, are genetically linked to almost all forms of life. We share 98 percent of our genetic code with the chimpanzee and 60 percent with the fruit fly (*Drosophila*), so we might expect to share some behavioral traits with them. In fact, human behavior is similar to that of many other social species, even to species with which we are not even genetically linked.[2] The explanation for why very similar cooperative strategies and social behaviors emerge in genetically distinct species is intriguing because it suggests that under certain environmental conditions, evolutionarily stable strategies (ESSs) have evolved repeatedly and in parallel in genetically distinct species. These ESSs are strategies of cooperation that are sufficiently stable that it is not in the interest of any party to defect from them. In other words, if any of their membership were to refuse to cooperate, all parties would be worse off.

Evolutionarily stable strategies are independently discovered by different species and are embedded in their respective genomes through trial and error over thousands of generations of evolutionary testing.[3] Certain cooperative ESSs are present in a variety of different social species: harvester ants, ravens, wolves, elephants, whales, bonobos, chimpanzees, and human beings. They appear to function as underlying laws—a kind of social physics—that govern collective behavior and cooperation, independent of any one particular species. Understanding what these laws might be has been the focus of research in evolutionary game theory, multiagent simulations, and models of artificial life.

Human beings, however, are unique in evolutionary history, partly because we have developed certain survival ESSs that no other species has achieved. It is as though we share the basic platform but have constructed some uniquely human expressions on top of it, out of the reach of the harvester ants and the other social species—as far as we know. It is not only important to understand how we are behaviorally similar to many other social species with similar social survival strategies, but also to acknowledge how we are uniquely different. Although the structure and operation of the human brain and limbic systems are similar to their reptilian, mammalian, and primate ancestors, there are new additions in the form of a neocortex, which is unique in its size and functionality. The human brain is composed of a large, ancient "legacy" system, which, like software code, is patched one layer upon another without any apparent design, but it is the frontal cortex that allows us to reason exceptionally.

For many years, anthropologists argued that what made human beings unique was their ability to make tools, with some anthropologists even going so far as to argue that *Homo sapiens* should more correctly be renamed *Homo fabens,* that is, "man the maker" rather than "man the thinker." More recently, it has been argued that it was the "language instinct," a human being's innate and unique ability to create language systems, that differentiates us from all other species. Yet as more and more research becomes available on the linguistic abilities of other species, especially primates, there seems to be no easily identifiable point divid-

ing human linguistic or communicative abilities from those of other primates.[4] This is not to say that humans do not have distinct linguistic capabilities or combinations of capabilities that make human language
distinctive and universal, but that it has proven difficult to identify what
they precisely are—and how they came about.

Now evolutionary psychologists and anthropologists offer a new explanation of the "human difference" that takes into account language
creation, toolmaking, *and* social cooperation. Until the mid-twentieth
century, evolutionary theory tended to look at natural selection as an individual and not a group phenomenon, and regarded competition—the
survival of the individual fittest—not cooperation, as the principal driver
of evolution. In contrast to Darwin's original writings, new theories of
evolution proposed that there was no selection for group traits. That
point of view is in dispute with many evolutionary biologists who argue
that now the evolutionary success of *Homo sapiens* can in large measure
be attributed to its ability to manage complex social relationships. In
other words, the ability of different species to function cooperatively has
tremendous survival value. Those that manage the most complex and
flexible forms of social cooperation enjoy a reproductive advantage.

Robin Dunbar and his colleagues conducted a study of the fossil record of
the brain sizes of hominids that showed that the size of the neocortex—the
part of the brain concerned with thinking and problem solving—increased
with the membership size of the hominid social groups. Dunbar argues that
the ability to coordinate behaviors and manage relationships in groups is
so important that it accounted for the growth of the neocortex not only in
primates but in other mammals as well:

All of our analyses so far had been built on the assumption that the
problem each animal has to face is keeping track of the constantly
changing social world of which it is a part. It needs to know who is in
and who is out, and who is friends with whom, who is the best ally of the
day. In the social turmoil, these things were in a permanent state of flux,
changing almost day-by-day. The animal has to keep track of all these,
constantly updating its social map with each day's new observations.

But there are other possibilities. One is that the relationship between the neocortex size and the group size actually has more to do

with the quality of the relationships involved rather than their quantity. This much is implied by the Machiavellian hypothesis itself, which suggested that the key to understanding brain size evolution in primates lies in the use primates make of their knowledge of other animals.[5]

In his analysis of the human neocortex, Dunbar predicted that the upper limit on the number of different relationships that people can manage is between 150 and 200. His predictions are borne out by the evidence of a variety of social groups: For example, groups as diverse as the Hutterites, the Mormons, the Anglican Church, military units, and Australian aboriginal clans all set an upper limit to their group size at around 150 members. Social groupings above 150–200 members become hierarchical in structure, whereas smaller groups rely upon personal contacts. According to Dunbar, most businesses seem to obey the 150–200 limit:

> Businesses with fewer than 150–200 people can be organized on entirely informal lines, relying on personal contacts between employees to ensure the proper exchange of information. But larger businesses require formal management structures to channel contracts and ensure that each employee knows what he or she is responsible for and whom they should report to.[6]

In contrast, many formal and *impersonal* reporting structures in large organizations are neither transparent nor trusted. Hence, much of the real work within large enterprises is still conducted through informal networks, as one would expect if people's behavior is governed by social protocols that are essentially innate. There is growing neurological and experimental evidence that many of the emotions associated with governing social behavior—shame, pride, anger, guilt, compassion—are also biologically based and characteristic of most mammalian social species, including wolves, and perhaps even vampire bats![7]

So why do we blink our headlights at perfect strangers whom we are unlikely ever to meet? It turns out that such altruism, for example, is not limited to human beings but is typical of many different social species.

Experiments with rhesus monkeys have shown that they will refrain from pulling a chain to deliver food if it delivers an electric shock to other monkeys. This suggests that empathy and reciprocity are not merely ideals, but rather ESSs that seem to be the encoded behaviors of many species. The highly respected neuroscientist Antonio Damasio has argued that social emotions have an identifiable physiology and measurable role in the behavior of the human brain: "Anger, fear, shame, indignation, jealousy, pride, compassion, gratitude, sorrow and joy appear to be part of an overall program of bio-regulation."[8]

One other compelling bit of evidence that social exchange is a universal trait for many mammals and all human societies is a study that compared the ability to detect deceit among Harvard undergraduates and the Shiwiar, an isolated Amazonian tribe of hunter-horticulturalists.[9] If the ability to identify cheating were the product of culture or economic development, clear differences in this competence would be discernible. But the study found that "cheater detection reasoning" was present in all of the developed and developing countries included in the study. The Shiwiar were just as adept at identifying a con as the Harvard grads.

This is significant because according to early research, cheater detection—along with our ability to recognize facial expressions, intentions, and emotions, our ability to make friends, our sense of loyalty and protectiveness, our ability to detect injustice, calculate our own self-interest, create a new language, and so on—has been identified as a specialized brain function. This finding by John Tooby and Leda Cosmides on cheater detection, however, has been challenged by subsequent research. However the capacity to detect cheaters is acquired, it nonetheless seems to be a specialized and universal competence of all peoples. If the regions of the brain that carry out these functions are injured, no other competencies are impeded—only these highly specific capabilities.[10]

This suggests that natural selection has indeed played a role in the gradual development of our specialized cognitive capabilities for enacting social exchange. Our competencies for social exchange (cheater detection, trust building, a sense of fairness, reciprocity, retribution) appear to be highly specialized and innate cognitive and emotional operations, rather than products of a general intelligence. The evidence from hunter-gatherer archaeology is that hominids have carried on social exchange for at least 2 million years. The history of cultures shows that social exchange *is* human history.[11]

Leda Cosmides and John Tooby were the first among a number of evolutionary sociologists and psychologists to have argued that social exchange algorithms, that is, the ability to reason about social contracts, are the innate competencies that enable massed humans to function as communities.[12] Such algorithms include a person's sense of justice and guilt, social reciprocity, gift giving, and an ability to interpret social cues:[13]

> This mutual provisioning of benefits, each conditional on the others' compliance, is rare in the animal kingdom. Social exchange cannot be generated by a simple general learning mechanism, such as classical or operant conditioning. . . . This strongly suggests that engaging in social exchange requires specific cognitive machinery, which some species have and others lack.[14]

This same point is echoed by Dunbar in discussing brain evolution when he argues that the "mind doesn't work like an all-purpose computer" but rather "consists of a number of separate modules, each designed to do a particular task."[15]

The evolution of equivalent brain circuitry has meant that we are in effect, of a common mind. During the 1990s, research by Giacomo Rizzolatti, Leonardo Fogassi, and Vittorio Gallese on macaque monkeys revealed that a certain type of neuron in the monkey's inferior frontal cortex responded when the monkey observed another macaque grasping and picking up objects.[16] Such neurons mirrored the actions of other monkeys. Similar neurons have been found in the Broca's area of the human frontal cortex (an area primarily associated with language), which makes it possible for humans to infer the intentions of other humans. According to the cognitive linguist George Lakoff:

> [W]e know from psychology professor Paul Ekman's research that configurations of facial muscles express certain emotions. Presumably, our mirror neurons fire when we see the same configurations of facial muscles on someone else that our facial muscles would make. And

that firing can activate our own emotional centers. In short, that allows us to empathize—to feel someone else's pain or joy . . . We have evolved to be empathetic (via mirror neurons and connections to the emotional centers of the brain) and to be connected to the world (via canonical neurons). Empathy and connection to the other and to the physical environment are central aspects of human nature![17]

Arguing about whether human social exchange behavior is selfish or altruistic misses the point.[18] We behave the way we do because it has survival value. The neuroscientist Damasio makes this point:

The biological reality of self-preservation leads to virtue because in our inalienable need to maintain ourselves we must, of necessity, help preserve others. If we fail to do so, we perish and are thus violating the foundational principle, and relinquishing the virtue that lies in self-preservation. The secondary foundation of virtue then is the reality of a social structure and the presence of other living organisms in a complex system of interdependence with our own organism.[19]

But the unique human evolutionary trait is not just a highly proficient form of social organization or the ability to manage complex social relationships. It is also the capacity to symbolize, that is, to construct new systems of meaning out of arbitrary terms, thereby separating the representation of a thing from the thing itself.[20] For example, the sound of some words can mimic the sound of the thing that they are referring to, such as *growl* and *bark*, but in most cases, the sound or the textual representation bears no resemblance to the thing referred to. It is totally arbitrary; neither the spoken nor the written word *horse*, for instance, sounds or looks like an equine animal. Even when humans use ideographics, as in hieroglyphic languages, they can communicate highly malleable ideas about their reality and experiences.[21] Steven Pinker[22] and Noam Chomsky[23] have argued that language is the artifact of an inherent language instinct. It seems likely that language began as a social coordination capability, a kind of rudimentary "handshake" that enabled multiple participants to create conventions for sharing information and coordinating their behaviors. Whereas many computational and generative linguists have treated language as a logical system for transmitting "well formed propositions," in effect, what is called its *depth structure*, the great bulk of linguistic apparatus—words, prosody, voice, modals, deixis, discourse, and thematic devices—are concerned with expressing social roles and relationships through variations in "surface structure," a fact not lost on Dunbar:

> We do seem to use language in establishing and servicing our relationships. Could it be that language evolved as a kind of vocal grooming to allow us to bond larger groups than was possible using the conventional primate mechanism of physical grooming? . . . If conversation serves the same function as grooming, then modern humans can at least "groom" with several others simultaneously. A second is that language allows us to exchange information over a wider network of individuals than is possible for monkeys and apes. If the main function of grooming for monkeys and apes is to build up trust and personal knowledge of allies, then language has an added advantage. It allows you to say a great deal about yourself, your likes and dislikes, the kind of person you are; it also allows you to convey in numerous subtle ways something about your reliability as a friend and ally.[24]

Many social species have what evolutionary biologists call assessment protocols, that is, rules for evaluating the threat of a predator, the strength of a competitor, or the health of a potential mate. In this respect, human beings are no different from other species in that we use both innate and socially learned assessment protocols to evaluate risks and opportunities. However, human beings are unique among all species in that we can construct new and arbitrarily complex conventions for coordinating the interactions between members of large groups. What separates humans from all other animals is an ability to extract a symbolic representation from a set of physical interactions and then give this symbolic representation its own social reality that can direct and orient behaviors independent of the physical objects or actions that gave rise to it in the first place. The most compelling examples of this are religious and shamanistic practices and rituals such as the "Eucharist," the mass, or an initiation ceremony whereby conventional objects define new realities and roles. This is what the noted philosopher and linguist John Searle sees as the critical function of language: the competency to arbitrarily construct what he calls *social* and *institutional* realities out of social and institutional facts. He contrasts "brute facts," such as the fact that the earth is 93 million miles from the sun, from "institutional facts," the fact that I am a citizen of the United States. Social facts are any facts involving two or more agents who have what he calls collective intentionality, such as animals hunting together or birds cooperating in building a nest. Presumably most so-called social insects such as ants and bees manifest collective intentions and have social facts:

> Human beings have a remarkable ability that enables them to get beyond mere social facts to institutional facts. Humans engage in more than just sheer physical cooperation; they also talk together, own property, get married, form governments, and so on.[25]

In order to illustrate his point about how institutional facts and realities arise out of linguistic abilities to symbolize human interactions, Searle cites the example of money. He argues that originally, currency entailed the negotiated exchange of objects of inherent comparable value—a barter system that was wedded to the inherent value of the physical object. The second kind of money was "contract money," which consists of contracts to pay the bearer with something valuable on demand. This entailed the exchange of valuable commodities such as gold and silver whose value was more "imposed," to use Searle's term, than intrinsic. Instead of exchanging objects that were highly cumbersome and whose comparable values were tedious to compute—100 bales of hay for one sheep, say—precious coins representing the value of the objects were used. And then, as the transport of these coins became cumbersome, another layer of abstraction was added, paper currency, which was a contract to redeem the face value of the paper currency with a tangible, precious metal. Next, "fiat currency" emerged, another invention of convenience and efficiency. This unit of exchange was not redeemable, but simply declared by an issuing body to be a currency. Just recently, there has been a further innovation in efficiency and convenience, the further abstraction and virtualization of money: digital currency, which is no more than 0 and 1 substitution symbols about the status of the relationship between agents to a transaction. Today, one can go online and transfer money in and out of one's bank account, secure a mortgage, or purchase an automobile without having to interact with a human being or transfer any physical object. Here, no physical object has to be redeemed at all, as the "social reality" is captured in the digital representation.

Evolutionary language theorists assert that language and syntax may have arisen as a means to stabilize social communications and render them less ambiguous. These theorists explore the ways a number of interacting agents might come up with a language that has the expressive powers of human language. For them, explanation entails being able to replicate the evolution of a human language from a minimum set of rules that characterize relatively simple social interactions. The elementary exchange rules are similar to those that Adam Smith identified as mankind's innate moral sentiments of empathy, self-command, and the predilection to bicker, barter, and exchange—governed by those same emotions that we share with the wolves and the bats. So is it possible that these innate moral sentiments not only gave rise to markets, but also to language as well? Some evolutionary game theorists argue very convincingly that when all members of a group have coincident interests and exhibit innate traits of cooperation, human language can naturally emerge. But what happens if people are not always cooperative and do not share common interests, and are, like the figure of Adam Smith's *The Wealth of Nations*, self-interested? Could language naturally emerge under these conditions?

The evolutionary biologist Carl Bergstrom believes so. He has argued that human language could have evolved as a highly efficient system that did not require full cooperation. He then makes a very significant point about the benefit conferred by language precisely when there is not full cooperation between the speakers, where there is doubt about reputation or trustworthiness. Language is a particularly useful tool, for both speakers, when the relationship between them is not collaborative but doubtful:

One reason to suspect that language may have initially evolved to use in coincident interest situations is that individual reputations—in which individuals become known as liars or as good sources of information—

may provide an important "cost" to deception in human communication. While reputations can emerge even without communal "discussion" of an individual's reliability, language certainly facilitates the spread of reputations by allowing individuals to share information about others' reliability.[26]

In this scenario, language allows us to assess honesty, because it makes it possible to communicate detailed signals about the reputation of the speaker. It is precisely because language allows one person to evaluate another who is not reliably cooperative that it is such an evolutionary asset; it commands cooperation even when there is no established basis for trust. Language allows people to share the histories of their experiences and to comment on the accuracy and value of what is communicated. Given that people are aware of the fact that the value and truthfulness of what they say might be reported upon, they can be highly motivated to be honest. As individuals develop reputations for honesty and usefulness, these reputations persist and function much like "social currencies" by giving them social standing and access to resources. No top-down governance mechanism is required, only the "invisible hand" of the social exchange value of an individual's reputation. All languages have built into them highly sophisticated mechanisms for communicating social standing, intimacy, mood, intention, approval, disapproval, and social emotions that can be highly effective means for invoking and enforcing social norms. Hence, languages have elaborate means for signaling and enforcing social reputations.

For much of the public, and this includes many prominent linguists, the notion that anything as complex and uniquely human as language could have evolved from simple rules of social interaction is preposterous. For them, such evolutionary arguments are reductive and, like arguments about the evolution of the eye and other complex organs, unconvincing. Indeed, full recombinant linguistic abilities are unique to *Homo sapiens* and are therefore seen by some as the characteristic that elevates us above all other species. It is a position with deep emotional roots, bearing on how we define and value ourselves, and consequently, not easily relinquished. Language is, for some, at the core of our identity as a species, and as individuals.

But others are not convinced that language is inherently human. John H. Holland, father of genetic algorithms, and his Chinese colleague Tao Gong[27] are conducting research to see whether it is possible to computationally evolve complex, human-like languages from simple rules. This work is in its early stages, but the initial results from such simulations and the experiments of evolutionary biologists are very encouraging. In the case of Holland and Gong's research, the intent was to simulate the emergence of a simple language from a proto-language that lacked any grammatical or logical properties.

John Searle and anthropologist Terrence Deacon contend that this unique human ability to construct social realities that result in highly sophisticated institutions is based upon some relatively simple rules that depend on language. Consistent with the arguments made by John Holland, Stuart Kaufman, Stephen Wolfram,[28] and other major figures in the complexity sciences, highly complex behaviors can come from the repeated application of simple rules. Languages, like biological systems, are always looking for ways to be more efficient. Biological systems adapt to conserve energy; languages conserve memory and communicative efficiency. Hence, language is always looking for opportunities to condense and simplify; terms get contracted when there is little risk of ambiguity and the thing or event being referenced is sufficiently stable or repeated that it can be given a new name. What may start out as a complex compound term—such as *automobile* or *horseless carriage* becomes an *auto* or a *car*. Moreover, as new terms are created, they still preserve the referential context of the older term, that is, the object is still the same, but the key distinguishing and salient features are different. For example, when it is no longer salient that the vehicle is self-propelled or that it is not pulled by a horse, then the complex term becomes condensed into a simple term—*auto* or *car*.

For Searle, a distinctive power of human language is to invent new social institutions.[29] He uses the example of a stone wall. Once a group of people has come together to build the wall, the idea of it remains even after it decays and all that is left is a line of sunken stones in the earth. This line is still acknowledged as a boundary: The act of naming it memorializes the function; the wall remains all the while that it is still referred to as a wall, irrespective of whether it exists as a meaningful physical obstacle. It is, in short, a living metaphor. Language makes it possible for the words or phrase describing the line of stones to count as a barrier and perform an analogous function in the social sphere. In other words, the line of stones, and the terms to describe the line of stones, replace the physical barrier for a range of social interactions. In effect, there has been a substitution of a symbolic relationship for a physical relationship. Over time, this symbolic relationship takes on a life of its own, independent of the original physical objects.

Another telling example is the use of tally sticks during the thirteenth century as receipts for payments.[30] When a payment was completed, the stick was split down its length and the larger part—the stock—was issued as a receipt, while the smaller part was kept by the Exchequer. Thus was born the first "stock exchange." Though the intent has been preserved throughout the centuries, the method by which value was created and protected has changed completely. But perhaps the most compelling example remains that of money itself. How did it evolve from "commodity money," which had inherent exchange value to "contract money," which "represented" exchange value through a contract to pay the bearer something of value upon demand, to "fiat money," which has neither inherent value nor contract value, only declared or perceived value. If fiat money were no longer perceived to have value—that is, if it could not be exchanged—it would cease to have any value. Such is also true of digital money—bank accounts, credit cards, stock portfolios. What gives them value is the efficacy and credibility of the financial institutions in enabling trade and economic exchange. Given that they have no inherent physical value, they are only as good as they are perceived to be. Hence, they are complete social constructions.

Searle makes the point that people not only have economic relationships, but institutional and social relationships as well—all an outgrowth of our ability to construct institutional realities within language:

> I have *money* earned as an *employee of the state of California*, and I have it in my *bank account*, which I use to pay *my state and federal taxes* as well the *bills* owing to the *gas and electric companies* and to the *contractor of my credit cards*.[31]

Notice that all the words that are italicized are not real in any physical sense, but rather social instructions constructed, expressed, and controlled through language. This is how Searle believes social institutions come into being. This process of substitution and layering within language makes it possible to add new kinds of salient knowledge to things that themselves are changing and evolving. Searle calls this the XYC rule, meaning that X can substitute for Y in context C. So in the case of the evolution of money, this rule says that a new term, "paper money," can substitute—that is, be treated the same, as an old term, for example, "coinage," in the social context of currency exchange. Searle argues that this process is responsible for the creation of "institutional structures such as governments, armies, universities, banks, and so on, and even such general institutions as private property, marriage, and political power."[32] Without this symbolic capability of language, Searle believes that there would be no human culture or social institutions:

> I believe that language is the fundamental human institution in the sense that other institutions such as money, government, private property, marriage, and games require language, or at least language-like forms of symbolism, in a way that language does not require other institutions for its existence.[33]

Terrence Deacon makes a related point, but from the vantage point of an anthropologist who has studied the evolution of language and the brain over a 2-million-year period:

> All symbolizing hominids are linked via a common pool of symbolic information, one that is as inaccessible to other species as are human genes. We are all heirs of symbolic forms that were passed down from one generation to the next, from one group to another, forming a single unbroken tradition. We derive all our symbolic "traits" from this common pool and contribute to its promulgation. Being a part of this symbolic information lineage is in many respects a more diagnostic trait for "humanness" than any physical trait.[34]

The XYC rule is intriguing because it hints at an explanation for how new layers of social organization naturally emerge and take on lives of their own. Searle's example of the evolution of money is only one of many social-institutional examples, such as the institutions of marriage and property rights, which began as one set of relationships and evolved over time to become something quite different. For example, marriage in early European societies, as it was for many societies throughout the world and is still today in many instances, was a social mechanism for preserving, securing, and acquiring property rights for a kinship group. It had very little to do with contemporary notions of marriage, where individual choices are based upon romantic attachment. This capacity to generate emergent layers of organization appears to be a capability unique to human beings and may underlie what some characterize as the "language instinct," the ability to generate an infinite number of sentences from a finite set of rules.

One capability that is both essential and challenging for human beings is how to communicate and infer intentions. According to Robin Dunbar and his colleagues, this requires having a "Theory of Mind" (ToM) shared with those with whom one is communicating.[35] Intention often is not literally expressed, but in many cases has to be inferred. One has to get in the "shoes" of people one deals with and try to see the world through their eyes, their histories and interests. It is a kind of mind reading. In short, to effectively, and socially understand and communicate with others requires being able to empathize with them. Like Searle, Dunbar recognizes that inferring complex intentions, like understanding complex social-institutional facts and relationships, entails being able to understand on more than one level. He argues that although primates cannot mentally process more than two levels of intentionality, human beings can comfortably manage up to five. In order to test this theory, Dunbar constructed theory of mind experiments to see how many levels of "embedded intention" people could understand. Subjects were asked to unravel up to six levels of nested intention:

Peter believes (1) that Jane thinks (2) Sally wants (3) Peter to suppose (4) that Jane intends (5) Sally to believe (6) that her ball is under the cushion.[36]

Most subjects can handle up to five levels and then fail after that. While this example is contrived and artificial, the ability to infer social intention, especially emotions related to those intentions, is a critical social skill. And these can be quite complex, as Dunbar's example from Shakespeare's *Othello* illustrates:

> In writing *Othello,* he intended (1) that his audience realize (2) that the eponymous moor believed (3) that his servant Iago was being honest when he claimed to know (4) that his beloved Desdemona loved (5) Cassio.[37]

In many of his plays, Shakespeare showed how the inability of people to correctly infer complex social relationships and intentions was the root cause of much misunderstanding and eventual tragedy. The research findings by George Miller over forty years ago that there was an upper limit to the number of different distinct digits or layers that human beings could retain in memory may point to an Achilles heel of human social cognition. Due to the difficulty and cost in calculating and communicating complex multilayered social intentions and relationships, human beings tend to trust the groups they know best and hence develop strong "in-group" biases.[38] People naturally trust and gravitate toward those they have grown up with or with whom they share common cultural and religious traditions.

It is in this failure of people to process social signals and correctly infer intention that the importance of a shared theory of mind becomes most evident. Dunbar makes this point in discussing the pathology of autistic children:

> The failure to pass ToM tasks even in adulthood has a number of implications for autistic individuals' social lives. Because they lack ToM, autistic children do not lie (or at least cannot lie convincingly) and they do not engage in pretend play. They do not understand what is means to pretend that a doll is alive and might be hungry or sad. They take the world exactly as it comes. . . . An instruction like "Pull the door behind you when you go out" will be taken to mean exactly what its says—remove the door from the hinges and drag it behind you.[39]

Language communicates intent and is both the product and the instrument of highly creative, dynamic, and social processes. The English language, for example, has two "registers" or vocabularies: a low register that is essentially the colloquial use of everyday terms that are "under-specified," and a high register often made of Latinate terms that are technical and highly specified.[40] The concept of "register" is based upon the classical notion of social decorum, whereby certain levels of usage are considered appropriate (or inappropriate) to particular topics and social situations.[41] The higher the register is, the more formal and prescriptive the term is. The register moves from slang and colloquial interpretations up to scientific and technical interpretations—which are the most "impersonal" and highly specified.

The following table contains examples of high and low register terms for "mad" behavior. The higher-register terms distinguish a dimension of the *type* of mad behavior (a kind of diagnostic distinction), whereas the lower-register terms reflect a kind social acceptance or distancing distinction, that is, the extent of the social anomaly. The higher register functions on rational distinctions—like the frontal cortex—whereas the lower register evokes emotional reactions as if it were influenced by the limbic system.

Often, in an attempt to be more precise and therefore less subject to misinterpretation, people adopt the high register in the mistaken assumption that the more specified a term is, the better communicative intent is conveyed.

In fact, more often the more effective and reliable course is to use low-register terms to resolve ambiguity and communicate intent. Low-register

Table 1 High and Low Register Terms for "Mad" Behavior References

High Register Terms	Low Register Terms
Melancholic	Demented
Hypochondriac	Insane
Catatonic	Mad
Manic	Mental
Schizoid	Bonkers
Non compos mentis	Cuckoo
Schizophrenic	Loony
Psychotic	Crazy
Neurotic	Nuts

terms provide signals, which encourage the recipient to respond imaginatively, whereas high-register terms connote literal observance of a rule or instruction. People can infer intent from a low-register signal because over tens of thousands of years they have evolved the ability to construct and confirm "common theories of mind" through shared experiences. Even more surprising is that in order to be convincing and have someone agree with or accept your proposal, low-register communications are essential. One would think that by making a rational, high-register argument, the rational actor would hear the logic of an argument and be convinced. But evidently, the willingness to accept new information or change one's mind is regulated not by the rational language system, but by the low-register emotive language system in which rhythm, voice, meter, tone, and inflection are paramount. It is argued by some, including evolutionary psychologists such as Steven Mithen and Alison Wray,[42] that there is an emotive language system that evolved from music that is most influential in shaping opinions and emotions. Rather than there being a single language system that is generative and compositional in a purely grammatical sense, there may be two complementary language systems: one that is grammatical and logical, and one that is emotive that relies upon emotionally charged phrases to convey emphasis and significance. Hence, we have the adage that if you want to sell a product of any kind or convince an audience, you have to tell a good story where the narrative contains the right combination, progression, and resolution of emotive phrases. Contrary to the practice of large bureaucracies that adopt a version of emotionally denuded language in order to seem credible and objective, really convincing communication comes through the use of narratives and accepted formulas. Such narratives make communication easier and more credible in synchronizing intentions and developing empathy. Or, put another way, I'm much more likely to agree with you if I like the sound of what you're saying.

What language allows is a short cut to trust. I am prepared to believe you on the basis of your words (and expressions)—you don't have to lay out concrete proof each time. I might even believe you even though I've never met you before, on the basis of what my friend, whom I've trusted for years, has told me about you. In the same way, we accept the language-based social institutions of invisible money. When fully appreciated, there may be ways to create new types of social technologies that build upon this capability. If we are naturally inclined to evolve new kinds of social institutions, as Searle has argued, and have over the last few centuries learned to create powerful forms of new kinds of financial institutions, then it may just be a matter of time before we are able to design and evolve more effective and trusted social institutions.

Then, just as it was once important to evolve reliable methods for assessing and managing financial risk before accepting symbolic currency, so it will be important to assess and manage social risk. The ability to correctly evaluate the quality of a social relationship is a precondition for building trusted social institutions. Trust is not an abstract moral virtue, nor can it be imposed by one person or institution on another. It is a network property—a by-product of the quality of interactions between parties—because it can only exist as a consequence of mutual expectations being fulfilled.[43] Trust requires measurement, feedback, and accountability. In most social networks, the consequences of low trust are high transaction costs, that is, constant monitoring, negotiation, bickering, and dispute resolution. For example, where there is little trust, there are rates of high "defection" and free riding, and hence, a need to enforce breaches, create alternatives, or punish offenders. The military is well aware of this, especially among their elite units, where peer trust is absolutely essential to achieve any kind of unit cohesion and effectiveness. In successful elite units, the "Rambos" and the individuals rated low in trustworthiness are quickly identified and culled from the group. If any members of a unit find that they have not been receiving their normal number of "grooming contacts," they can correctly infer this as a rebuke, a signal that they will need to re-earn the group's interest and trust.[44] The ability to build and leverage trust among members of a group builds *social capital* and significantly reduces transaction costs. For example, an organization with low-trust membership might have to invoke explicit legalistic methods where the intentions of the parties cannot be reliably inferred or depended upon. But because high-trust social networks are mutually interdependent, with all the parties having a common stake and a shared theory of mind, they require low coordination and low enforcement costs.[45]

As biological, evolutionary, and neurological sciences are rapidly developing a scientific and rigorous understanding of how people think, feel, interact, and conduct themselves as social beings, scientific knowledge is replacing speculation and superstition. New forms of intervention—genetic, cognitive, pharmaceutical, and social technological—are beginning to greatly enhance our ability to create more effective social organizations and institutions. Instead of relying on moral judgments and invocations, we now have scientific insight into learning styles and disabilities, personality traits, and emotional states and this has made education, training, and management practices much more efficient and effective. Our brain and our emotions are no longer an impenetrable black box. The mapping has begun. Fields such as neuro-economics and evolutionary psychology are reshaping our understanding of human nature and revealing the neuroscientific and evolutionary significance of reputation, trust, social signaling, and risk-sharing behaviors. Eventually, these sciences will inform the construction of more effective, efficient, and trusted social and economic institutions. Already, behavioral and neuroscience analyses are being used to develop powerful predictors of human financial and marketing behaviors to mitigate risk. This trend will only get stronger and involve other areas such as capacities for trust and cooperation. There is some urgency in our need to embrace this opportunity. Such is the speed of change in our world that we may not be able to adapt quickly enough without the support of technology. Evolution, after all, usually takes place over millennia; we may not want to wait that long.

In contrast to well-entrenched economic and organizational models that operate on the assumption that human beings are selfish, individualistic rational actors, the new sciences are showing that human beings are also innately cooperative, with highly evolved and highly adaptive strategies of collaboration, trust, and reciprocity. By understanding how such innate human social exchange competencies function, it becomes possible to design and implement the next generation of post-Enlightenment institutions. Based on the new understanding of how human trust functions in social groups, these organizations should be able to accommodate anywhere from small groups of 150 members to millions of members, creating conditions that nurture rapid learning and easy adaptation to change.

Chapter Six

A New View
of Human Nature

ONE HUNDRED AND NINETY-SEVEN THOUSAND OF HUMANKIND'S
200,000 years on earth have been spent surviving the raw challenges of
nature: disease, famine, climate, natural disasters, and fellow predators.
The varied colorations, shapes, weights, and immune systems of the races
of mankind reflect 200,000 years of struggle and opportunistic adaptations. A mere 60,000 years ago, the continued survival of *Homo sapiens*
was in extreme jeopardy, dependent upon the luck and pluck of just 200
ancestors.[1] Due to extreme drought, these few survivors traveled along
the coast of Africa to eventually repopulate the entire planet with their
offspring. Only within the last 400 years—just one-fourth of 1 percent of
the human record—has the global population of humankind exceeded
500 million. Until the Enlightenment, population levels ebbed and
flowed. Nature was still the unconquered adversary, forever curbing human hubris and blindly enforcing its rules of fitness and survival. Encoded
in our bodies, brains, and cultures is this 200,000-year survival struggle.

Then something happened, as dramatic, pervasive, and irreversible as
the Cambrian Explosion 500 million years ago. Neither our species nor
the planet have been the same since. Science and technology emerged in
the West, wresting control away from nature and depriving it of its

culling and governing powers. Nature became subject to the whims and aspirations of a species, eager for abundance, comfort, health, control, recognition, and longevity. Within the last 200 years, this trend has accelerated exponentially in scope and depth. It is a transformative event in the life of a planet.

The engine of this transformation is not the product of Mother Nature, but her offspring, human nature. Humankind has invented new flora and fauna, permanently altered the landscape and climate, leveled rain forests, altered the earth's atmosphere, and triggered some of the most extensive extinctions of species in the planet's history.

Humanity has been propelled into a role of ecological responsibility for which it is ill prepared. In geological time, it has occurred in a mere blink of an eye: One moment everything was familiar; the next, the world had utterly and irreversibly changed. We have, through our own inventiveness, rapidly changed our circumstances. Yet we have failed to adapt our own evolutionary survival strategies to match the world that we have created. We have paid too little attention to our collective identity—our shared human nature—in the West for the last 250 years, preferring instead to let an extreme form of individualism run rampant.

So human nature remains largely a mystery to us. What worked out well for the Pleistocene past of 200,000 years ago seems profoundly out of place in a rapidly evolving technological world. Highly adaptive survival mechanisms in low-density, slow-changing environments based upon hunting and gathering and rudimentary agriculture are ill suited to an interconnected global ecosystem and digital culture. So the challenge is not only to understand the mechanics of human nature but to see how they might be redirected and adapted to the realities of the present environment.[2]

Yet is it really possible, or even desirable to study human nature the way we study the physical, botanical, and biological worlds and the behavior of other animals? Can human thoughts, emotions, aspirations, intentions, and values be reduced to the same scientific laws that describe inanimate physical and chemical forces, the behavior of bacteria and chimpanzees?

Even among the scientifically venturesome, there can be a visceral discomfort in equating human behavior with that of other life forms. One hundred and forty-five years after the epochal and precedent-setting debates between Thomas Huxley and Bishop Samuel Wilberforce over the theory of evolution, the controversy over human uniqueness and irreducibility still persists. Antipathies are still as strong today as then. Attacks by both the Left and the Right on any form of biological and evolutionary explanation of human social behavior testifies to the immediacy and combustibility of these issues.

What is especially disturbing to some is the notion that much of human social activity is neither unique, nor rational, nor conscious, but rather subject to the same physical and biological principles that govern all forms of life. To suggest that there is a science of human nature is in many quarters to cross a line, to trespass on some sacred ground. Western religious traditions have set "Man" apart from "Nature," giving him "dominion" over nature. But science has increasingly demonstrated our interdependency and direct lineage to all forms of life. The argument for human exceptionalism appears to be weakened with each significant scientific advance in genetics and neuroscience.

But scientific explanation does not have to be at the expense of humanism; by attempting to quantify and explain aspects of ourselves, we don't have to be reduced to those aspects. Adam Smith's work is especially relevant in this respect. He was a philosopher—a seeker after truth—and an economist in an age when the tools of economic measurement were primitive compared to today's. Perhaps because the tools were crude, he never lost sight of the larger issues. As a result, the story he told about human nature and culture was expressed in terms not overburdened with technical detail. It's a story that continues to resonate. Not only did he anticipate many of the key ideas of neuroscience and evolutionary theory, he also fashioned a vocabulary and framework that is still meaningful. His notion of the "invisible hand" not only continues to be intuitively compelling but has become a foundational narrative in the West to show how we see ourselves. His theory of moral sentiments as "moral instincts" anticipated Darwin's writings on instinct and emotion, as well as the discovery of "social emotions" by evolutionary psychologists and neuroscientists in the twenty-first century.

Because there was no way in the eighteenth century to measure "moral sentiments" or the "invisible hand" of natural regulation, the accounts of Adam Smith and his contemporaries were speculative and "pre-scientific."

Now, though, science is opening up the human brain for public inspection. The mechanisms and pathways of "moral sentiments" can be measured, and identified, as parts of the brain with known behaviors. We need not rely upon the useful "fiction" of the "state of nature" nor the ideal of the "noble savage." Such inventions can be replaced by exhaustive behavioral studies of primates and cross-cultural studies of highly diverse cultures. Evolutionary biology provides a theoretical basis for understanding why certain types of moral sentiments evolved, how they are triggered, and how they improve or compromise an individual's and group's survival. Given the foundational importance of Smith's thinking for contemporary economic and social institutions, it is not surprising that some of the more innovative work in this field is now being undertaken by a new generation of behavioral, evolutionary, and neuro-economists.

Their work shows that many forms of social change and innovation are not the result of "visible," conscious, large-scale economic forces, policies, geographic factors, or charismatic leaders. They are, instead, often the result of myriad, invisible, and unintended exchanges of contending interests and relationships. Among these contending, unconscious quests are urges to establish trust, combat fears, assert dominance, and build reputation, and they are often more important than other conscious pursuits in shaping outcomes, whether in business or government.

The shift in perspective is similar to the one that occurred following the discovery of bacteria and microorganisms as the source of disease. Until the invention of the microscope by Anthony van Leeuwenhoek in 1683, illness was thought to have been caused by an imbalance in the four humors—yellow bile, black bile, phlegm, and blood. It was not possible to posit a modern theory of disease and contagion until people could actually see the swimming microbes. The electron microscope and molecular biology were necessary to understand the genetic underpinnings of certain forms of disease and thereby provide for a whole new class of treatments. In each phase in the progression of medical knowledge and treatment, it was necessary to go beyond surface descriptions and plunge into the depths and complexities of processes that were initially invisible. The forces responsible for the transformation of societies remain largely "invisible" to most people, but new scientific insights and new technologies are beginning to show how they work. One story from the Enlightenment, arguably the modern birthplace of science, provides a classic case study of a social transformation whose roots were once baffling but are now becoming visible.

Throughout human history there have been many powerful and successful cultures—Chinese, Japanese, Indian, Hellenic, Persian, Egyptian, and Ottoman. And yet, it can be argued, none of them has had the enduring effect of the Enlightenment, and in particular the Scottish Enlightenment, in laying the foundation for modern scientific, social, economic, and political institutions. In a period of seventy-five years, Scottish metropolitan society was transformed: an intolerant, hierarchical, and dogmatic culture became a model for open inquiry, skepticism, and democratic participation. A traditional, feudal society became not only the progenitor of contemporary, democratic institutions, but also brought a radically different understanding of human nature and the role of authority.

Prior to 1720, Edinburgh, situated on a monumental sacred rock, was a provincial town lacking any industrial base. It was noted more for its stench and drunken barristers than for any consequential public architecture. Sewers were few and civic order minimal. The preferred way to resolve differences was with the fist and sword, on the streets and in the taverns. At ten o'clock in the evening, it was the custom of each household to pour "its waste down the street, where it lay all night till scavengers came at first light to collect it. Citizens burned sheets of brown paper to neutralize the smell."[3]

Yet in just fifty years, Edinburgh had undergone an astonishing transformation from a filthy, alcoholic, poor, backwater, quarrelsome parochial city of 40,000 into the "Athens of Europe," lauded for its civic society, fashion, good conversation, and learning. Adam Smith, David Hume, and fellow Enlightenment peers were not only products of this transformation, they were its most eloquent advocates.

It is hard to appreciate how radical a transformation the Scottish Enlightenment was. Adam Smith's famous insight in 1776 that wealth creation was guided not by a single authority, not God, not a monarch, not even human intention, but "by an invisible hand to promote an end which was no part of his intention" would have been a capital offense just seventy-nine years earlier. This indeed happened on January 8, 1692, to Thomas Aikenhead, then only eighteen years old, who was hanged for simply questioning the literal truth of the Bible.

At that time in Scotland's history, no form of religious dissent was tolerated. All the powers for criminal prosecution were concentrated in the hands of a single lord advocate, who could imprison anyone at will. Power was centralized and hierarchical. After three failed harvests and decades of extreme poverty, the standard of living of the Scottish Highlanders was below that even of the Miami Indians of Ohio.[4] There was constant warfare between the Jacobites, who supported a traditional Catholic Scotland, and the Presbyterian Protestants, who challenged the authority of the church hierarchy. The Jacobites were an artifact of the Middle Ages: feudal, honor-based clans, parochial and pastoral. The Presbyterians, on the other hand, were more urban and secular. Although they had a very severe Calvinist religious code at the beginning of the eighteenth century, they espoused beliefs that were less medieval and more egalitarian—beliefs that would become the social and political foundations of the Scottish Enlightenment.

Until the mid-1700s, the Highland Scots lived by a "culture of honor," typical of many patriarchal and pastoral societies. As cattle and sheep— the principal form of capital in nonurban Scotland—could be easily stolen, Highland men would resolutely respond to threats to their property, person, or reputation with their swords and daggers. The credibility of a man's willingness to enforce his threats and protect his honor was an essential instrument for preserving a social order that had no reliable judiciary or constabulary.

This culture of honor had its roots in ancient Anglo-Saxon traditions that included the use of combat to settle disputes between contending parties. Known as *judicium dei* (the justice of God), combat was seen as a divinely sanctioned means for resolving disputes. Might, it was assumed, would be Right. These habits spanned generations. This mindset is not just limited to traditional pastoral societies but is also found in the American South, where Scottish honor code traditions are still prevalent.[5]

After 1720, Edinburgh began to harvest the fruits of its extensive intellectual climate and the numerous battles it had fought over religious and civil rule. Edinburgh had not only resisted English efforts to impose

Anglican religious reforms, but it had equally resisted divine-right monarchy and the Roman Catholic Stuarts. The Lowland Scots, as exemplified in their Presbyterianism, had a long and distinguished tradition
of resistance to religious and governmental hierarchy: Within a short
period of time, the citizens of Edinburgh awakened to their own unique
identity and began to express their newfound cultural, intellectual, and
political identities. They began to drain their lochs, curtail public duel-
ing, discourage public drunkenness, and build bridges, sewers, public
ways, libraries, cobblestone streets, new squares, and parks. The slovenly
and gaudy styles of the old gave way to a new sense of self and etiquette,
whereby women, once commonly abducted as wenches, were courted
as ladies.

No single factor accounted for the dramatic transformation of Scottish
society. Clearly, the long struggles to break the authority and hierarchy of
the monarchy and the church played a critical role. But at the same time,
this was a time of educational reforms, new freedoms for women, advances in medicine, civic participation, extensive travel, external influ-
ences from the Continent and North America, and a new appreciation
for the sciences. As both centralized political and clerical authority di-
minished in influence, a new secularism took root. Throughout the eighteenth century, Scottish society grew more open, heterogeneous, and
cosmopolitan, and through its international trade and commerce, it came
in contact with different cultures and traditions, thereby engendering
greater tolerance and receptivity to new ideas.

Alongside the new mindset a new kind of authority took root—not of
blind obedience or submission, but based on peer acknowledgment and
rationality. Gone was the need for a higher authority figure in either religious or civic affairs; the special privileges granted to the human proxies
for God and monarch were soon revoked or ignored.

Reason and the physics of nature came to replace theology and divine
intent as the preferred means for explaining natural and human events.
From this perspective, Adam Smith's analysis of market behavior and
moral sentiments as products of our innate nature seems less precocious
and surprising. Nonetheless, what Smith managed to do, better than anyone else at the time, was frame the question about how natural forces
might control and influence both markets and social behavior.

Smith saw a vibrant balance between two innate moral instincts, that for self-regard and self-preservation, on the one hand, and that for reciprocity and the common good on the other. Smith understood these as complementary moral instincts governed not by conscious rationality but unconsciously triggered by collective self-regulatory mechanisms, such as manners, "sentiments, shared norms, and a sense of the 'common stock.'"

Like Darwin after him, Smith used the example of breeds of dog to contrast with human collaborative ability:

> The strength of the mastiff is not in the least supported either by the swiftness of the greyhound, or the sagacity of the spaniel, or by the docility of the shepherd's dog. The effect of those different geniuses and talents, for want of the power or disposition to barter and exchange, cannot be brought into a common stock, and do not in the least contribute to the better accommodation and convenience of the species. Each animal is still obliged to support and defend itself, separately and independently, and derives no sort of advantage from the variety of talents with which nature has distinguished its fellows. Among men, on the contrary, the most dissimilar geniuses are of use to one another; the different produces of their respective talents, by the general disposition to truck, barter, and exchange, being brought, as it were, into a common stock, where every man may purchase whatever part of the produce of the other men's talents has occasion for.[6]

Smith, like other contemporary Enlightenment thinkers such as Locke, Rousseau, and Hume, struggled to find a way of describing mankind in a natural state independent of the circumstances of history and culture. Lacking a theory of evolution, they had no way of explaining why people had certain moral sentiments.

Humankind did not, of course, evolve in a vacuum. What Adam Smith and his contemporaries hadn't grasped is the notion that human beings are born incomplete. There is a deep evolutionary expectation that as humans interact with other human beings and their environment, certain developmental responses are triggered. Some are predetermined and some are not. Evolution counts on the external world to help carry the burden of development and differentiation—what the philosopher and biologist

Andy Clark calls the "scaffolding."[7] Clark makes the point that every genome depends upon external factors to activate developmental processes,
because there is insufficient information in a genome to specify the full
complexity of a mature organism like a human being.[8] DNA alone cannot
fully specify all the detail needed for the full development of a human being. So evolution makes extensive use of regularities in the environment—
the scaffolding—to provide the requisite information to complete the
growth of a full human being. Change the scaffolding and you change
the human being. There is no prototype of human nature and never has
been. Life coevolves with its environment, with nature and nurture each
reflecting and embedding the other.

During the first 197,000 years of human history, humankind functioned
in small hunting-and-gathering bands. Early human society was not unlike primate society. We can therefore ask: What clues are there in primate society to explain how the human might first have behaved socially?

Primates show a mixture of self-interested behavior and genuinely
collaborative traits.[9] They can be extremely aggressive with one another,
although aggression is generally moderated even among alpha males.
Smaller males form coalitions with other males and even alpha males,
indicating that even among primates there is the ability to develop cooperative strategies. Food sharing and cooperative hunting are other
examples of cooperation and the capacity to create "joint payoff" among
primates. Human beings are unique in their degree of willingness to
share food; it is a universal value among all human groups that food is
shared among the nuclear and extended families. The sharing of food
with strangers is also common among many traditional societies—hardly
indicative of a singular preference for self-interest.

So strong are the survival values of reciprocity and trust that they have
become embedded as a permanent function of the brain. Human beings
receive chemical rewards for engaging in reciprocity—substances called
positive neurotransmitters. A significant part of the brain, the nuclear cau-
date, is dedicated to thoughts, emotions, and behaviors associated with
trust. Trust is not simply an abstract idea, but a kind of circuit of neural responses that seek and reward reliability and reciprocity. It is no less a
"fuzzy" concept than self-interest or aggression. In evolutionary biology,
one rule of thumb is that what has become physically encoded in the

brain—whatever behavior or emotion—offers a real evolutionary advantage. The brain is a big consumer of energy, and evolutionary forces are very miserly about what gets put into "neural hardware." So, emotionally encoded behaviors are a significant evolutionary endorsement. The fact that reciprocity and trust are two forms of social interaction that are encoded in the brain is strong evidence of their evolutionary importance. They are as much a distinctive part of our human nature as are our hands or our bipedalism, or our larynx and language capacity. They are one of the unique adaptations that make us human.

There is, however, considerable variation in how much people are willing to trust and reciprocate. An estimated 25 percent of human beings act exclusively in their own self-interest and are impervious to incentives to reciprocate (called MACH IV behavior by neuro-economists).[10] The neurological evidence suggests that the capacity to trust and reciprocate is a genetically linked trait that varies among populations and has been selected for and against over the course of human history. The fact that it is so prevalent across time and a spectrum of cultures, and is so deeply encoded in the brain, is indicative of its enormous and persistent survival value. Trust and reciprocity are core social emotions. In the evolutionary framework they both represent evolutionarily stable strategies.[11] They persist among the most advanced social species; evolution has not dislodged them but rather endorsed them.

Evidence from recent behavioral studies, evolutionary game theory simulations, and cross-cultural studies has shown that when there are "free riders"—people who simply act in their own self-interest at the expense of the group—the overall outcomes or fitness benefits for the group are reduced because its members are less willing to reciprocate with acts of cooperation.[12] However, when free riders are punished or ostracized, then the cooperative behaviors return. Free riders are not punished or purged as an act of moral censure, but out of rational concern for the overall welfare of all members of the group. Punishment is less a moral condemnation than an evolutionary necessity. The ability of a small group to appropriate for itself the benefits created by the cooperative efforts of all the members would jeopardize those benefits for the entire group.

Given the importance of "fairness" and the danger of free riders to a group's survival, it is not surprising that a specific region of the brain may

have evolved that is dedicated to detecting cheaters.[13] Even more remarkable, innate personality traits seem to have also evolved to detect
and punish cheaters in social networks. The evolutionary justification for
reciprocal behaviors is that they distribute risk. It is in one's own self-
interest to attend to the interests of others—even those who are not kins-
men.[14] In the case of some hunting-and-gathering cultures, the likelihood
of a hunter bringing back a large bounty of protein is no more than 4 percent. This gives hunters a keen interest in reciprocating acts of sharing.[15]
It diversifies their risks and increases their ability to survive.

This conclusion of a growing number of evolutionary scientists runs
headlong against the classical laissez-faire economists and some traditional evolutionary biologists, who contend that only individual self-
interest, the "selfish gene," is the primary motivator of human activity.
For them, everything revolves around self-interest and the individual,
and it is individual selection—not group selection—that is the principal
agent of natural selection.[16] Both these points of view, however, are becoming progressively less tenable. Dan Kahan of the Yale Law School is
scornful of the traditionalists:

> The main—indeed only—selling point for the conventional theory of
> collective action is its assertion of behavioral realism. Individuals, it
> tells us, are inherently self seeking. Accordingly, we can't count on
> them voluntarily to subordinate material interests to the good of soci-
> ety; rather we must alternatively bribe and threaten them through a
> costly regulatory process. It turns out, however, the conventional
> theory isn't right. Individuals in a collective action setting might not
> act like saints, but they don't behave like fiends either. They can be
> counted on to contribute to collective good, the emerging literature
> on strong reciprocity shows, *so long as they perceive that others are in-
> clined to do the same.* Bribes and threats are not nearly so necessary as
> the conventional theory would have us believe; the law can instead
> enlist our cooperation by furnishing us with ground to *trust* one an-
> other to contribute our fair share to society's needs.[17]

The prevalent presumption among "political realists" and free market
economists that the only tenable means of promoting cooperation is

through coercion and the lure of self-interest subverts the very conditions for social stabilization that they say they are trying to encourage.

That is why the example of terrorism is germane. In the vast majority of cases, terrorists have no "self-interest" in becoming international outcasts. They tend to be well educated and financially independent—and yet are willing to sacrifice their lives for people they don't know. In terms of evolutionary science, the best explanation for their actions is not self-interest—but the logic of "strong reciprocity."[18] They are aggressively defending their group. The strong neurotransmitter rewards—chemical inducements—for cooperative behaviors, are, in a purely physiological sense, equivalent in potency to the compulsions of sex or drugs. It may seem far-fetched to assert certain social emotions—affinity, identity, esteem, and cultural standing—can be bound to acts of faceless violence and self-destruction. But motivated by reciprocity and punishment—the need to purge free riders or, in this case, infidels—that may be what happens.

The moral imperative in honor cultures, such as many Arab cultures and the pre-Enlightenment Scottish Highlands, to correct an insult or a wrong is arguably something that young men are wired by evolution to do. In neurological terms, such acts of sacrifice may be a way the ambiguity of youthful identity is resolved by the certitude of a heroic, socially sanctioned recognition. It is not surprising that the U.S. government is blind to the motivations of such young men. The government is itself so committed to perpetuating its own code of honor, self-interest, and materialism that it cannot gauge its alienating impact upon others. The sad paradox is that the U.S. government has adopted those very policies that exacerbate the conditions it is trying to eradicate.

During the last decade, there has been an explosion of research by such pioneers as Antonio Damasio and Giacomo Rizzolatti that challenges the commonsense notion that emotions are an alternative to cognition. Even in the scientific community, the Cartesian separation of reason and emotion, the irrational and the rational, has long been accepted as a given. This convenient divide is now shown to be simply wrong.[19] It turns out that even the cerebral cortex—the bastion of high-level cognition—is infused with neurons from the "older" and "lower" brain region, the amygdala, where the emotional responses are located.

Emotions are themselves a kind of intelligence. They signal what is important, desirable, and dangerous, and act as motivators and governors of cognitive and physical activity. Circuits of neurotransmitters have evolved that motivate and reward many forms of behavior—competition, play, curiosity, grooming, empathy, disgust, humor, trust, sexual attraction, hoarding, and aggression. Emotions provide positive and negative kinds of rewards—a sense of well-being or shame and guilt, as regulated by neurotransmitters such as oxytocin and serotonin, and the high of an adrenaline spike or the sense of power and aggression from testosterone.

One of the most disturbing traits of human beings is their behavior in crowds and mobs. Seemingly rational and compassionate individuals, when placed into a group and acting collectively, can assume a monstrous group personality. What transforms independent and thoughtful individuals into unreflective agents of a group will? This dynamic is not confined to the "madness of crowds" situations but can be found in the "groupthink" of a distinguished board of directors that approves actions that each person individually knows to be wrong but seems incapable of checking when acting as a group member. In the 1935 Leni Riefenstahl film *Triumph of the Will*, the scenes of faceless crowds of men, women, and children jabbing their arms in unison to salute their führer is an iconic reminder that a seemingly civilized people can become possessed. Variants of such scenes continue to be repeated in Serbia, North Korea, and Iran.

When groups of people "swarm," or interact as a single unit, or seem to exhibit a "group mind," it is often due to the overwhelming power of social signals that trigger collective responses—often of fear and immediate flight. The "threat calls" of birds and other species show a similar pattern. Some social emotions are triggered when members of a group identify an outlier, a free rider, or someone who simply does not belong. The responses triggered can be cruel enforcements of group norms, ranging from the "mean girls" of teenage cliques to "ethnic cleansing" and genocide. Such emotions are not "rational" in the sense that they are not reflected upon. They are generated at a preconscious level, a sign that an ancient survival mechanism has been activated.[20]

Social emotions seem to fall into two groups, those that regulate self-interest and aggression, and those that promote group interest and empathy. The first set of social emotions are coercive and aggressive—and are triggered and reinforced by testosterone and adrenaline. These social emotions are most prevalent in highly volatile and competitive societies in which there is low sustainable group trust. Game theorists liken such circumstances to a one-shot game in which players have little incentive to cooperate. Societies of this sort have difficulty marshaling societal resources and cooperation. Any economic and cultural successes tend to be episodic and caused by a "Big Man" leader type.

The phenomenon of the "Big Man" is prevalent across cultures and time. It is an organizing principle for geographically diverse traditional societies, from the Haida of British Columbia to the Yoruba of Nigeria, as well as for more "modern" societies, such as organized crime families, kleptocracies, terrorist networks, and the despots of failed states. The Big Man concept is also the organizing principle for laissez-faire capitalism, which valorizes the entrepreneur and the investor as the leader whose risk taking and property rights should be protected from the "parasitism" of the group. They are given the lion's share of not only the initial value created but any ensuing secondary and tertiary benefits. The assertion of "fairness" is based on the presumption that without the heroic acts of the Big Man, no value would have been created. In effect, all value creation is an individual act; and most of the time, the individual that matters is the Big Man. Social networks centered around the Big Man idea are often governed by principles of honor, loyalty, and a kind of feudal fealty. They are structurally archaic, with limited specialization, and find it difficult to grow. They are the antithesis of "civil society."

However, modern communications and the increased lethality of weapons can amplify the powers of the Big Man form of social organization, thereby undermining more civic forms of authority and power. From an evolutionary perspective, there is no presumption that a more archaic and violent form of organization could not displace a more "civilized" and cooperative one. History is replete with examples of Big Man forms of organization—bands, tribes, hordes, guerrilla networks—overthrowing highly differentiated and prosperous societies. A stable civil order that we take for granted is always vulnerable to free riders and disruption, and eventual prolonged chaos and disorder.

There is, however, another important countervailing set of social emotions—those built upon empathy and reciprocity. Just as mirror neurons[21] enable one to experience what others are experiencing and thereby help facilitate the rewards of reciprocity, affinity, and trust, the second set of emotions rewards the idea that an individual's welfare is interdependent with that of others in the group. In most cases, the inducements for trust and reciprocity are positive rewards, such as the release of oxytocin, a neurotransmitter associated with female bonding to children and trust building. Groups based upon these cooperative emotions, such as many religious communities, sports teams, business teams, and special forces, are essentially peer networks that function cooperatively on principles of trust and reciprocity.

It is not surprising that in many traditional societies where the social emotions of cooperation and reciprocity are paramount, it is the women who run the markets and the economic affairs. Yet even among male groups, such as hunting parties and military units, the social emotions of bonding and reciprocity can be extremely strong. In such cooperative forms of peer organization, the more "feminine" social emotions of trust, empathy, and reciprocity are required—hence, the importance of oxytocin and serotonin rewards over adrenaline and testosterone. Although it is tempting to link social emotions to gender differences, the truth is much more complicated. Neither sex has a monopoly on certain types of social emotions. Even intense male activities such as combat and hunting are regulated by the social emotions of trust and empathy. Activities that tend to be primarily female, such as the nurture of the young and food gathering, can be governed by testosterone and adrenaline.

In this sense, natural selection is gender blind. It is willing to assign a variety of social emotions to any gender in order to assure survival. Hence, traits that are typically thought of as male or female are but loosely sex linked, and can vary by culture and circumstance. One might conjecture that in the case of cooperative social emotions, natural selection is at a group level, and possibly of more recent origin.

As the tasks for a group become more and more specialized, complex, and interdependent, then the individualistic, Big Man forms of social organization become less scalable (or measurable), viable, and adaptive.

Yet there will always be a tension between the two poles. The challenge to any executive or public policy maker or anyone responsible for the welfare and efficacy of a large group is how to modulate the balance between the two.

There is a need for the initiative and efficiency of having a Big Man, an alpha leader. Yet networks based upon the principle of the Big Man can become too personalized, too dominated by the interests and personality of the Big Man. Hence, effective social networks have a variety of roles and checks and balances on the powers of their members. Highly evolved social networks have specialized relationships whereby members have socially designated roles. Social scientists think of relationships in social networks as the "links" and individual roles as the nodes. Social networks are therefore not meaningfully measured simply in terms of the sheer number of links separating individuals—their "degrees of separation"— but rather, it is *how* people are linked and in what *contexts* they are linked that affects the quality of the network.

The marking of types of links and nodes is accomplished through "tags." Tags are virtually any way of marking or labeling people, places, events, actions, or things that highlight a significant difference. Tags are ways of creating Searle's social and institutional facts. Tags are also social signals, thus how one dresses, moves, or speaks are tags. Likewise, so are honorifics, titles, ranks, roles, hats, degrees, haircuts, beards, scarves, even perfumes. They are an integral component of any self-organizing social network. They signal through sound, sight, and smell to those in the network who someone is and how they should be responded to. The importance of tags is largely underappreciated: They are the singular means by which rewards and punishments are given and control is transferred in all complex networks.[22] Judgments of worthiness and performance—moral judgments—are expressed through the assignment of tags. In social networks, tags define the conditions of membership and participation through titles and names. On the other hand, in the human immune system, which is one of the most sophisticated self-organizing networks in nature, tags are used to defend the body against pathogens such as the HIV virus by detecting and countering false signals, rapidly evolving defensive mechanisms as sophisticated as any designed by man.

Change the nature of the tags and you dramatically change the nature of the network. If the network is human society, one way to change it is to reallocate decision rights—which are the tags. In highly patriarchal pastoral societies, for instance, decision rights over property, marriage, and trade are typically vested in the oldest male. However, as in the case of Scotland in the eighteenth century and many developing countries in the twenty-first century, when rural societies become more settled and urbanized, decision rights that were once vested in the male elder become dispersed to male heirs—sons, cousins, in-laws, and in some cases to wives and daughters. The circumstances of urban living, with its inevitable exposure to other social networks, produce a diffusion of decision rights. That is an unanticipated by-product of urbanity. Consequently, many older forms of feudal hierarchy did not successfully transfer to urbanized environments. The reverse may also be true: If the cities disperse people to suburban ghettos, which reduce the exposure to a variety of social networks, old patriarchal habits may reassert themselves in the absence of any other viable social tag. In cities, the fact that children may have more alternatives and be less dependent upon the core family unit results in a renegotiation of privileges and powers. The modernization and urbanization of China today seems to have had such an effect on the Confucian values of filial piety and parental authority, and would suggest that a new, more distributed form of social control is emerging. Can the control of the Communist Party really function in a quasi-market economy, with rapid technological changes, with strong ethnic differences and a population of 1.5 billion people?

One of the most powerful tags in any network is reputation, because it is so directly linked to the social emotions of trust and reciprocity. The Net over the last decade has demonstrated the power of rating systems in affecting how purchases are made online. Yet the power of rating and reputation systems was not so much invented on the Net as "revealed," because rating and reputation system are a natural and universal artifact of all forms of human cooperation. A reputation is really the collection of tags that are assigned to an individual or entity to reflect assessments of his or her competence. In eBay, for example, sellers acquire a reputation score given to them by their buyers. High reputation-score levels not only make it more likely that newcomers will do business with them but confer a certain status among other members of the eBay community. Credit scores are another form of reputation that is now integral to not only receiving credit but participating in the society and the economy at large. It is something that is independently calculated, based upon financial behavior that in turn is thought to predict likelihood of default or delays in payment. Reputation systems are linked to all aspects of human endeavor—to sports with its performance statistics, to education with its grades and degrees, to social standing with its board and club memberships. In the online world, online games depend upon accumulated scores, levels, roles, and ratings to encourage participation, as do various online peer-production undertakings such as Wikipedia, Slashdot, and open-source software development.

In closed societies, once a reputation is acquired, it may be very difficult to change. Honor-based societies depend upon reputation tags as the principal governance mechanism for defining and enforcing a social order. "Honor killings" of a violated daughter or sister to preserve a kinship reputation brutally demonstrate the cost and power of reputation in a closed social network. Even in online social network communities such as Xanga, Flickr, LinkedIn, Facebook, and MySpace, people take very seriously the ratings of the other members and such explicit and implicit reputation ratings can affect their social mobility, access, and standing. Identity itself is closely determined by reputation tags in social networks: Who you are in many networked environments depends on how others see and rate you.

Reputation tags also affect an individual or group's ability to participate within and across different networks, thereby becoming the basis for granting or revoking certain privileges and decision rights. Since reputation tags can be measures of competence by a socially credible third party—be it religious, educational, financial, political, trade, or professional institutions—they play a very powerful role in governing social mobility and enabling or thwarting the interactions between different social networks. By providing information about information—who or what it is, where it came from, as well as marking the rights and privileges for accessing, exchanging, altering, or forwarding goods, services, and information, tags are the true control points in self-organizing networks.

The reputation score acquired by an individual in a particular social network—analogous to achieving celebrity status or being on the "A-List"—is called a social currency; social currency states how valuable you are within the network. It is a universal propensity of all human beings to exchange information, services, and goods, and implicitly and explicitly calculate their social and economic "debts and credits" with one another. Adam Smith correctly saw this propensity to "truck, barter, and exchange" as a primal impulse for the division of labor and specialization so essential for efficient production:

> The division of labour, from which so many advantages are derived, is not originally the effect of any human wisdom, which foresees and intends that general opulence to which it gives occasion. It is the necessary, though very slow and gradual, consequences of a certain propensity in human nature which has in view no such extensive utility; the propensity to truck, barter, and exchange one thing for another.[23]

Celebrities in sports and film are an excellent example of how public status in one form of social network is readably convertible into the social currencies of a variety of other social networks—social, business, and political. Arnold Schwarzenegger is big box office—in both movies and politics. His social currency is broadly valued in both networks. Different social networks have their own social currencies, reflecting their reputation and membership rules. Scientists, artists, technologists, and academics may have criteria for calculating and rewarding social currencies and reputations that are not easily accessible to those outside their networks, and therefore, it is difficult to calculate a conversion rate between these more obscure and private social currencies and the more public currencies of public celebrities. However, highly proficient members of social networks, those who know how to truck, barter, and exchange, can accumulate their own form of social capital—favors, obligations, goodwill—that in many cases can convert them into the social currencies of other social networks. The more open and diverse a society is, the greater the likelihood that reputations will be transferable across social networks, leading to increased social mobility and innovation, something that is rarely possible in closed societies.

So the role of Big Men must be circumscribed. The personalization of power, the subordination of institutional and societal interests to those of privileged individuals, are earmarks of the inroads of tyranny over democracy. This is something both the Romans and Greeks foresaw but could not prevent. John Adams, the architect of the oldest functioning constitution, the Commonwealth of Massachusetts, recognized the importance of curbing the powers of the Big Man and protecting the rights of the community:

> No man, nor corporation or association of men have any other title to obtain advantage or particular and exclusive privileges distinct from those of the community, than what arises from the consideration of services rendered to the public.[24]

The Scottish Enlightenment would not have succeeded had not Edinburgh and Glasgow possessed a rich repertoire of potential combinations of roles and relationships, as centers of learning and exchange that were well connected to not only England, but to continental Europe and North America. Likewise, the Italian Renaissance, which will be discussed in greater detail in the next chapter, would not have succeeded had it not been for the rediscovery of Italy's rich Roman tradition, which offered legitimate new models for not just architecture and the arts, but engineering and civic organization as well. It was not simply enough to break with the old medieval political and religious hierarchies; alternative forms of technology, and social and economic organization had to be generated that actually outperformed and displaced the older order.

Since then, the human challenge has been to find the means within ourselves and in our political and culture inventions to transform closed, theocratic, hierarchical, and traditional societies into open, dynamic, self-directed, and self-sustaining societies.

This chapter refused to invoke the hallowed canons of "democracy" and "free markets" as solutions because these are artifacts of particular cultures at specific times in history and are not universally applicable. By contrast, the science of evolutionary biology and the field of self-organizing networks is a genuinely universal concept. Although the perspective may appear to be somewhat technocratic, it is rooted in the work of Adam Smith and is supported by a growing body of research. Smith, after all, regarded social and economic behavior not as the product of conscious choice, omniscient policies, or rational deliberation, but as the products of self-interest and cooperative moral sentiments working together: That was where the guidance of the "invisible hand" came from. As it turns out, Smith was prescient about Darwin's theory of natural selection and the neuroscience of social emotions and self-organizing networks. Perhaps the most productive way to begin a new discussion is to ground it in some deep, empirical scientific reality. We need a vision of an economic, political, and cultural order that builds on such a source. Any viable long-term vision must aspire to become an evolutionarily stable strategy that can grow, persist over time, and assure the diversity of life. The migration of so many aspects of economic activity, politics, and culture to the Net is, in this sense, a very hopeful sign. The online world provides a marvelous petri dish for experimenting with, and closely scrutinizing, new modes of human interaction and governance. Software architecture can be easily modified and tested. Huge amounts of meta-data can help organize human economies and communities. The viability of certain scenarios can be tested in fairly rapid, low-cost ways, based on the actual needs and sentiments of human communities. All of these features should be of immense value as the human species seeks to find a new, more scientifically grounded, politically effective, and ecologically benign vision for its future.

Chapter Seven

Transforming Trust: Social Commerce in Renaissance Florence

So, HOW CAN WE OVERCOME THE SHORTCOMINGS OF HUMAN NATURE to transform closed, theocratic, hierarchical societies into open, dynamic, and self-sustaining societies? Societies have done it before, but not without luck and at enormous cost. One of the most spectacular and well-studied successes is the Italian Renaissance, especially in Florence, from the thirteenth to the fifteenth centuries.

The events of more than 500 years ago are still relevant today. At a time when global security and ecological sustainability are tied to the transformation of hierarchical and closed societies into more tolerant and open societies, there is disappointingly little understanding of how such changes might actually be achieved. Yet transformation on this scale was achieved during the Italian Renaissance in two phases, 1200–1400 and 1450–1500.

For historians, economists, art historians, and political scientists, the Italian Renaissance is a trove of historical material. It was an eruption of social, economic, political, architectural, artistic, scientific, and literary innovation in which many of the blueprints for Western cultural, civic, economic, and political institutions were laid. In many respects, the Italian

Renaissance offers the perfect, contained, concentrated case study of how closed traditional, clannish, violent, and hierarchical societies were transformed into significantly more open, progressive, inclusive, and less violent societies in relatively short periods of time. These changes were more inadvertent than intentional. They were not the consequence of any deliberate "democratizing process"—such as elections, universal suffrage, legislation, or even enlightened rulers—but rather the result of extending trust networks beyond locality and familial relationships.

The period is well documented through the many meticulous letters and records of some of its principal actors. As a consequence, computerized data analysis techniques developed over the last two decades to permit us to analyze the accounting and demographic records of Renaissance Italy in order to test a variety of hypotheses about how proto-modern social and economic institutions and practices might have emerged during this time.

Two of the pioneers in this effort are John Padgett, a political scientist at the University of Chicago as well as a research professor at the Santa Fe Institute, and Paul McLean, now a Sociologist at Rutgers University. Padgett led a highly ambitious fifteen-year research project to study the period 1300–1500 to determine, among other things, how business partnerships, commercial credit, capital formation, double-entry bookkeeping, and civic institutions emerged during the Renaissance.

As part of his multidisciplinary project, Padgett and his associates collected data on over 50,000 Florentines, which they then used to construct social network models and analyses of the relationships among leading families, neighborhoods, business partnerships, merchant banks, and political groups. Also gathered and examined were many documents, such as family memoirs, personal letters, and commercial correspondence that provided variegated evidence of the Florentine mindset. Among the sources for this evidence was the immense archive of documents left behind by the highly successful merchant and banker of Prato, Francesco Datini (1335–1410). The team also compiled lists of several hundred partnerships formed between the mid-1300s and the 1420s, and a vast data set of commercial relations between companies available for one period of time—1427, the year of the so-called *catasto*. The *catasto*, much of whose content was computerized by David Herlihy and Christiane Klapisch-Zuber (1985), is a tax-related census of over 9,700 households in the city of Florence, and countless more in the surrounding countryside. Each household provided a list of its members, their place of residence, their agricultural holdings, their commercial involvements, their debtors and creditors, and their shares of the public debt. From these records, Padgett and his associate Paul McLean were able to compile, for example, a list of commercial credits transpiring among 406 Florentine firms at a specific moment in time: July 12, 1427. These data, essentially comprising a high-resolution snapshot of the early Renaissance Florentine economy in all its intricacy, were used to build an input-output economic model of commercial relationships of the period.[1]

One of Padgett's research goals was to test how different social networks—commercial, kinship, friendship, neighborhood—evolved and combined to create new kinds of economic partnerships and social alliances. One hypothesis that he and McLean wanted to test was whether neoclassical perfect competition economic models could explain the rise of Florentine capitalism. According to this theory, the reason that Florentine capitalism took root and helped launch a new age of international trade and finance was its abandonment of old notions of personal exchange and group loyalty in favor of the uninhibited pursuit of rational self-interest. Classic economic theories credit the rise of modern capitalism and finance to the innovation of "impersonal" exchange. According to this hypothesis, the invention of double-entry booking and the ability to calculate profits laid the foundation for modern capitalism.

What Padgett found, however, was that the classical economists were wrong. The majority of Florentine business partnerships were not impersonal, highly competitive, or transactional. Rather, they were highly personal and relational, and only mildly competitive. Instead of trying to drive one another out of business, partners acted to "make" one another— that is, to help one another through extended credit and cooperation. Rather than acting out of narrow self-interest, businessmen acted through what Padgett has called "reciprocal credits," which resulted in each extending credit and support to the other. Whereas during the 1200s there was little commercial credit or trust among merchants, by the late 1300s, the Florentine merchants and bankers were famous for their willingness to do business through oral agreements and on a handshake. Padgett explained how such high levels of trust came about:

> Behind the words "oral agreement" lay a vast social-network of credit arrangements and understandings. "A French satirist, in the fifteenth century, marveled at the ability of the Italians to do business without money. In dealing with them, he said, one never sees them touch any money; all they need to do business is paper, pen and ink" (de Roover 1944, p. 381). This innovation of course was central to the Italians' capacity virtually to monopolize international markets all over Europe in the thirteenth, fourteenth and fifteenth centuries. Goods (including bills of exchange) flowed freely among Florentine merchants, with cash settlements being delayed sometimes for short, sometimes for long periods. . . . Full settlement, indeed, could indicate termination of the trading relationship, almost like a divorce. The capacity of Florentine international markets to generate high-volume throughput was founded directly upon this informal "social exchange" system of credits among Florentine merchants.[2]

The only constant in the Italy of the 1200s was chaos: Italy didn't exist as an entity but was an amalgam of warring city states, feuding families, nascent industries, limited trading partners, high religious and social intolerance, social stratification, and struggling civic institutions. Autocratic and violent patriarchies, opportunistic and heavily armed feudal magnates, and princes of the church prevailed over the interests of merchants and the *popolino*—the little people. Warfare was incessant, with clans fighting clans, city-states against city-states, gentry against gentry, merchants and tradesmen against both the gentry and the church.

Advancement in business was familial and generational. Sons had to wait for their father's death and inheritance before they could run their own enterprises. Wealth was consolidated in the hands of the clergy and nobility, who, in many cases, could both demand loans from banks and default at their will. An immutable social hierarchy prevailed, with limited and fixed social roles and duties. Hereditary nobles stood at the top; propertyless workers were permanently entrenched at the bottom. Capital was illiquid, hoarded, and concentrated in the hands of the few and the titled.

Within 150 years, Italy, and Florence in particular, became one of the most innovative, influential, wealthy, humanistic, civic-minded, and vital societies the earth has ever seen. How? There was, after all, no omniscient ruler. There was no sudden windfall of wealth, no transformative technological invention. It was hardly a time of peace and stability. The period was plagued by major wars, bankruptcies, workers' revolutions, a counterrevolution, and the Black Death of 1382, which killed nearly 60 percent of the Florentine population. And yet, during this brief time, some of the greatest "geniuses" of Western society were produced. In art, Giotto, Masaccio, Donatello, Botticelli, Michelangelo, da Vinci; in architecture, Alberti, and Brunelleschi; in literature, Dante and Boccaccio; in political theory, Machiavelli, and Petrarch in philosophy. It was also the time of the "invention" of the modern individual, the "Renaissance Man," "so talented in so many domains at once that he stood above them all as a role-free individual."[3] It was a time of unfettered curiosity and inquiry, during which stylistic experiments into new aesthetic styles and modes of personal expression essentially invented modern Western art and culture.

Strictures on personal expression were relaxed. Beginning with Giotto and progressing through Michelangelo, artists of all types—poets, painters, architects, sculptors—began to progressively emancipate themselves from religiously imposed canonical forms of human depiction. Unless the period contained a "perfect storm" of genetic brilliance—hardly likely—it was culturally, economically, and politically fertile circumstances that allowed the genius of the everyman more easily to blossom.

Like the Scottish Enlightenment, the Florentine Renaissance saw a transition from hierarchical to distributed authority. Insular and closed social networks gave way to the intermixing of multiple networks. Highly restrictive roles and relationships dissolved and led to the invention of new roles and relationships.

It was also a singular point in economic history. In the course of the lifetime of one of Italy's most successful businessmen and prolific letter writers, Francesco Datini, (1328–1420), Italians succeeded in transforming merchant banking, inventing new forms of business partnerships, and aided in the widespread diffusion of newly-available technologies such as double-entry bookkeeping, overdrafts, and current accounts.

During the 1200s, there were clear differences in interests among the papacy, the gentry, and the merchant and artisan classes in Florence. It was also a time when regional authorities—clergy and hereditary rulers and princes—were displacing the influence of the Pope and the Holy Roman Emperor. Their powers resided in the preservation of hierarchy and the exercise of force, in this case, private feudal armies to protect and advance their hegemony.

The merchant and artisan classes, on the other hand, banded together to mitigate the violence of the "magnates" and pave the way for more civil and cooperative civil institutions that could assimilate new members based upon merit and performance.

Newly important were the *cives*—the propertied, city-based merchants, engaged in trade, moneylending, and the textile industries. The cives recruited the popolino—the day laborers, serfs, poor artisans, petty tradesmen, servants, and domestics—to counter the powers of the nobility and the vested merchant classes. The cives, however, were to benefit most from a redefinition of the Italian social and economic order. Their powers were neither positional nor inherited but derived from their proven skills and abilities as merchants.

One of the catalysts for change during the 1300s was the shortage of skilled workers of all types and classes, given all the warfare and plague. The strictures of a hierarchical social and moral order had to be relaxed if any work was to be completed, in the same way that World War II liberated women to join the workforce to replace the missing men, which in turn led to a new expression of feminism. So, the combination of disasters broke down traditional social networks. Enterprises needed new "blood" and new roles. Distinct social networks—not only different strata of society, but different domains of society—church, banking, families, neighborhoods, guilds, business partnerships, civic bodies—interacted and recombined to create new social roles, and new norms, new business, social, civic, artistic, banking, and kinship identities and institutions.

This was also a time of experimentation in virtually all aspects of Florentine life, as much out of necessity as anything else. Social controls became more "secular" and pragmatic out of efforts to negotiate rather than fight over differences. Rather than turn to arms to resolve differences, as had been the reflex in the past, conflicts were resolved through formation of laws, councils, and courts, to facilitate and accelerate commerce. This approach among the merchant-based republics and guilds stood in contrast to those Italian city-states that were dominated by the Big Men rulers, the *signori,* and the authoritarian rule of the old gentry and the church. One of the signature achievements of the Florentine Renaissance was the emergence of cooperative and affiliative institutions—guilds, communes, voluntary associations, and city councils—that resulted in the rise of a plurality of social roles and a social identity that was multiple and self-defined: the Renaissance Man. Yet the guilds were not democratic and open in any modern sense, but rather were used by the tradesmen and merchants to limit the power of the popolino and secure and further their own interests. According to Paul McLean, "one of the signal contributions of the consensual elite that spurred so much innovation in the 1380–1430 period was the 'dismantling' or de-fanging of the guilds and the concomitant rise of the 'businessman' as someone engaged in multiple industries simultaneously and using holding company structure and dowries-cum-startup capital to pull it off."[4]

Although powerful patrilineages dominated commerce and politics, with the passage of time, the power of the "patriarch" came to be diffused. First sons, then son-in-laws and apprentices became business partners, their advancement based more on merit than simple kinship.[5] The combination of the privileges and roles of old families with the skills and energy of the new merchant families allowed for the invention of new social, cultural, and economic roles. Men like Francesco Datini, who were born of low social standing, could through their business accomplishments, church and political alliances and well-connected marriages become men of significant public reputation and standing. Through the combination of different social networks, a new array of social roles, norms, and forms of alliance and partnership became possible.

The rise of business partnerships based on merit—and not purely upon gender and kinship—opened the way for mentor-apprentice and patron-client models that became a primary engine of Renaissance creativity and vitality.[6] Dowries became transformed from a means of preserving social stratification to a means for generating "seed capital" to finance new business ventures.[7] Even during the latter period, 1380–1434, when the older families were able to reassert their control, they retained many openings for including and sanctioning venturesome and successful new members.[8] Innovation and social mobility became motifs of the time.

The Renaissance Florentines had a highly developed talent for reciprocity, using the favors and reputational gains acquired in one social network to gain entry into other social networks. Florence, like many other Italian city-states, had seeds of a rich civic society. There were a large number of "social markets"—reflecting the plurality of trades and professions, among them goldsmith, wool and silk merchant, banker and financier, mason, mercenary, sculptor, and architect—whereby individuals could acquire public reputations and eventual entry into the gentry and ruling councils. Trading in these reputational favors created a kind of "social currency" that greatly facilitated social mobility. Success in Renaissance Florence depended upon acquiring relationships, skills, and status in one arena and using them to achieve prominence in another. For this reason, these different social networks mirrored one another in their mores and roles. Social currencies enabled the accounting and exchange of privileges across social networks; social currencies acquired in one setting or context, such as business, could be exchanged for access and privileges in other social networks, for example, in "polite society." The competition among "new men," those of newly acquired wealth and status, and even established families, to achieve reputational standing and recognition drove commercial, civic, and artistic invention. The fact that individuals did not stay in single professions or business partnerships for very long, often no more than six years, meant that an entirely new "circulatory system" of social interaction came into being.

During the Renaissance, art was developed as an instrument of human self-awareness and emotional expression. Public art became a form of public medium for commentary, expression, civic identity, public recognition, and social rivalry. Italian art enjoyed an especially high degree of technical virtuosity, in part because it grew out of the highly accomplished artisan traditions of goldsmithing and silk dying. Another contributing factor was the rigorous apprentice programs of the trade and artisan guilds that typically began when a boy was very young. Many of the great Florentine and Italian painters were architects, sculptors, and painters (Brunelleschi, Donatello, da Vinci, Ghiberti, Michelangelo). All forms of public art became vehicles for individuals, communes, guilds, and city-states to express and reinvent themselves both to their peers and their competitors. New artistic vocabularies and forms for civic, religious, scientific, literary, and commercial expression were invented and experimented with and these enabled new forms of communication. The prevalent medieval social emotions of guilt, shame, fear, and humility were often re-interpreted and given new artistic expression. Biblical figures were represented more classically and naturalistically. The very human gods and goddesses of antiquity were often painted and sculpted with an enthusiasm not accorded biblical religious themes.

The modern and very Western emancipation of the arts from religious dogma began at this time. There were no *a priori* criteria for deciding what combinations of ideas, sentiments, emotions, or inquiries were permissible. The final judgment resided in the success or failure of the artistic outcome—not in any adherence to an overriding moral code. In this respect the Renaissance Florentines were far ahead of many of their contemporaries. Even the arts were governed by the invisible hand of moral sentiments—not by the authority of any single institution, credo, or individual. Likewise, there was an opening up of a new kind of pluralistic identity that was derived from individual effort and achievement.

The merchant of Prato, Francesco Datini, was particularly representative of the values and tastes of the time, the perfect example of a man whose status and social standing was not set by birth, but something he created by his own efforts. Through his prolific letters and meticulous records, one can glimpse an intimate and detailed portrait of Italian business and banking practices from the mid-fourteenth century to the early fifteenth century. Datini is credited by some scholars with being the inventor of the modern business partnership, which he managed through double-entry booking. Datini, the son of a tavern keeper who died from the plague when Datini was a small child, was the epitome of the self-made man, the "new man." Lacking title, social position, and inherited wealth, everything Datini later acquired, he set out on his own, at a time when the gentry, the magnates, and the church monopolized a limited pool of wealth. In many respects, he was neither an exceptional nor a heroic man. His most remarkable trait appears to be his devotion to his business and his record keeping. Reading his letters, one gets the impression of a man ill at ease with himself and in constant fear of a financial or political catastrophe.[9] Despite becoming one of the most prominent men of Prato, his painted portrait reveals a frowning brow and an expression of anxious anticipation.

Datini mastered and advanced the organizational and financial technologies of his time, first, through his incessant use of letters to manage every detail of his far-flung enterprises, and second, through his use of double-entry booking to calculate his profits and to form and dissolve his many partnerships. Datini's career mirrors the tumultuous events of his time, showing a man frantically escaping outbreaks of the plague, bank collapses, revolution, and inter-city and papal warfare, and then, opportunistically pursuing business opportunities brought about by the changing circumstances throughout Italy and Europe. His letters reveal a man whose social and commercial roles were in transition from medieval notions of custom and hierarchy to the more individualistic and opportunistic attitudes of an international merchant and banker. A religious man, he regularly attended mass and was fond of biblical admonitions, and yet he fathered a number of children out of wedlock and was not civic-minded until late in life. As was the custom for men of his social standing, he had a conversion experience and went on a pilgrimage toward the end of his life. He was exceptional, however, in the magnitude of the gift of his estate and the 70,000 florins that he left to the poor in his native Prato.

He started business in 1358 as a merchant trader in Avignon, the seat of papal government, staying until 1382. He then moved to Florence to take advantage of the new business climate. In Pisa, Genoa, and later in Catalonia, he developed new business partnerships, and at the same time he founded a bank. He was able to manage these commercially and geographically diverse partnerships though "financial controls," that is, the calculation of accounts and profits.

A few years later, he formed a holding company, an arrangement that had legally distinct partnerships with branch managers for each location. For each branch there were separate account books, which enabled Datini to centralize control and diversify his business risks and exposure. Although he was one of the leading commercial practitioners of his time, he was not unique. The "invention" of partnerships and financial controls in this period was less the result of individual genius than the inevitable discovery of many merchants and bankers.

> Viewed as a partnership contract, the partnership system was an innovative way to protect capital from risk. Viewed as industrial structure, the partnership system was an innovative route to establishing diversified cross-industry ownership and "financial conceptions of control." Viewed as the economic-network component of the Florentine elite, the partnership system (along with marriage) was an innovative logic for social integration of the political and the economic elites, in response to challenge from below. Ultimately all levels reinforced each other in reproduction.[10]

Throughout the 1200s–1400s, there was a constant jockeying for power and influence as social networks, roles, and norms kept being redefined by the various upheavals. The ability to broker between different networks—in effect, to act as a converter and exchanger of social currencies—resulted in the creation of significant new power bases.[11] The ability to have multiple identities and to span diverse social networks gave oligarchs such as Cosimo di Medici so much of their power and influence.[12] Hence, influential gentlemen sought to become participants and players in many networks. Padgett notes that Cosimo di Medici was especially adept at such manipulations: "Cosimo did not create the Medici party, but he did shrewdly learn the rules of the networks around him. Rather than dissipate this power through forceful command, Cosimo retreated behind a shroud of multiple identities, impenetrable to this day."[13]

Florence's government was a constitutional oligarchy where political participation was limited to the privileged few and public office was a vehicle to advance familial and business interests. The rule of law and the independence of the judiciary and the legislature was not sufficiently strong to prevent families like the Medicis from indirectly but effectively ruling Florence. Unlike the case of commercial world and business partnerships, there was no robust political basis for governance by rule of law. Alliances among the oligarchs were personal, relational, and often covert. In an attempt to limit the concentration of power, office terms were limited, and the highest magistracy of Florence, the priorate, rotated officeholders every two months. However, special, small ad hoc councils wielded much of the real power and were often reserved for especially connected or experienced men. Control over eligibility and nominations was one of the means that the oligarchs were able to use to retain their power and influence.

During the fifteenth century, the experimentations and liberties of the prior century were somewhat curbed as the established social, economic, and political interests reasserted themselves. Yet through their patronage of the arts, the Medici continued to advance artistic experimentation through the support of Michelangelo, da Vinci, Botticelli, Ghirlandaio, and many others. Although Florence was a republic, political participation remained limited to the wealthy merchant and aristocratic families. The Big Men, the Medici, and other merchant and banking families were able to gain control over the political processes. Patronage and corruption raised the powerful families above the law in much the same way that the gentry had been above the law 200 years before. Therefore, rather than developing independent, cooperative institutional powers, the latter part of the Renaissance devolved into Big Man and family-based powers and rights. Once the ruling families tightened their grip on political, cultural, and commercial networks, the vitality and creative spontaneity of the Renaissance began to wane.

The transformation of Renaissance Italy holds many lessons for our current global circumstances. It provides a rigorously researched snapshot of how vital social, culture, economic, and political institutions arise from conditions of great uncertainty, conflict, and cultural constraint. What is especially striking during this period of civic and financial institution building was the role of social networks in extending spheres of public trust and opening up new social roles and forms of participation. Furthermore, it was not a democratic process in any sense, since it was the elites who were the principal instruments of change. Contrary to current prescriptions for "nation building" and democratization, it was not through innovations in political institutions per se that resulted in a new kind of civic society, but rather innovations in social and financial mechanisms of trust and equity.

The example of the Renaissance should not be understood as recommending that developing societies ought to ape Western institutions and mores. Rather, we should consider the importance of creating the conditions from which different traditions can evolve their own viable, open institutions. The case study of Renaissance Italy suggests what some of the formative forces and preconditions might be, but it makes no assumption of what kinds of specific institutions might emerge. Renaissance Italy had many particular advantages; it had a highly successful prior historical tradition, that of Rome, 1,000 years earlier, from which to learn. It also had natural resources—literacy and well-developed trade and merchant traditions—thanks to its location at the heart of the Mediterranean. Although it is impossible to say what conditions *guarantee* that a traditional closed society will become an open society, it may be possible to identify the necessary preconditions without which it will not happen. The Renaissance would not have happened had there not been so much chaos to crack open the feudal order. Had the feudal order worked, as it had in China for thousands of years, and had the different classes not been forced to work together through the decimation of warfare, plague, bankruptcies, and revolts, it seems unlikely heterogeneous and vital social and commercial networks of the Renaissance would have emerged. In short, significant crises and pain are needed to overturn an established older order. Throughout the Middle East and Central Asia, there are hierarchical social and economic social models in place that have remained unaltered for 3,000 years. Such social models appear to be ultra-stable even under a variety of very trying conditions. In many respects, it was the Italians' skills as tradesmen, bankers, and merchants that opened up Italian society and supplanted archaic feudal institutions. It was the values of cooperation and joint payoffs that eventually out-competed the values of hierarchy and zero sum conflict. One of the key findings of Padgett's research is that it was not just "free markets" per se, that is, pursuit of unmitigated self-interest that resulted in civic society, business partnerships, international banking, and civic institutions, but a kind of "social commerce," one that is balanced by "reciprocal" credits that built "common stock."

Another scholar of this time period, Luca Fantacci, makes a similar point in his analysis of the two currencies used for domestic and foreign exchange. During the thirteenth century there were two kinds of currencies introduced into Italy and throughout much of Europe. One was essentially a local currency that was "debased" in the sense that the precious metal content, principally silver, was unreliable. Fantacci calls this "black money," comprised of small coinage that was intended to be in circulation to control for inflation and deflation. Black money is in effect a form "reciprocal credits" in that it preserves social cohesion and cooperation by adjusting its value in order to enable economic and social exchange. Fantacci notes, "All these uses hint to the distributive nature of small coins, and provide a further explanation of the irrelevance of its content in precious metal. It was not made to be kept[14] but to circulate; hence it was not indispensable for it to be precious, but to be dispensable. In transactions reserved to each was to be determined with reference to the community as a whole, according to the principle of distributive justice." "White money," on the other hand, was purely transactional and was based upon the gold standard, and as in the case of the florin, first minted in 1252, was not debased. It was not a communal currency but intended to be used outside the community or the city. Therefore, its trust value was dependent upon the purity of its gold content. Fantacci goes on:

And gold coin provided the medium of payment [for] inter-regional long distance trade, even beyond the frontiers of Christendom. In this case, the intrinsic value was important, since it was the only warrant for the equity of the transaction. In transactions among merchants, that by definition did not belong to the same community, the parties had to exchange goods of equal value, according to the principle of commutative justice. The gold and silver of large coins, of established weight and fineness, provided the necessary counterpart for dispatching an order of precious merchandise. However, even in this case, money was not meant to be kept, but only to favor the circulation of goods. A confirmation of this is given by the peculiar form of money that the Renaissance merchant-bankers adopted since the [twelfth] century: the bill of exchange. These were letters of credit, issued in payment for a transaction, and then circulated among merchants, thanks to their greater convenience and security compared to specie transfers—yet not indefinitely. All bills of exchange were either compensated for or paid out, once every three months, at the seasonal clearing fairs. It was expressly prohibited to carry over credits or debts from one fair to the other.[15]

This complementary currency system, which allows for both "social commerce" and impersonal commerce was not just a financial invention for managing risk, but a form of social invention for extending trust within and without a community.

On the other hand, under conditions of extreme disorder, when warfare and uncertainty prevail, a kind of social ecology emerges that is highly distrustful and risk adverse. It favors individuals who are aggressive, ambitious, and willing to assume risk for themselves and others. The Renaissance illustrates this well, with the proliferation of risk-taking leaders in all aspects of social, cultural, economic, and political life. Without such aggressive "alpha" leadership—which seems to be contingent upon a breakdown in the old order and hence, a time of crises and stress—the emergence of new civic leadership models that favored consensus, rule of law, and civic participation would not have been possible. The challenge to creating sustainable civic institutions, however, is making the transition from personal power to independent institutional power. During the earlier phases of the Renaissance, especially in Florence, there was a decentralization of power and the curbing of the power of the magnates and the gentry. However, as Florence was an oligarchic republic with only 2 percent of the population with a political voice, it wasn't long before the Medicis or their equivalent took over.

The transition from governance through fear, coercion, and personal exchanges to independent, voluntary, institutional exchanges is one of the great and unfinished challenges of all societies. What is clear from the example of Renaissance Florence is the power of reputation and social currencies in creating civic, cultural, and economic wealth. The importance of how, when, and by whom reputational benefits are given and revoked is very much underappreciated in many "nation-building" ventures. In Iraq, for example, the transition from an honor-based social hierarchical social order to one that is open and merit based is a prerequisite for building modern civic institutions. The transition from reputational benefits being conferred by fixed social or bureaucratic rank to the independent, invisible hand of social commerce is very likely pivotal to creating open, inclusive, and stable societies.

Elections and universal suffrage are reputed to confer such rights and capabilities of participation and representative influence. However, if

democratic processes are merely a cosmetic overlay on an existing feudal
network, as they are in Iraq and Afghanistan, voting behavior will mimic
feudal obligations and controls. Before elections or other democratic processes can be effective, there first needs to be an open, independent, credible, and mobile reputation system. That is, there need to be independent,
transparent, and accountable measures of performance that are not be-
holden to a Big Man or special interest. Successful civic societies "invent"
new roles and relationships that can be maintained through credible reputation metrics. In this respect, digital technologies could play a transformative role in opening up societies and enabling the development of
trusted social and commercial institutions. The computerization of the
banking and financial markets not only increased the flow of capital on a
global basis but also created the opportunity—yet to be fully realized—for
the democratization of capital in the form of microfinance, mortgages,
credit scores, and a variety of other metrics to manage risk in financial exchange. Digital technologies can be applied to making social and political
institutions more transparent, accountable, and responsive. Likewise, new
forms of digital complementary currencies that combine the benefits of
"white money" and "black money" offer another avenue for affecting positive forms of social, financial, and political transformation.[16]

Renaissance Italy borrowed from classical Greek and Roman notions
of art as public expression and took it to another level. Because of the
importance of public art and the powers or patronage, the arts became a
relatively unfettered arena for self-discovery, public debate, commentary,
and social invention. Through the arts during the Renaissance, there
could be a competition of ideas. Through public competitions, the arts
also set very high standards and expectations, and consequently, accom-
plishment was respected and recognition highly sought after.

Had not it been for prior Roman traditions that were tolerant, open,
and immensely successful, there might not have been a Renaissance at
all. Today, it is an open question whether societies that have no significant traditions of openness and experimentation can truly develop open
civic and economic institutions and still retain a sense of their indigenous identity.

Current debate on security and democratization issues still tend to be
framed in ethnocentric, moralistic, political, and cultural terms. Implicit

in the debates over global security is the presumption that disenfranchised peoples can somehow make informed, rational choices about what their social, political, and economic institutions should be, even when they have never experienced such institutions before. It is further assumed that having made their choices, they can then embrace institutions that have no natural precedent in their societies and cultures. But can you elect a parliament or congress, say, and expect it to work, without ever having seen one in operation?

The evolutionary sciences and the associated technologies of self-organizing networks are culturally neutral, like physics or other branches of the sciences, they do not have to be embedded in a particular culture in order to make predictions or create viable technologies. Hence, they offer the promise of a more rigorous and testable accounting of social and economic processes than do notions of "democracy" or "nation-building" and do not presuppose any specific ideology or tradition.

From this perspective, there is no basis to argue for the inevitability of Western democratic and economic institutions. Little differences, local differences, historical precedents, even random differences can result in massive, nonlinear, irreversible changes and extinctions. Different cultural traditions do not necessarily "mutate" or recombine into more open societies where the fundamental Western-style building blocks of social-exchange relationships are absent. A complex brew of religion, culture, personality, history, economics, and geopolitics can produce very different outcomes for societies that superficially seem the same. Just as there is no inevitable "progress" in nature, so there is no inevitable progress in human affairs; successor societies are not always better than their predecessors. The Renaissance was followed by two centuries of political retreat in Italy, with much of the innovative energy of the Renaissance moving out of the country.

So, can current highly traditional, closed, and highly parochial societies, which in many core respects have not changed for thousands of years, make the leap to modernity in the course of seventy-five or 150 years, as did eighteenth-century Scotland or fourteenth-century Florence? Could Kabul become an Edinburgh in 2100? Can Iran recapture its Persian past, as Italy did with its Roman past, and bring it into the twenty-first century? Are there legitimate seeds of "openness" and tolerance in each of these traditions—as there were in the cases of both Scotland and Italy—or are their historical social identities so wedded to fixed and inflexible identities that they simply cannot change at all? Even in the cases of the Italian Renaissance and the Scottish Enlightenment, where there were prior, respected traditions of openness from the classical traditions, the transitions were bloody and chaotic. In those times, there was no highly destabilizing force of accessible and relatively inexpensive weapons that in time would enable small bands of zealots to hold nation-states hostage. Technology has wholly altered the equation, and it will take new generations of technologies designed specifically to create new kinds of equitable, transparent, and effective social and commercial institutions to make the transition to a new kind of global community viable. But technology also offers the promise of positive transformation: In Kabul, it is possible to watch the images of the rest of the world on CNN and the BBC. The best of the wider world's traditions and cultural expressions are available (as are some of the worst), thanks to the Net. It is almost impossible now to be a citizen of the world and not have some sense of the range of diversity within it, the opportunities it can confer. If there are Renaissance virtues anywhere, they can be projected everywhere eventually.

Chapter Eight

Prospects for Digital Trust

ONE THE MOST REMARKABLE QUALITIES OF FLORENTINE BANKERS during the Renaissance was their ability to secure a transaction with a handshake. Prior to the Renaissance, there really was no functioning banking system. Corruption and violence were so rampant that merchants and business members only trusted family members and those with whom they had a history of dealings. But after the fourteenth century, Florentine and Venetian bankers were financing projects around Europe and the Mediterranean. There was a trust explosion.

Trust is often treated as an individual quality or value. One routinely says, "That person is 'trustworthy'"—without mention of the conditions under which a person is trustworthy or why one thinks so. The position taken here is that trust is a consequence of how relationships in social networks are managed by members of the network. In this sense, trust is not so much an intangible personal virtue as a group property, the consequence of social emotions such as empathy, reciprocity, and the capacity of the group to recognize and sanction those who are not trustworthy. Because trust is a combination of individual and group skills for managing risk, it should be replicable and scalable.

The United States Marines manual offers the following definition of trust:

> Trust is the cornerstone of cooperation. It is a function of familiarity and respect. A senior trusts subordinates to carry out the assigned missions completely with minimal supervision, act in consonance with the overall intent, report developments as necessary, and effect the necessary coordination. Subordinates meanwhile trust that the senior will provide the necessary guidance and will support them loyally and fully, even when they make mistakes. . . . Trust has a reverse side: it must be earned as well as given. We earn the trust of others by demonstrating competence, a sense of responsibility, loyalty, and self-discipline.[1]

Trust is the currency that drives and holds together highly successfully military operations. You cannot assign a monetary value to the risks or the likelihood of death that combatants incur, nor even promise the reward of status and glory, because many of the most valorous and critical actions go unnoticed. The reward is the trust of the unit. Militaries around the world and throughout time have long understood the power of trust and have adroitly exploited the willingness of soldiers to sacrifice and fight for their peers to achieve broader military or political goals. As Brigadier General Thomas Druade, USMC, narrated in a Vietnam War documentary, "Marines don't fight for their country, and they don't fight for the Marine Corps. They don't fight for apple pie, motherhood, Sally Lou, or Lost Overshoe, Iowa. They fight for their buddies."[2]

Thanks to the innate proclivity of young males to compete, bond, and assume risks, military organizations have long had the basic ingredients for the formation of networked organizations—peer trust. But this trust does not extend naturally beyond the immediate group. It is well known that soldiers fight and die for their comrades—not their division or their country. The challenge is to create trusted institutions by understanding how the conditions for trust naturally emerge and can be reinforced.

Whether in business, warfare, or personal relationships, trust is often cited as the most important attribute for success. Yet how trust is to be formed and sustained when few of the parties know one another is one of the great challenges confronting large-scale, dispersed organizations. This is especially true for cross-organizational alliances and partnerships, such as disaster relief or multinational peacekeeping organizations that require not only cooperation among the different services and agencies, military and civilian, but also cooperation among coalition partners who have different perceptions, goals, values, capabilities, cultures, and traditions.

Trust under these circumstances would seem unlikely at best, as it is generally regarded as an intangible social value that is difficult to inculcate, harder still to replicate, and virtually impossible to scale. Yet as the U.S. Marine Corps recognizes, trust is essential for moving beyond a strictly hierarchical command and control model to one that that is agile, flexible, and networked:

> The aim is not to increase our capacity to perform command and control. It is not more command and control that we are after. Instead we seek to decrease the amount of command and control we need. We do this by replacing coercive command and control methods with spontaneous, self-disciplined cooperation, based on low-level initiative, a commonly understood commander's intent, mutual trust, and implicit understanding and communications.[3]

The question then becomes: how can large-scale social networks be created so that they are spontaneous, self-disciplined, and guided by mutual trust? Small-scale social networks of peers can be terribly effective at controlling and synchronizing themselves through subtle forms of peer pressure. As we have seen, groups of up to 150 members human beings have built-in algorithms for directing their members' social behavior and cooperation.[4] However, in groups of more than 200 individuals, our innate capacity to track and enforce social relationships breaks down.[5] Among the qualities lost is the ability to trust broadly.

Digital technologies offer unprecedented opportunities for amplifying our innate ability to track and manage social relationships by providing virtual methods for assembling, tagging, and rating one another's behavior, and thereby achieving new forms of visibility, accountability, and hence trust and cooperation. Peer-to-peer networking technologies—from e-mail to instant messaging, to various forms of "peer production networks" and the open source movements—have demonstrated that networks of trust and cooperation can be created from digital peer-to-peer networks. In other words, thanks to technology, trust and cooperation may be expandable beyond the natural network limit that the human brain equips us for.

Pierre Omidyar, the founder of eBay, has always believed that trust was the foundation of human social exchange and community.[6] He founded eBay on the untested, unproven notion that total strangers could come to trust one another sufficiently to engage in significant financial transactions. In contrast to the assumptions of *Homo economicus* in classical economic theory, which holds that man is innately selfish and distrusting, Omidyar believed that people naturally want to trust one another and are not guided by Hobbesian notions of greed and narrow self-interest, but rather by principles of reciprocity and community. In a letter to the members of eBay, Omidyar characterized eBay as a "grand experiment . . . creating an open market that encourages honest dealings . . . to make it easier to conduct business with strangers over the Net."[7] What made eBay such a phenomenal success—Levi Strauss & Co paid $46,532 for a vintage pair of its own jeans, bought on eBay and reported by *Forbes* magazine—however, was not starry-eyed idealism but a genuine insight into the *mechanics* of how people formed their identities within communities where their actions were visible:

> A feedback system was created to accommodate members' evaluations of one another. EBay solicited feedback from the participants after each transaction. Buyers and sellers rated one another as positive, negative, or neutral, and often appended a brief comment in their feedback. These ratings became a permanent part of each user's membership file on the site.[8]

Members were able to achieve standing in their respective communities through their service ratings and by their contributions to the chat rooms associated with their product categories. Members could achieve a unique kind of social status, influence, and visibility not normally accorded to them. The eBay mechanisms for building trust were so successful that in 2001, of all transactions, fraud registered less that 0.01 percent, taking trust to the point where a Corvette was sold on eBay every three hours.[9] By 2005, eBay had over $1 billion in profit. Over time, schemes to defraud customers and to "game" the reputation have grown in sophistication, and eBay has had to develop progressively more sophisticated fraud detection, dispute resolution, and enforcement mechanisms. But that reflects the growing sophistication of an untrustworthy minority, not a fundamental misjudgment by Omidyar.

Early on, eBay had many competitors, including Amazon, Yahoo! and OnSale. However, what accounted for eBay's long-term economic success was not its prowess as a fierce competitor or proficient auctioneer but its seemingly uneconomic emphasis on community and trust:

> After using eBay for just a short time, users became actively involved in e-mail dialogue, their reputations on the system were built as other users observed their actions and rated their reliability, and users came to know the ins and outs of the system. The community was also self-policing, and users frequently formed "neighborhood watch" groups to help guard against user violations of site etiquette . . . Stories about eBay users helping one another prevailed. For example, during the 1998 holiday season, eBay started the Giving Board for people to post stories about people in need . . . The response to the board was so overwhelming that a committee of eBay members was formed to help coordinate charitable efforts of the Giving Board.[10]

Many of eBay's competitors tried to compete on traditional economic grounds, not recognizing that the success and lure of eBay resided in its commitment to build communities where members were connected to one another and were empowered to shape the offerings of the company. Meg Whitman, eBay's CEO, was clever enough to recognize this from the beginning and has identified it as one of eBay's unique competitive advantages:

> OnSale's view of the world was the following: it's auctions and it's economic warfare. This isn't about auctions. It's about community commerce. Auctions are the enabler. I don't think they understood that. It's not economic warfare; in fact, it's the opposite. It's about you and me making a connection over a shared area of interest.[11]

Ironically, the hardheaded pragmatism and economic orthodoxy of eBay's competitors blinded them to what the real objectives or effects of their competition were: satisfied customers and suppliers who identified with the company. In other words, eBay's competitors were fighting the wrong war; they presumed that their customers were rational economic actors, maximizing their own self-interest. The eBay model is such an anathema to conventional economic wisdom that it is not difficult to see how it was misunderstood and even discounted by its competitors as a dot-com aberration. However, what makes eBay so important is that it was the first commercial organization to successfully scale trust as a network property and capture it as an economic and organizational asset. Furthermore, the principles and the mechanisms it developed are inherently simple and widely applicable.

The eBay example is also important because it is the first economically successful model of a "post-market networked enterprise," which is to say that its success did not derive solely from pure economic principles and motives, as most of its competitors presumed, but from the creation of community principles with its customers. In short, its customers were *members* who were both producers and consumers, and the value that eBay created was in enabling the exchange of goods and social assets in a safe context. Whenever eBay tried to lay claim to the ownership of the eBay space or impose its will and directives on its members, it was met with immediate and overwhelming negative responses ("flaming" and rebukes) from the membership.

Trust is vital to any meaningful collaboration. During a collaboration, the trust depends not on a transaction, but on certifying the quality and extent of a individual's contribution to a common effort, and thereby providing for the equitable allocation of rewards. In collaborative work, poor quality and free riders are the agents of distrust.

Nowhere is collaboration more important than in software development. Software development is an idiosyncratic, social, collaborative activity that is more art than science. It is also a highly complex, arcane, and expertise-intensive undertaking that can be hugely costly. The billion-dollar overruns on software projects undertaken by the leaders of the field (IBM, Microsoft, Oracle, and SAP) are legendary and well documented. Here again, experience contradicts accepted wisdom: Open source software, that is, the voluntary development of software by tens of thousands of programmers, most of whom have never met each other, can produce more reliable and robust software than that produced by commercial enterprises. It is a global movement, widely embraced by European, South American, Asian, and developing governments eager to get out from under the yoke of predominately American software vendors, and it encompasses all types of software, from the famed Linux operating system to browsers (Firefox), server software (Apache), Web hosting applications (PHP), grid services (Globus), Web services (WC3), and debuggers (Bugzilla).[12] The open source software movement is so pervasive and potent that it may do something that neither IBM nor any other commercial software vendor could do: dethrone the software hegemon, Microsoft. According to Professor Steven Weber, an expert on the open source software movement, "[T]he notion of a proprietary operating system will seem quaint in the near future."[13]

One of the most extraordinary successes of the open source movement has been Wikipedia, a free multilingual online encyclopedia, which is a "wiki," meaning a Web site that anyone can edit. Instead of being written by experts, anyone who registers can make an entry to the wiki, where it is reviewed by editors who amend, augment, and edit the entry. There are over 4.5 million articles or entries in approximately 150 languages. There have been a number of controversies about Wikipedia because it is free, voluntary, and does not use "experts" or claim copyright for its content. There have been numerous examples where false, highly biased, and promotional information has been entered. But in most cases, the Wikipedia community is self-organizing and self-correcting, and the quality and range of the entries is quite extensive and thorough.

This vision of the future of software has been adopted by IBM, which has aggressively embraced the open source software model. IBM has been the champion of open Java standards, Linux, and the Globus grid-services software. Instead of investing billions of dollars in developing proprietary software in competition with other commercial vendors and the open source software movement, IBM has become a proponent of the commons model, whereby even competitors recognize that their long-term commercial success depends upon the creation of common software assets that they can in turn adapt to the special needs of their customers.[14] In effect, the open source movement is creating a new form of common software resource that can then be adapted and appropriated for private commercial gain much more efficiently than if all parties acted independently on their own behalf.

Like eBay, the open source movement has developed highly sophisticated methods for building trust among large numbers of scattered actors. Protocols for how to evaluate, rate, and incorporate new software and covenants for its use and reuse, developed by the commonwealth of producers and consumers, have been successfully worked out in sufficient detail that they have now become the accepted norm of software development. The Eclipse Foundation, originally founded by IBM with an investment of $240 million, is now a wholly independent open-source foundation with over 1 million registered developers. The classic strategy of locking in customers through enormous licensing agreements and proprietary "hooks" is being phased out through the proliferation of high-quality free software that is supported and extended by the commonwealth.[15] Even Microsoft, which had perfected the practice of proprietary software lock-in, is having to come to grips with the reality of open source. Instead of selling and licensing software products, the monetization of the value software will be achieved through highly specialized value-added Web services. Microsoft's announcement about opening up its identity software for identity management, CardSpace, for third parties makes a major shift in its policies toward interoperability of software and openness.

The success of the open source movement has been propelled by the power of peer review, which is achieved through the same combination of visibility, ratings, and accountability that worked for eBay. For software innovators, monetary reward is secondary to peer recognition, reputation, and access to consumers. What is especially instructive in this example is how quality is judged and rewards allocated. Trust is earned through a demonstrated competence with one's peers, and trust is given if subordinates know that their "leaders or governors will provide the necessary guidance and support them loyally and fully, even when they make mistakes."[16] In technologically defined commonwealths, technical proficiency is more easily gauged than in less-measurable environments, though it is by no means without ambiguity and controversy. Therefore, it is vital that the performance of corporate or group leaders be subject to independent ratings that are credible to the commonwealth at large. Distrust and mayhem will occur where the rating systems of the peer networks and the governing networks are not aligned. The more hierarchical, formal, and opaque an organization is, the more likely this undesirable outcome becomes. Military organizations function best when commanders are respected and trusted, not simply feared and obeyed. Effective peer networks have very clear definitions of their common purpose and are able to rate senior and subordinate contributions accordingly. This is especially true of undertakings that can include many different partners, each of whom has a distinct organizational agenda and reward structures. When rewards become based upon politics over performance and rank higher than competence, and the ability to manipulate the system trumps genuine contributions, then trust breaks down and with it, the capacity for any organization to be effective. When the rot of distrust sets in, each party retreats into its own narrow interests, becoming noncooperative and contributing to the cost of inefficiency.[17] To have robust trust and genuinely collaborative networks there must be complete transparency and accountability, and the interests of the commonwealth, to use John Adams's terms, should trump individual claims of "advantage" or "exclusive privileges."

Recent scientific research on trust and the success of trust-based peer organizations such as eBay, Wikipedia, and the open source movement indicates that trust is a highly expandable network property. Yet in order for trusted networks to evolve, there must also be trusted leadership roles. Leadership is a critical ingredient for any organization, and like trust, it is especially difficult to capture and quantify. Here, too, evolutionary biology provides insight into the purpose and nature of different types of leadership roles, defining leadership as both a network property and an individual trait. This takes us to the central question of whether leaders are born or made. And if made, who makes them?

Chapter Nine

Toward a Literacy of Natural Leadership

DO THE TIMES MAKE THE MAN OR THE MAN THE TIMES? ISSUES OF leadership strike at the heart of a central theme of this book: the interplay between the individual and the group. A leader is—by all the usual definitions—single, distinct, a contrast to the group in every way. But if, as this book has argued, there is no absolute distinction between the individual self and the group, where is there room for leadership?

In human history there have been rare moments of individual and societal genius, when an unexpected combination of factors resulted in a burst of creativity and social invention, where leaders in the arts, sciences, and politics—Giotto, Datini, Darwin, Michelangelo, Genghis Khan, Caesar, Alexander the Great, Confucius, Mohammed—seem to come out of nowhere to shape a new cultural and civic order. Small, technologically backward societies, in today's terms, have produced leaders in virtually all categories in greater quantities—certainly on a per capita basis—than has been achieved in the last hundred years.

Equivalent to the two centuries of creative and commercial innovation that began in thirteenth-century Florence is the period that began in fifth-century B.C. Athens. It had a population of around 30,000 citizens, out of a total world population estimated to be 250,000. From this small group and the other city-states of Greece emerged Socrates, Aristotle, Pythagoras, Plato, Thucydides, Sophocles, and Aristophanes, and the foundation for Western democracy. By contemporary standards, Athens was a poor and backward society lacking the infrastructure of technologies and amenities that are now deemed essential for building institutions of enlightenment and education. And yet principles of culture, science, and governance were discovered then that are still active today, and the men who made these discoveries are still studied and exhibit a level of intellectual rigor and refinement that is hard to find among their contemporary "peers."

A more recent example of an era of explosive transformation and abundant leadership is America from 1750 to 1810, the era of the founding fathers of the American Revolution. Not since then has America seen such an extraordinary collection of talents among its civic and political leaders. During that time, there were no more than 2 million inhabitants in the American colonies. Yet it apparently produced more leaders from this small base than has contemporary America with 150 times the population! The first of the uniquely American "self-made" men was the entrepreneur Benjamin Franklin, who was also a world-class scientist and diplomat. The writings of Jefferson, Madison, Hamilton, Paine, and Adams are still fresh and relevant today. These men, like their Florentine counterparts, were Renaissance Men, public men, broadly and deeply self-educated, enthusiastic and responsible architects of their country's future. They were forward looking, eager to break the historical shackles of the authorities that sought to limit free thought and assembly.

How is it that such comparatively small and technologically disadvantaged societies such as Athens, Renaissance Italy, and revolutionary America produced such extraordinary achievements and leadership? Might it be in how people interacted with one another? The ways in which they developed trust, collaborated, competed, learned, and expressed and defined their roles and identities? Might all these societies share certain underpinnings, social norms, values, and structures that might account for their extraordinary successes?

The influence of Greek and Roman traditions, specifically the importance of civic virtues, slices across these different time periods and societies. The Romans imitated the Greeks, the Italians emulated the Romans, and the Americans used the Romans, the Italians, and the Scots as models. Within these societies were firmly planted views of a broader social purpose, ideals about the republic, the subordination of self-interest to the public good, notions of virtue, honor, truth, and character. Such terms appear somewhat quaint today, artifacts of a more innocent and simpler age. Yet these values, combined with a real reverence for aesthetics and truth, were decisive.

When the founding fathers—as privileged and unrepresentative a group of older white males as there ever was—were putting their lives and fortunes at risk to found a more just society governed by laws and not men, their success was due primarily to their shared qualities as a closely knit group of "gentlemen" whose values were inspired by Roman republicans of 2,000 years earlier. Joseph Ellis, in his portrait of the "revolutionary generation," makes this point in discussing why the "founding brothers" were so successful:

> Honor matters because character mattered. And character mattered because the fate of the American experiment with republican government still required virtuous leaders to survive.[1]

What is so striking about the founding of the American Republic is how much this class of leaders had read and assimilated the major works and lessons of the Roman republic. Alexander Hamilton, who was a harsh political critic and opponent of Thomas Jefferson, nonetheless came to Jefferson's defense in his run-in with the scheming Aaron Burr. Both Hamilton and Jefferson realized Burr was a man of few scruples, willing to sell out the struggling republic in order to advance his own interests. In a speech, Hamilton castigated Burr in the same terms that Cicero used to rebuke, Catiline, a notorious conspirator against the Roman republic:

> His private character is not defended by his most partial friends. He is bankrupt beyond redemption except by the plunder of his country. His public principles have no other spring or aim than self-aggrandizement. . . . If he can, he will certainly disturb our institutions to secure himself permanent power and with it wealth. He truly is the Catiline of America.[2]

Cicero's attack on Catiline was well known to Hamilton's peers, and the values implicit in the condemnation well accepted. The pivotal point here is that the values of Roman virtue were governed by informal codes of conduct and honor that were in turn accountable to a common good. These codes existed in networks of persistent social relationships—not transactions—in which leaders were accountable to one another for the general welfare of the network. Leadership and virtue in this context meant a willingness to be accountable to such principles and place the common good over personal advantage. The common theme among the examples of Greece, Rome, Florence, and revolutionary America is the "social technology" of personal virtue, valued social relationships and honor as modeled in the person of Cicero.

It was these virtues that made George Washington the most respected leader of his generation. Although the diminutive John Adams noted that Washington was "always the tallest man in the room," it was the presence of his character that made men want to follow and obey him, as noted by a contemporary, Benjamin Rush:

> He has so much martial dignity in his deportment that there is not a king in Europe but would look like a *valet de chambre* by his side.[3]

Each of these societies recognized and rewarded the desire to serve a greater cause than self-interest. It was not coincidental that the experiences of the Romans were the models for both the Renaissance Italians and the founding fathers. The Roman general Cincinnatus, who after defeating the Carthaginians, gave up his role as dictator and returned to his farm to complete spring planting, was a direct inspiration to General Washington and many of the other officers who served in the Continental army. Like Cincinnatus, Washington resisted offers of absolute authority and in doing so, made possible the birth of a republic at a politically fragile moment. It required a kingly presence to overcome a royal authority, but crucial to Washington's lasting authority was his willingness to give it up once the job was done.

Many of the societies that have shown the greatest bursts of creativity, talent, and leadership have done so in opposition to hierarchical networks of hereditary leadership: the Greeks in response to their own "tyrants" and the Persians; the Romans against "dictators"; the Renaissance Italians against the church, the gentry, and foreign kings; Enlightenment Scots against the church and the king; and finally, the American revolutionaries against George III. They all succeeded by replacing or modifying authoritarian, rigid, hierarchical, hereditary, and theocratic networks. They replaced them with less hierarchical leadership networks in which the exercise of power was based more on merit and was more transparent and accountable. In all these cases, the identities and roles of "elites" became redefined and became more heterogeneous as they came to adopt many of the civic virtues captured in classical writings. It would be a stretch to say that all social revolutionaries could quote Cicero. But many of them did. Indeed, many of them still do, perhaps without realizing it.

Marcus Tullius Cicero was the unparalleled champion of Roman virtue and as such, he was one of the most influential of classical political thinkers and writers for Renaissance Italy, Enlightenment Scotland, and colonial America. His speeches and aphorisms were widely taught and became the models for virtuous conduct for fledgling republics. This aphoristic common sense, nearly 2,100 years old, still rings true, from "The first duty of a man is the seeking after and the investigation of truth" and "The strictest law often causes the most serious wrong" to "Freedom is participation in power" and "Virtue is its own reward."

Aphorisms like these have such enduring appeal because they reveal a constant in human nature. Such virtues are time-tested, self-directed methods for building sustainable and equitable forms of cooperation that can raise individuals from warring mobs into civic society—as they did in Renaissance Italy and eighteenth-century Scotland. Cicero's civic virtues are examples of time-tested, universal principles for civic leadership. His aphorisms are as interesting for their efficacy as social algorithms (for building trust, openness, and flexibility) as they are as moral philosophy.[4]

In the same way that religious doctrine on the subject of food and hygiene was once, and sometimes still is, a form of camouflaged health care—it isn't a good idea to eat seafood in hot climates far from the sea nor to eat uncooked pork that might harbor trichinosis; yoga and vegetarianism are medicinally advantageous in many circumstances—so aphorisms contain certain truths that encourage civic virtue, or a healthy society, which only now are being revealed through neuroscience and the evolutionary sciences. Many moral and religious precepts, grounded in the collective experiences of what worked to make societies prosperous and viable, could not explain why they were needed or how they succeeded. As a consequence, they, too, had to be imposed as rules. In this respect, religious, social, and political practices, along with political institutions, have been historically linked. What is exceptional about the Romans, and Cicero in particular, is that they evolved secular practices around governance that have a universal application independent of a particular culture. As more and more is learned about the evolutionary and neuroscientific basis for different types of human morality, then as in the case of medicine, it should be possible to design new social technologies that rely not upon blind obedience but upon scientific proof and practice. The aphorisms of Cicero are a good starting point. They are not narrowly prescriptive but instead treat leadership virtues in such a way that they are open to scientific testing.

So Cicero's statement, "The first duty of a man is the seeking after and the investigation of truth," although so familiar that it may seem vacuous, sets a very pragmatic requirement for effective leadership. It is every bit as "realistic" as Machiavelli's advice to the prince. This is a virtue that if properly pursued, instills high degrees of trust and loyalty. In sociological terms, a leader who is accountable to principles of truth that are outside his control lowers social friction, thereby increasing efficiency. It seems possible to test the efficacy of this virtue and to conclude whether it could be replicated in the design of leadership networks. The leader's pursuit of truth can be regarded as just a more traditional way of advocating for an open network of leaders who are not captive to any single point of view. Online experiments using social network models could be designed to test whether such openness has an impact on the success of leaders in achieving the goals of a group.

Similarly when Cicero coined "Virtue is its own reward," he invented not only a popular aphorism but a way of speaking to the importance of self-command. Incentive and reward systems that reward virtue with financial or status incentives will fail. This view is very much at odds with market-based incentive structures for leadership, especially exorbitant compensation to corporate leaders. In designing new forms of leadership networks, it is a testable proposition. The neuroscientific studies of trust and empathy by Ernst Fehr and his colleagues bear this out: People playing trust games with monetary rewards receive oxytocin rewards for trust and empathy. For them, virtue is its own reward. In contrast, the offer of compensation and formal rewards can diminish the value of the incentive for altruistic behavior.[5]

"Freedom is participation in power" is a definition of freedom that reflects a Greek perspective on democratic processes, in a society where the citizen did not expect to be served by the state but was expected to participate in the exercise of government, and hence power. Contemporary American democracy takes an opposite view and regards freedom as being free from the interference of government; rather than being a source of freedom, government is viewed as a necessary irritant that needs to be minimized and avoided. Again, this is a proposition about human governance that is eminently testable and hence subject to scientific exploration.

Many of Cicero's aphorisms highlight the contrast between real and assumed authority ("The nobler a man, the harder it is for him to suspect inferiority in others") and the qualities inherent to great leadership ("True nobility is exempt from fear"). Most intriguingly memorable are those constructions that are subversive, and several draw attention to qualities that are reputational or trust based: "A man's own manner and character is what most becomes him." Cicero used the aphoristic style to get to the essence of virtue; he was, in his time, trying to model ideals of leadership and social behavior. That's why his words endure.

People have tried in different eras to discover the essence of leadership in different ways. Today, one way we study "natural" leadership cultures is through the example of how our closest relatives, primates, act naturally, independent of human intervention. Leaders in this context are the alpha males and females, who by virtue primarily of their size, beauty, aggressiveness, and sometimes, guile, dominate and hence lead other members of their group. Yet even among this group there is a spectrum of "leadership" types or roles, from savanna baboons to highland gorillas and tree-dwelling rhesus monkeys to forest chimpanzees.

Sometimes primates provide mirrors on our own behavior. Yet even among primates, there is no pure Hobbesian state of nature. Leadership among primates is not solely a question of dominance and size; other capabilities count as well. These include coalition building, food sourcing, vocalization, grooming, and dispute resolution, each a complex social skill that depends on empathy. Size plays a role, but it is not definitive. Although undoubtedly there is intense competition among highly social primates for physical fitness and dominance, there also appears to be natural selection for social traits of cooperation and relationship building. In both cases, competing males seem to learn from imitation, and research has shown that chimpanzee bands can have their own cultures and histories, depending upon who their leaders are and what specific traits seem to succeed.

In all primates, humankind especially, some degree of leadership is conferred on an individual who embodies a kind of ideal form, who is an exemplar of fitness, beauty, strength, endurance, calm, bravery, and loyalty, all important qualities in a warrior leader, meaning one who can lead and protect in times of war and conflict. For much of human history, political leaders typically came with a military pedigree, even in recent years when it is inherited or ceremonial. Long after 1945, the British were selecting as their members of Parliament those who demonstrably had had "a good war"—in other words, had a distinguished military record—even though it was obvious the country had no intention of fighting another one. Given this long evolutionary history, it is no surprise that people tend to follow and obey those with a martial bearing. Specific physical traits of height, broad shoulders, strong chin, deep voice, and a deliberate and unflappable manner are probably anciently encoded social signals that reflexively trigger deference and loyalty. Although enormous credit is properly given to the brains of Jefferson, Adams, Madison, Franklin, and Hamilton, someone had to be the liberating military figure. That is what kept the Continental army and the country together. Washington had prepared himself in the British army, was a man of discipline and ambition, and seldom got sick, even when drenched with the frigid waters of the Delaware River. He once threw a stone 215 feet over the Natural Bridge of the Shenandoah Valley, something other men watched and noticed.

Yet the qualities of a truly successful leader, one to whom other men and women would entrust their lives, are as much about character, intelligence, daring, and trustworthiness as they are about physical strength. Lord Nelson and Napoleon Bonaparte were petite men by any standard. Yet both possessed great courage, self-confidence, charisma, and military intuition. So, primal leadership is not simply a matter of physical stature. There are specific traits of character that matter, that reflexively invoke loyalty, respect, and trust. In his "Ode on the Death of the Duke of Wellington," Alfred Lord Tennyson imagines many of the qualities of character so essential for both a military and a civic leader: sacrifice, decisiveness, courage, initiative, and modesty:

> . . . Mourn for the man of amplest influence,
> Yet clearest of ambitious crime,
> *Our greatest yet with least pretence,*
> Great in council and great in war,
> Foremost captain of his time,
> *Rich in saving common-sense,*
> And, as the greatest only are,
> In his *simplicity sublime* . . .

> . . . *Who never sold the truth to serve the hour,*
> Nor palter'd with Eternal God for power;
> Who let the turbid streams of rumor flow
> Thro' either babbling world of high and low;
> Whose life was work, whose language rife
> *With rugged maxims hewn from life;*
> Who never spoke against a foe;
> Whose eighty winters freeze with one rebuke
> All great self-seekers trampling on the right.
> *Truth-teller was our England's Alfred named;*
> Truth-lover was our English Duke;
> Whatever record leap to light
> He never shall be shamed. . . . *(emphasis added)*[6]

A good leader exemplifies the best qualities of a group, but he does not try to elevate himself above the group. By doing so, he makes his qualities the group's qualities, thereby enabling its members to perform at a level that they could not attain on their own. He brings honor and distinction to his company, brigade, or division, not to himself. These qualities of "simplicity sublime" and "truth-teller" are parts of the best of military culture.

They are hard to transfer from the field of battle into bureaucratic and administrative assignments or civilian life, where often different kinds of codes of conduct are rewarded. Those who succeed on the battlefield but fail to adjust to the rules of a bureaucratic organization are often the casualties of a culture that does not respect true leadership. Civilian codes of success are often at variance with those of the battlefield. In some bureaucracies, leadership is politicized to favor the subordination of the interests of the group to the promotion of the individual, the iconic representative of a certain policy or success. Under such circumstances, the leader in bureaucratic groups becomes a marker, a kind of shorthand, for the success or failure of an issue, policy, or campaign—not the exemplar of the group. This kind of quasi-leadership can absorb much of the credit and little of the blame, thereby undermining the very principles of transparency and accountability upon which effective peer networks depend.

Many of the traits Tennyson imagines in Wellington—sacrifice, courage, modesty, truth-telling, earned competence—are all virtues that make a social network trustworthy, effective, and robust. There is no deceptive signaling, there is no deception of the network; it is transparent and authentic. The acclaimed military leader is always true to his word; he does not leave his dead behind. For the United States Marine Corps, whose motto is *Semper Fidelis* (Always Faithful), the retrieval of the dead under the most perilous circumstance has a very practical purpose. It is a highly trustworthy and authentic signal that the group will always stand up for the individual under all circumstances. Once you are in, you are in. One for all, and all for one.

Martial competences have been selected for thousands of years, and as a consequence, it is very probable that they are innate. From the success of Spartan phalanxes in maintaining their coherence and ferocity under impossible battlefield conditions to the common format of small bands of highly trained and mutually dependent special forces, trustworthiness and a willingness to sacrifice oneself for the group are persistent traits of military leadership. Risk taking and peer accountability have been proven to be evolutionarily stable strategies for building and sustaining reciprocal social relationships that ensure mutual security under maximum duress. Given their prevalence, these traits are most likely embedded in neurotransmitter circuits that specialize in rewarding social emotions that build such bonds. Such circuits are likely to be triggered by testosterone and adrenaline—chemicals responsible for the highs and sense of power and invincibility that fighters get in moments of combat. The qualities of a natural leader can be learned to some extent, but to some people they come instinctively as a natural part of their personality. Those individuals can read and create the social and physical signals that can be trusted and relied upon. Other soldiers instinctively know from body language, timbre of voice, posture, eye-to-eye contact, excitability, and use of language whether an officer is worthy to follow into battle. His reputation confers upon the officer his authority; on his own, he can only demonstrate his rank.

The transition from primal leadership to group or networked leadership is an important transition in any society's development. It represents a kind of role specialization not dissimilar to Adam Smith's observation about the specialization in economies. Similarly, this leadership shift depends upon a distributed kind of control, the kind produced by Smith's invisible hand of moral sentiments.

Leadership that expresses and enforces these moral sentiments can be broken down into at least seven types, of which even the most obvious—the standout natural leader—ultimately proves incomplete. This is because leadership requires specialization and flexibility as groups grow, shrink, or simply alter over time.

As networks begin to increase in size, the skills of even natural leaders need to be disaggregated, and more specialized leadership roles identified and assigned to others. Leadership networks are in effect peer-to-peer networks in which leaders have specialized leadership roles, each with their own social protocols; when these are combined, they provide a highly robust and effective network. In such a network, no single leader has total power but instead exercises his or her power in the context of the respective leadership role. The challenge for any emerging community or society is how to progress to the point where the talents of the Big Man, that rare individual who may personally possess all the requisite leadership skills, can be explicitly institutionalized, so that the group itself is no longer dependent upon the single leader. For example, the leader who acted in the role of truth-teller, or enforcer, or gatekeeper no longer holds that function as a personal role; the role then becomes "specific institutional," an impersonal role, carried out by an auditor for truth-telling or a judge or policeman for enforcement.

Alpha Leaders.   Most social networks, whether they are military, recreational, adolescent, criminal, terrorist, artistic, professional, or athletic, are anchored by individuals who exemplify the ideal standards and qualities of the network. These are the role models that others imitate. Sometimes their role can be simply symbolic, even ceremonial, but they are nonetheless important in establishing the tone and culture of an organization or group. Successful and charismatic founders of new organizations, from Bill Gates, Steve Jobs, and Sam Walton to Osama bin Laden and Aum Shinrikyo, all embody values and personalities that become the defining values of their organization. These leaders also set the standards for becoming a member of a network. In the military, each service sector has its own types of exemplars: pilots and Seals for the navy; Green Berets and Rangers for the army; and fighter pilots for the air force. They embody what is considered the most arduous and admired professional qualities that set that service apart. Similarly, different corporate cultures value different talents and skills in their workforce.

The alpha leader commands respect not because of any inherent leadership or moral qualities, but because of his or her extraordinary talent—as a warrior, athlete, technologist, or scientist. In some cases, alpha leaders can be maladroit in dealing with people, self-interested, and lacking in judgment, but nonetheless, because of their preeminent skills, others want to be in their company, to learn from them and model themselves after them. They are "alpha" in the sense that an alpha male dominates his competitors through physical superiority. Yet in human society, physical dominance is only one limited arena of competition. Alpha leaders are not necessarily broadly competent in the sense that they can effectively manage the dynamics of building, governing, and protecting the interests of a particular group or network. In a sports team, a conspicuous star player may inspire and attract other great players but be a poor leader in the "clubhouse." The real leadership for the team is provided by a player of lesser physical talent but greater natural people-talent.

Exemplary Leaders.   Some leaders are just good leaders, comfortable with themselves, responsible for themselves in setting and adhering to their own values and standards, and at the same time, acting as stewards of the interests of the group. They are able to empathize with all the others within the group and are able to create a shared theory of mind for the group, a shared code of conduct and belief that gives the group its own identity, character, and purpose.

The importance of having an exemplar as a leader, whether of a country, company, or cause, cannot be overstated. Given the historical scarcity of such leaders, exemplarship also appears to be the rarest of all leadership qualities. Despite all the leadership talents of the founding fathers of the American Revolution, there really was only one who had this particular quality in requisite abundance to match the challenges of that time: George Washington. Not only was he an alpha leader in his bearing, courage, and military achievements, but he exemplified the moral sentiments of self-command, empathy, and a shared purpose needed to forge a new identity for a country.

Washington was the palpable reality, the man who clothed the revolutionary rhapsodies in flesh and blood, America's one and only indispensable character. He was the core of gravity, the one who prevented the American Revolution from flying off into random orbits, the stable center around which the revolutionary energies formed. As one popular toast of the day put it, he was "the man who unites all hearts. He was the American Zeus, Moses, and Cincinnatus all rolled into one."

The Visionary.   The visionary imagines futures, determines what is limiting about the present, and shows what is possible. Visionary leaders such as Steve Jobs, Winston Churchill, Walt Disney, Craig Venter (a pioneer in human genomics), Billy Mitchell (inventor of the modern notion of airpower), and Thomas Edison were a constant fount of new ideas and were "at war with the present." Many high-tech start-ups have been founded by visionaries, but are often not run by them. Visionary leaders imagine new possibilities, creating new institutional facts and realities, and therefore play a critical role in mobilizing their constituencies in new directions. This is an absolutely critical role in the start-up or crisis phase of any undertaking, and yet it can also be highly disruptive in circumstances where continuity and execution are critical to success.

Visionaries are like the prophets in the Old Testament or the *Iliad*. They can see the future before others do, but often they are not believed. Visionaries tend to live outside the mainstream and, as a consequence, do not abide by the prevalent norms. They observe offbeat or ignored trends, and gather and interpret facts differently. They have strong peripheral vision and connect the dots in ways that others ignore. The Nobel laureate Richard Feynman, for example, was celebrated for his ability to think outside the box, not only in physics but in a variety of endeavors; most notably, he was lauded for his ability to spot the failure of "O" rings in the destruction of the space shuttle *Challenger*.

A visionary may not only anticipate the future, but construct novel ways of resolving old problems. During the Italian Renaissance and the Scottish Enlightenment, it was not always a matter of inventing new technologies and ways of constructing buildings, governments, and public spaces, but was rather a matter of reapplying older, neglected ways—what the Romans had already achieved. It was the equivalent of removing the blinders: New possibilities were both imaginable and possible. That sense of potential was, of course, shared by many American immigrants in the eighteenth and nineteenth centuries. America represented a way of escaping the confines of class, religion, and monarchy in Europe and exploiting the open resources of land and social mobility in the New World. In this respect, the success of immigrants in America was in no small measure not just an emancipation from physical, social, and economic bondage, but an emancipation of the imagination, the capacity for anyone to imagine and build alternative futures without the heavy hand of past legacies. They had a vision.

The Gatekeeper. For every network there are membership rules, criteria for being included, retained, elevated, and excluded. The gatekeeper decides who is in and who is out. In congressional politics, the party leadership plays this role by deciding who gets which committee assignments and whose bills take precedence in a legislative agenda. This is a role that President Johnson as the former majority leader of the Senate understood brilliantly, whereas President Carter—an outsider, visionary, truth-teller, and moralist—never fully appreciated. In military organizations, the drill sergeant often plays multiple leadership roles, acting as alpha, enforcer, and gatekeeper. He weeds out recruits whom he believes fail to meet the standards of his unit. The gatekeeper role is especially important for elite units that seek to maintain their exclusivity by demanding exceptionally high standards of performance.

In corporations, the gatekeeper role is often expressed through formal and informal hiring practices and policies. In well-managed organizations where the real assets are the people and the corporate culture, the gatekeeper's role really is what protects and sustains the identity and character of the entire enterprise. As a consequence, how people describe themselves through their résumés, references, relationships, clothing, and manners are all social signals that are processed by gatekeepers.

The Truth-Teller.   In every organization, someone has to keep the network honest, identifying free riders and cheaters. In media and information-driven networks, the role includes ferreting out half-truths, spin, blunders, and lies. Such a leader can easily be compromised. As with the accounting function in a corporation or the judicial function in the legal system, if truth-tellers lose their independence they become ineffective. The role of the truth-teller is often the first to be jettisoned in times of stress; successful leadership is exemplified by independence, transparency, accuracy, and candor in the face of enormous pressure. As Tennyson's ode to Wellington[7] astutely expresses, truth-telling and resistance to the "lure of fame" go hand in hand and are a critical and enduring signature of effective leadership. One of the arguments for modesty in leadership is that the lure of celebrity and its attendant rewards can compromise independence and hence, credibility. For truth-tellers to be effective, they must also be credible; even a hint of self-dealing, or using inside information to profit, can undermine them.

The challenges faced by truth-tellers are especially acute and consequential within military organizations. If credibility breaks down, trust soon becomes the next casualty, followed by the overall effectiveness of the chain of command. The admonition "Don't shoot the messenger" is taken from military experience and reflects the high potential cost of reporting unwanted information. In response to such pressures, the military developed the doctrine of "ground truth" after the Vietnam War. The "truth-telling" goal is to provide authenticated and accurate reporting of the outcomes of missions. It can take enormous courage to resist the inevitable pressures of peers and superiors to report what they want to hear rather than the truth of the matter. Being a truth-teller can be highly unpopular and can result in a long road to advancement.

Given the high cost of "speaking truth to power" in any network or organization, it is important that truth-tellers be protected from retribution and reprisal. As more and more organizational activities become digital, new kinds of anonymizing technologies can be used to authenticate that truth-tellers have the expertise and clearances that they claim, and to protect their specific identities from being exposed and punished. This is the same type of problem that anonymous sources have in the news media. But given the power of new anonymizing technologies, there may be ways to have anonymous but authenticated sources for covering leaked stories. Anonymizing technology, for instance, could be used to make it possible to authenticate a source as having the required expertise or access to write a story without having to disclose the full identity of the source.

One of the great weaknesses of large-scale bureaucracies such as the Pentagon and the CIA is the ease with which senior leadership can punish and marginalize those who do not say what the organization wants to hear. That was the case in the Bush-Rumsfeld Pentagon, which officially espoused a doctrine of decentralized decisionmaking and network centric warfare. In practice, however, decisionmaking of any political consequence was highly centralized and politicized. Dissenting intelligence officers and generals have been marginalized and forced into early retirement. Although all bureaucracies are subject to such politicizing forces, the extent of such practices in the DOD under the Bush administration has been unprecedented, and should it continue, it will further undermine national security.

The Fixer.   Fixers know how to get things done and measure themselves not by how many people they might know, but rather by how well they can get things done that others cannot. Such individuals are results oriented. They "know where the bodies are buried" and what "makes people tick." In politics, they are the operators. They are all about opening and closing loops—getting tasks done. In Tennyson's words, they abide by the "rugged maxims hewn from life." They are illusion free and are inherently pragmatic. They may interact with a range of other network leaders—visionaries, truth-tellers, and connectors—but always with a concrete outcome in mind.

Within the military, there is the archetype of the "scrounger," an individual who is highly skilled at finding and assembling "found" materials, people, and resources to solve a variety of human and mission needs, from chocolate and silk stockings during World War II to scrap iron as armor plating for Humvees in Iraq. Fixers are gifted improvisers, what the French call *bricolagers*, people who take common available materials and turn them into something useful. In contrast to those who work through formal channels and depend upon approved procedures, fixers are typically "rule benders" and work through informal networks.

The Connector.   The connector's role is to participate in multiple social networks, connecting with a large number of highly diverse members. They are known for having numerous friends, relationships, and contacts. Like the visionary leaders, they can introduce variety and options into a network through the diversity of people with whom they interact. They are critical for identifying and accessing new resources and helping to get a message out. By building links across network boundaries, they can help a organization break out of the "lock-ins" of closed networks and introduce greater diversity, and hence robustness.

"Rainmakers" in professional service firms are often those senior partners who are great connectors. They attend many events, social and professional, and are skilled at leveraging their relationships in one social network to get things done in others. They are often great gift givers and gossipers. They know people's birthdays, favorite foods, personal likes and dislikes. They connect with many different people because they know what personally matters to them and how to make them feel valued. They are highly skilled at recognizing and validating how people see themselves and how they construct and support their identities, and they use this perceptive ability to good advantage. Natural-born politicians such as William Jefferson Clinton, Franklin Delano Roosevelt, and Ronald Reagan have a naturally gregarious manner and are responsive to people.

According to some research, women use gossip to build social cohesion and are better interpreters of social signals than most men and consequently are more accomplished in roles and professions where the connector type of leadership is important. Connector skills are especially critical for any diplomatic function that entails bringing together and introducing important players from diverse backgrounds and interests. Society "hostesses" such Pamela Harriman and Alice Roosevelt Longworth played this role at Washington, D.C. dinner parties, bringing together heads of state and different power brokers to address difficult issues that could not be dealt with in other settings.

During World War II, as supreme commander of the Allies, General Eisenhower developed a reputation as a highly accomplished connector by virtue of his ability to relate to the different interests and cultural styles of the other commanders. He was able to make and sustain connections among contending parties in order to keep the alliance together and on course. He was also able to exercise significant control over those whose primary allegiances were to different military organizations.

The Enforcer.   In smaller networks, the role of the enforcer is often combined with that of the gatekeeper and even the truth-teller. However, in larger networks it becomes an independent role, similar to the eventual separation of policing powers from judicial powers. Enforcement can mean physical coercion, but more often it entails social or peer pressure. As in the truth-teller function, independence and transparency are critical for overall network effectiveness. Coercion and physical force are the enforcement methods of last resort, but they are necessary to buttress lighter forms of enforcement, such as shame and legal redress. Most networks have their own forms of redress and enforcement that entail some form of exclusion or expulsion. The power of ostracism in Greek city-states, for example, was extremely effective because it not only removed individuals' right of protection but also destroyed their social identity as citizens.

Within larger bureaucracies enforcers have many subtle means at their disposal, not least of which is the denial of access to influential superiors, restrictions on budgets, travel, and authority, assignments, job reviews, and so on. Accomplished politicians such as Representative Tom DeLay, the former Speaker of the House of Representatives, are highly proficient in meting out rewards and punishments. DeLay was known as the "Hammer" because of his willingness to use virtually any and all means, legal and even otherwise, to enforce his will. Censorship and ostracism, when leveraged by respected peers and pillars of a leadership network, exerts enough pressure so leaders will abide by personal codes of conduct and stay accountable to these codes and their own sense of honor and decency. This is a more effective instrument than a legal process, which can be slow, crude, and compromised. Even the abuses of power by the infamous Senator Joseph McCarthy were not checked so much by legal means as by the shaming and humiliation of his peers in the Senate. For this reason, codes of conduct and models of public virtue set by exemplary leaders are critical to achieving robust and honest leadership networks.

Like trust, leadership is tangible, and it emerges from the ways individuals interact in social networks. Good leadership requires a composite identity, including both the individual and the group, that coalesces around a collection of different network roles. In this respect, leadership failures are not necessarily moral failures, or the result of individual character flaws, or the absence of requisite training, but instead can be seen as a design failure, an inability to create and fulfill leadership roles with the right mix of the requisite types.

Successful leadership fuses individual identity with group identity. It is a crowd of one. Yet our ability to foster true leadership remains episodic, accidental. But this may change. As our scientific understanding of how people trust, reciprocate, motivate, and initiate evolves, there is the real prospect that we can consciously and successfully create the conditions for cultivating high-quality leaders. We already test for cognitive and emotional competency, and businesses, schools, and governments have become much more proficient in screening and testing applicants. Yet such tests are still quite primitive, especially the measurement of personality and social emotional traits related to leadership. However, as the neuroscientific understanding of the social signaling mechanisms involved in building and governing social groups progresses, so too will the testing, screening, and training for leadership skills. It will become a science. Hence, character will no longer be seen simply as a moral aspiration, but rather as an essential trait of both leadership and social identity.

The qualities of character that Cicero and the leaders of the Renaissance, the Enlightenment, and the American Revolution valued and emulated may become a required social literacy for effective participation in a modern, civic society. By making leadership tangible and placing it in social context, a science of leadership can develop to make it a teachable competency. This is not to say that all people can become great leaders. Rather, by understanding the conditions that cultivate leadership, a society or organization could markedly increase its "yield" of high-quality leaders. However, doing this on a societal basis would require making leadership virtues and roles a part of a collective social identity. This is also demonstrated to some extent in the military, where leadership is a core value and part of one's rank and identity. Some of the most remarkable and successful leadership programs are within the military. For example, recruits who are disadvantaged can be trained in the course of a relatively short period of time to become highly effective and respected leaders. To be successful on a societal basis, however, those qualities that build character and leadership need to be reinforced by the appropriate identity narratives and become part of a shared social identity.

Chapter Ten

Negotiating an Identity:
One of the Crowd

I MET HIM IN A PRIVATE DINING ROOM IN ONE OF BOSTON'S OLDEST and most exclusive clubs, overlooking the Boston Commons. He was introduced to me by a highly congenial business friend, who was also the head of the Harvard Club in Boston. Mark Emerson Spangler, graduate of the prep school Buckingham, Browne and Nichols, and Harvard University, and the Wharton School to round out his business education, had all the earmarks of an old-line Bostonian. He was a patron of the Handel and Hayden Society, an avid sailor, a sponsor of Tanglewood; he summered in Nantucket and had season tickets to the Boston Symphony. Within Boston, Mark was one of the "rising stars" of new money managers, and according to an article in the *Boston Globe,*

> Spangler's name was appearing in the best of places. In the newspaper *USA Today* he was rated one of the nation's top money managers. . . . In 1984 Mark Spangler's money-managing business began to take off. He registered with the SEC and moved to One Boston Place. The Spangler Group was claiming rates of return on money placed with it ranging from 18.6 percent to 86.4 percent.[1]

Those who met Mark were invariably impressed. A *Boston Globe* article quoted two of his clients, a trusting retired couple from Vermont:

> "It's so good finally to meet you and Marie," the Millers recall Spangler saying, and he seemed to mean it, too. He ushered them by rows of offices and computers and into his corner office overlooking Boston Harbor, quickly slipping into a dark suit jacket. "Now there's a proper gentleman," Marie Miller thought.
>
> For more than two hours, they questioned Spangler at his antique desk and looked over computer printouts detailing their investments. They left impressed.
>
> "We felt lucky to know a man like this," Mrs. Miller says.[2]

But Mark was not what he appeared to be. I, like the Millers, had no idea who he really was. It took James Dupey, a retired Texas retailer living in Naples, Florida, to uncover the real Mark Spangler:

> Dupey got Spangler's name from a list ranking top money managers that had been supplied him by Ralph Goldman, a financial consultant and broker for Shearson Lehman Brothers Inc.
>
> Contemplating placing "a substantial" amount of money, he flew to Boston to meet Spangler in person. "I was really sold on him," he recalls. "I thought he was a neat guy. I really did."
>
> After the meeting Dupey asked Spangler to send him copies of written certification of his earnings record, as well as recommendations and background material.
>
> Spangler, he says, sent him a letter purportedly from Arthur Young & Co., the accounting firm, attesting to the group's claimed investment results. He also got the material listing Spangler as a Harvard and Wharton School graduate, where he said he finished third in his class.
>
> "I said, 'Fine, I'll do my homework,'" Dupey says, and he started making what he thought were routine calls to verify the claims.[3]

Dupey's homework revealed that nothing that Spangler sent him stood up. Not only did Spangler not graduate from Harvard, he didn't graduate from any college. He was kicked out of Buckingham, Browne and Nichols and never attended Wharton. He had forged the letter from Arthur Young & Co. He wasn't an investment adviser. It turns out that being registered as a money manager is not a certification of proficiency or even legitimacy—as one might assume. "Anybody," according to Peter Flynn, the assistant regional administrator of the Boston office of the SEC, "can register as an investment adviser. There are no entry standards or testing requirements."

That was a painful and expensive lesson for me. It was little consolation to his defrauded clients that even his wife had no idea about her husband's true identity. So then who was Mark Emerson Spangler? He certainly was not who he said he was. Nor was he who his colleagues said he was, nor who the head of the Harvard Club said he was, nor who USA Today said he was, nor who the SEC implied that he was, nor who the list of rated money managers said he was, and not who the Shearson Lehman broker said he was. And finally, he not who his wife—whom I had met—thought he was. Mark spent a lot of time, effort, and other people's money acquiring costly markers of status and credibility—from his antique furniture and club memberships, his sponsorship of the arts, his manners and dress, business address, and the references of his colleagues. It took a real leader, a "truth-teller," someone outside the chummy network of colleagues and "peers" to practice the required self-discipline, even when he didn't think it was necessary to research Spangler's record.

Mark grew up in wealth. His father was a well-respected Boston physician, and the family lived in Weston, the most expensive suburb in Boston. The trappings and behavior associated with social status, wealth, and achievement came naturally to him. The problem was that he was incapable of achieving them on his own. Not only was Mark Spangler not the trustworthy professional that he appeared to be, but neither were the many people and credentialing institutions that vouched for him. His inauthentic and untrustworthy reputation corroded the reputations of those who had vouched for him.

Mark took his identity from those around him, and he used his relationships to make himself appear to be more than he was. His crowd of one was a deliberate attempt to invent himself in such a way as to give him the standing and access he was otherwise incapable of achieving. He was wholly, calculatedly, and probably compulsively, inauthentic. His every intent was to appear what he was not. That was his true identity.

Mark Emerson Spangler did not commit identity fraud in the typical sense. He never appropriated another person's name, password, or bank account. Rather, he falsely represented his reputation, first through the artful and altogether legal orchestration of appearances, circumstances, competences, relationships, and affiliations, and then, through the illegal falsification of records and documents. He knew that high-status credentials and possessions implied competency, access, and hence, trustworthiness. He also knew that in appearing to possess and attain those things that were difficult and costly to achieve, he would gain the trust of those whose respect and financial means he needed. He realized that once he was in the right social network, he could leverage his relationships and standings in sailing and the arts to gain access and credibility as a money manager. Once trust was given in such circles, he knew it was not questioned, and that through a kind of Ponzi scheme of personal references, he could build his reputation. Mark was a con man in a blue blazer and Nantucket "reds."

This kind of reputation-identify fabrication happens all the time in human exchange. Not to the degree in Mark Spangler's case, thankfully, but such identity deceits, challenges, and tests are an everyday part of social life. Knowing who you are dealing with and what they can be expected to know and do, is fundamental to all forms of human interchange. Knowing how to read the social signals, to determine whether someone is really who he or she appears to be, knowing how to detect and counter deception is a competency of everyday life. Institutions such as the courts, legislatures, administrative agencies, insurance companies, and banks were invented precisely to certify and test, and to enforce the authenticity of representations of identity and reputation. Without such institutions and credible social methods for asserting and authenticating people's identity and reputation, civil society ceases to function.

This interplay of identity, reputation and social signaling is not only integral to human social exchange but is fundamental to the survival of all living things. What we experience as an everyday social occurrence— that is, our struggles to appropriate the proper social markers and credentials to be credible, trustworthy, and secure—are but the manifestation of a timeless, deeper struggle. All forms of life, from the simplest to the most complex, are engaged in a primal struggle to preserve their definitions of themselves against an onslaught of competitors and predators. From the perspective of the evolutionary biologist, everyday human concerns with identity, status, honor, trust, reputation, rejection and acceptance, cooperation and defection are all part of a larger evolutionary drama to survive those forces attempting to nullify or subsume the uniqueness of an individual or a species. The triumph of survival is to preserve and replicate a species across successive generations, and that in itself is an identity-preserving act. Our collective struggle to preserve our identity is the history of our species. That grand narrative is what the simple act of giving a person a first and last name builds toward. It is the first step in marking "me" as both a part of and distinct from the group.

For the majority of contemporary Western democratic societies, identity is an inalienable attribute of the individual, closely associated with his or her freedoms and rights. By comparison, some Enlightenment depictions of a state of nature imagine the individual as a kind of irreducible social atom from which all social and political institutions are constructed. The presumption exists that if individuals did not have to defend themselves from the tyranny of the many, and hence, seek the support of the state, they could happily, freely, and prosperously live in a benign state of nature. Collective institutions are portrayed as necessary evils, arising from a tragic fall from a state of individual grace.

Implicit in this notion of atomistic individuality is the belief that identity is self-asserted and self-referential. One does not have to depend upon any others. But this Enlightenment conceptualization of identity is a profoundly different notion than was constructed by earlier feudal- and kinship-based institutions. The individualistic notions of identity that were espoused during the Enlightenment were indeed revolutionary and were a reaction to the highly restrictive, hierarchical, and static definitions of self, roles, and relationships of feudal Europe. Prior to the Enlightenment, identity in the West was defined in a manner that remains typical of many of the world's cultures: principally, in terms of one's relationships to others in a social and religious hierarchy. Surnames were typically derived from a trade, a physical trait, achievement, place of birth, or paternal kinship. The word *surname* is even defined in these terms in the *Oxford English Dictionary*:

> **Surname as in sure-name or sir-name:** A name, title, epithet added to a person's name or names, esp. one derived from his birthplace or from some quality or achievement.

People living in feudal societies had very little choice over how they could be seen by others. Their freedom of self-expression in the most fundamental sense was determined not by them but by their communities. It was very difficult to be a "self-made man." Such choices were made for you. Until relatively recently in human history, only the gentry had the status and hence, the need for a full family name, whereas peasants, serfs, and tradesmen were identified principally by their place of birth, for example, the name Minsky, meaning "from Minsk"; or the trade-designated Miller, Smith, Farmer, or Baker; or paternal kinship names denoting son of: Ivanovitch, Johnson, Frederickson, bin Laden, Anderson. Even among the gentry, names could be brutally descriptive and less than flattering—Olaf the Stout, Karl III the Fat, Otto the Indolent, Mikael III the Drunkard—further indicating that the assignment of a name was not self-asserted but the prerogative of the group. Within the West, after the seventeenth century, surnames became commonly associated with the other names one bore in common with members of one's family and kinship group, hence the emergence of the "family name," one's unique persistent family identifier. Family names were to be distinguished from the first name, or in Western societies, the *Christian* name. The combination of the two names resulted in a unique combination for *an individual* just about the time of the Enlightenment, something that did not occur until much later in many non-Western cultures.

So what we take for granted today in Western democratic society, the right to have an individual identity, which to a significant measure is the right and property of the individual, is principally a product of the Enlightenment. In many respects, Enlightenment thinkers had to overstate the importance of the role of the individual in order to separate themselves from the rigidity and communality of feudal social categories. However, this overstatement has carried over into the present, notably in the United States, in the form of a lingering distrust of anything collective, especially the state.

The notion that the individual is the principal agent of his or her own identity is a principle championed by today's Libertarians and social conservatives. It is one of the premises upon which they base their arguments for the primacy of individual property rights and against progressive income taxes, minimum wage, and government regulation, for they believe it is through the agency of the individual alone that social and economic value is created. Yet scientific evidence says otherwise. People neither grow nor develop in a social vacuum. As a species, human beings are fundamentally dependent upon benign interactions with others to develop and mature both physically and psychically.

Well-documented examples of children raised in extreme isolation and in a true state of nature show that when there is neither suitable early intervention nor rehabilitation, isolated and feral children fail to acquire even rudimentary language ability and any sense of self or personal identity. They invariably suffer from "psychosocial dwarfism" and are roughly one-third or less the body weight of a normal child. So severe is the deprivation of those raised in a true state of nature that they fail to develop those traits that we uniquely associate with being human. The famous taxonomist Carl Linnaeus, in his *Systema Naturae* (1758), did not believe that feral children were human and classified them as a separate species: *Homo ferus*. According to studies of feral, isolated, and confined children,[4] the absence of normal human interaction and social stimulation results in irreversible damage to the brain. What it means to be human depends on an intensive and prolonged socialization process. Without that process, the intelligence, language, and social behavior we associate with being human simply do not materialize. In a very real sense, one's humanity materially depends not only upon genes but upon a prolonged socialization process that triggers complex, developmental processes. These examples of feral children illustrate unequivocally how personal identity is derived from a group identity, and hence, how the one and the crowd are inextricably interdependent.

Charles Darwin, a student of the Scottish Enlightenment, was greatly influenced by Adam Smith, Adam Ferguson, Francis Hutcheson, David Hume, and others. He also adopted some of the same artificial distinctions between the individual and group in developing his theory of natural selection. By separating out the organism from the environment, much in the same way his political theorist predecessors separated the individual from the group, Darwin perpetuated a false dichotomy that has hampered evolutionary biology ever since. Many of the debates over "altruistic" versus "selfish" behavior or between "individual selection" versus "group selection" arise from distinctions that are carryovers from a natural philosophy and have no place in evolutionary science. This is what the Harvard evolutionary biologist Richard Lewontin has characterized as Darwin's "alienation of the outside from the inside" for evolutionary biology. In proposing a new way to think of evolution and adaptation, Lewontin also offers a new evolutionary model to account for the social construction of social identities:

> Darwin's alienation of the outside from the inside was an absolutely essential step in the development of modern biology. Without it, we would still be wallowing in the mire of an obscurantist holism that merges the organic and the inorganic into an unanalyzable whole. But the conditions that are necessary for progress at one stage in history become bars to further progress at another. The time has come when further progress to or understanding of nature requires that we reconsider the relationship between the outside and the inside, between organism and environment. . . . But the claim that the environment of an organism is causally independent of the organism, and that changes in the environment are autonomous and independent of the changes in the species itself, is clearly wrong. It is bad biology, and every ecologist and evolutionary biologist knows that it is bad biology. The metaphor of adaptation, while once an important heuristic for building evolutionary theory, is now an impediment to a real understanding of the evolutionary process and needs to be replaced by another. Although all metaphors are dangerous, the actual process of evolution seems best captured by the process of *construction*.[5]

If one replaces the word *organism* with the word *individual*, and the word *environment* with the word *group*, the same argument can be made about understanding the construction of social identities and social institutions. Then, there does not need to be any sharp dichotomy between the individual and the group; rather, they can be seen as coevolving, mutually constructing, complementary identities.

Like progress in evolutionary biology, progress in the social and economic sciences may similarly depend upon abandoning a severe either-or distinction between the outer and inner, the individual and the group, and adopting a more evolutionary approach that does not succumb to the "mire of obscurantism" that has characterized such approaches in the past.

From a biological perspective, the root purpose of identity is survival and reproduction. If one's personal struggles with identity, trust, social boundaries, and signals at times feel like primal battles of life and death, it is with good reason: They are. They mimic in remarkable detail the everyday battles our immune systems incur in keeping us alive and free from the assaults of omnipresent and ingenious pathogens.

Being alive means that every organism must at a minimum successfully distinguish between itself and its "other"—the environment; every organism must have a rudimentary way of recognizing what is friend, foe, or food, and act on these differences. By virtue of making even these simple distinctions, every organism has a rudimentary sense of identity. This it does by *identifying* itself as being similar to or different from something else. To recognize the self, it needs to recognize the "other." They are interdependent.

The most sophisticated and effective security defenses ever to have been invented evolved to sustain biological identity. In a very real sense, the immune system biologically defines who you are. It is the barrier between you and the outside world. It works very hard to sustain and protect your unique biological identity. The human immune system, particularly the acquired immune system, defines what is unique to the individual and a species by identifying *what it is not, rather than what it is.* The immune system's definition and protection of an individual's identity is expressed as a negative, or as the complement of the outside world. It does not assert who you biologically are, only what you are not, and from that derives the definition of who you are.[6] Sometimes the immune system makes mistakes by attacking its own cells and tissues, causing an "autoimmune" response.

Type 1 diabetes, multiple sclerosis, psoriasis, rheumatoid arthritis, and asthma are examples of such an autoimmune response. If it intrinsically knew who it was, it would not make such a mistake.

If social identity is derived from the same principles that shape biological identity, then social and individual identity, like biological identity, is formed in opposition to external competing identities, those that blur the boundaries between one's own social niche and that of others. This might explain the intensity of a group's needs to reinforce in-group and out-group distinctions in order to clearly demarcate the boundaries of one's own social niches. Just as animals can be very aggressive in protecting their different breeding and feeding territories, so humans are aggressive in protecting their social territories, as these niches are fundamental to securing who they are. It is not an accident that names are derived from locality, trade, and kinship, all of which demarcate boundaries of identity and survival.

Examples abound in everyday life. The competition among cliques of adolescent girls and the ferocity with which in-group membership is defended and social boundaries marked by fad and fashion suggest that this is a normal path of identity formation. Likewise, the clashes between immigrant groups and indigenous low-income groups in urban areas are fueled by the need to have distinct markers in clothes, dress, music, and manners that are identity preserving. As soon as one group begins to mimic another, the other will do the opposite and introduce a new fashion variant. Being able to control an identity boundary is equivalent to carving out a social niche and is as critical to social survival as an ecological niche is to environmental survival. What is at stake is not just status and stability, but access to social and economic resources. Hence, it is not surprising the many of the bloodiest conflicts—between Hindus and Muslims, Serbs and Bosnians, Turks and Armenians, Catholics and Protestants, Tutsis and Hutus, Arabs and Jews—are those between ethic groups that had been sharing complementary, even symbiotic, social boundaries that have subsequently shifted. Whenever identity boundaries, for example, social niches, are altered and put into competition, our human nature responds with a primal fury. Nothing is more basic than the need and hence, the right to say who you are and what you can and cannot do. Therefore, there are no more primal challenges, and apparently, no more primal triggers that can easily overwhelm all rational attempts to contain it.

The notion that the most evolved and efficient mechanism for protecting identity should have a "negative" definition of identity runs counter to common-sense notions of personal identity. Yet much of the information about who you are comes from your reaction to those around you. Indeed, throughout life, we are continuously discovering ourselves through relationships to others. This could not happen if your identity were fixed and defined in the positive. Since neither physical nor social identity can be defined that way, there is no bounded definition as to who you are—both individuals and societies have the potential to be highly adaptive, and that is a great survival advantage.

Another reason for not having a single, explicit "identity code" that totally defines an individual organism is that if that code were ever breached, pathogens could locate and then destroy the individual. Given the enormous sophistication of biological pathogens, such as the HIV viruses, in disguising themselves and mutating, the immune system has evolved highly sophisticated mechanisms for detecting and destroying alien proteins without revealing what it is that it is protecting. One of the most complex things the immune system has to do is generate credible signals among its antibodies in order to locate pathogens, verify signals, and coordinate efforts to destroy them. This it does even while the pathogens themselves are changing and attempting to mimic benign proteins and cells, sending out confusing and deceptive signals. For millions of years, immune systems have evolved solutions to problems the computer industry is just now confronting—the biological equivalent to "malware" spyware, "phishing," "pharming," "denial of service attacks," "worms." The online security industry is now beginning to learn from the immune system and to appreciate the security power of negative identity. In one sense, a negative identity is like having a persistent but anonymous identity online; it is never disclosed in full, it reveals just enough of itself to enter into a relationship, and only it knows or experiences all its potential layers. By having a persistent anonymous identity, it is possible to authenticate parts of the identity so as to have trusted relationships without disclosing the full identity. A Web site, for example, does not need to know your birthday, only that you are over twenty-one, to let you purchase alcohol. Likewise, to sell you shoes, a merchant does not need to know where you live or even your name; only your size, preference, and credit are necessary. Given the importance of negative identity in the biological world, it should arguably be extended to the digital world, become the "default" for identity online.

The more social a species is, the more individual identity becomes aligned with the social signals used to communicate and coordinate the species' social behavior. In this respect, the line between the individual and the group becomes blurred, and the principle of the crowd of one takes effect. Whether it is at the cellular or at the cultural level, highly complex strategies have evolved for signaling, constructing, enforcing, verifying, and coordinating social identities. What becomes striking from the example of the immune system is that identity is not an inalienable, irreducible set of individual qualities or attributes, but rather a composite of attributes derived from interactions and reactions to other bodies. In other words, there is no single, unique, irreducible "identity," but rather many different "identities" that have evolved in different social niches.

Take the example of Mark Spangler again. He really wore "many hats," and he was able to use credible identity in one niche, his birth into a wealthy, recognized family, to undertake a deception in another niche, business and money management. He was born into a position of status and privilege. This was part of his heritage, derived from his social position, and beyond dispute. Yet he wanted to compete in a business, money management, where status markets were performance based and not positional. Since many of the same social markers of trustworthiness and competence were used in both worlds, he was able to deceive his investors. Social status signals became confused with competency signals. In short, he used deceptive social signals to become a "free rider," without the consent or the knowledge of those for whom he was parasitic.

Mark was successful in his deception because he had mastered techniques for signaling that he was someone of status and achievement, and was therefore worthy of trust. He knew how to penetrate the defenses of the social immune systems of not only his clients, but of formal and informal authorities—those who were traditionally chartered to protect others in the social networks, much like T cells, from social pathogens. Mark had feigned all the "high-cost" signals, a solid reputation of achievement, exclusive and competitive schools and degrees, the recommendations of trusted third parties, and yet in the end, none of these were sufficient to disguise his real identity and intent.

From an evolutionary perspective, social identity and reputation are part of a larger evolutionary dynamic in which individuals and species signal among one another their fitness for cooperation, competition, and reproduction. As the complexity of the social interactions increases, so does the richness and diversity of signaling and coordination strategies. To study these phenomena, there is a field within evolutionary biology called signaling theory that studies signaling behaviors in all forms of life, from the simplest bacteria to extended human groups.

Like economists, evolutionary biologists are especially attuned to cost. Species don't adopt behaviors or evolve structures unless they are cost-effective. In the majority of cases, nature is a harsh taskmaster and seldom tolerates structures or behaviors that consume resources without yielding commensurate reproductive benefits. That is why some forms of signaling behavior are so intriguing. Why does the peacock have such a large and extravagant tail? Like Spangler's antique desks, sponsorship of the arts, and exclusive business address, the peacock's tail would seem to offer no particular adaptive advantage, and yet it consumes significant resources to sustain it. Likewise, the antlers on the now extinct Irish elk were enormous to the point where they really didn't help in rutting competitions with other males, but nonetheless, they survived for millions of years. Large antlers, like large tails, seem to be a naturally sanctioned extravagance. Evolutionary biologists have discovered, however, that such excesses confer some evolutionary advantages. They are an example of "costly signaling," and what has come to be known as the "handicapping principle."[7] By expending all those resources on growing and supporting enormous tail feathers, the peacock signals to the peahen that he indeed is a very healthy specimen, and therefore, a worthy mate. Moreover, by being so costly and not easily faked, this social signal is highly credible and hence, to be trusted. In this case, the signaler, that is, the peacock, absorbs all the costs of the social signal, and in this manner he is "handicapped," and the female and offspring are the beneficiaries.[8]

Examples of "handicapping" abound outside of the realm of evolutionary biology. Consider the case of the bank with the huge stone edifice with Doric columns and cornices. The elaborate edifice is not required to protect the money, but the social signal that it took so much money to construct gives sufficient comfort to potential depositors to conclude that the bankers will not skip town with their money. By virtue of the money required to build the edifice, the message is communicated that the bank is not a fly-by-night operation and will be around for a long time. Other examples include acquiring advanced degrees at elite universities where admissions are highly competitive, the curriculum rigorous, and the tuition costs high. Again, these are credentials, themselves social signals, that are difficult to fake, where verification is possible. Under these circumstances, the credibility and desirability of graduates from such institutions is high for both employers and future mates. Spangler was no evolutionary biologist, but he intuitively understood all these signals and used this knowledge to construct a reputation and identity that could penetrate the defenses of his clients and colleagues.

What would happen if the cost of producing a social signal were not high? Would that mean that it could not be trusted? Evolutionary biologists have looked at this problem as well. A biological example that has been studied extensively is that of the male house sparrow (*Passer domesticus*) or Harris sparrow (*Zonotricia querla*).[9] In contrast to the peacock, the male house sparrow has a relatively low-cost plumage variation, in this case, a black bib, which is indicative of aggressiveness, fighting ability, and dominance. In experiments where researchers added an artificial black bib to a nondominant sparrow, the sparrow briefly won dominance interactions. But the deceit was soon exposed, and the other birds mercilessly attacked and eventually killed the impostor. In the cases of both the peacock and the sparrow, they were signaling some aspect of quality, but in the case of the sparrow, it was up to the receiver, much like the investor in the Spangler case, to verify the integrity of the message.

The cost of the signal was in effect borne by the receivers, who would then enforce the integrity of the signal by attacking the offending bird. So, the evolutionary biologists found that socially imposed signal costs—such as retribution by the deceived birds—allow for cheaper signals that are more resistant to breakdown over evolutionary time.[10] When the cost signals are low and under the control of the receivers, as in the case of the sparrows, there is no evolutionary incentive to destabilize the signaling system. As a result, a robust signaling system emerged that accurately communicated the identity of dominant male members to the evolutionary advantage of the species.

This insight also applies to humans as well. Humans also signal through physiological means—facial symmetry, smooth skin, clear nails, upright posture, size, muscle tone. All those things that cosmetics, dress, and exercise are designed to enhance or obscure are associated with physical health and hence, reproductive success. Estrogen-induced signals such as full breasts, thick lips, and ample hips are fertility signals and attractors, whereas strong chins, large shoulders, toned biceps and chest, and upright posture are testosterone-related signals indicative of male strength, aggressiveness, and health. If anyone doubts the power and importance of these innate physiological social signals today, they only need to look at the racks of magazine covers in a newsstand to see that the vast majority of images are the human equivalent of the peacock's plumage. The pictured embodiments of these archetypal ideals are the "celebrities" who act as role and status models for the less endowed. These signaling systems are high cost in that they cannot be easily altered or faked—even through cosmetics or plastic surgery.

Like other primate groups in which social status is determined by innate social signals of dominance and hierarchy, human groups also use strong physiological signaling cues to create hierarchical and exclusive groups. In this case, social identity is closely associated with group-valued physiological attributes such as physical markers of health, fecundity, and athleticism. Given that these attributes and the social groupings associated with them are costly, physiological, and innate, they can change only over evolutionary time through generations of biological reproduction. However, what would happen if the cost of social signaling were low and the ability to generate and select new signals could occur in "social" time? Would this not give an enormous evolutionary advantage to those species that could rapidly mutate their social identities and signaling systems to both exploit environmental opportunities and avoid environmental risks? For instance, instead of having to rely upon fixed markers of quality and health, such as physical size and symmetry, people could invent their own criteria and metrics, such as rating systems and measures of quality. This clearly is what people do, and through their cultural signaling systems, they devise a wide variety of markers through different forms of dress, ornamentation, speech, and behavior to signal social status and trustworthiness.

Evolutionary forces favor those species that both increase their options for responding to environmental changes and reduce the cost of testing, communication, and implementing those options. That is what good signaling processes do. Those signals that have low production costs and at the same time give the "receiver" of the signal control over the acceptance of a signal generate low-cost options for reducing costs and mitigating risks. Given the adaptive advantage of a rich and versatile signaling system, it would seem that the emergence of human language or its equivalent was virtually an evolutionary inevitability.

The evolutionary biologist Carl Bergstrom thinks so. He has argued that the example of the house sparrow demonstrates that a set of low-cost signals, such as human language, can evolve as a highly efficient system that does not require full cooperation. Moreover, this allows for the "arbitrary assignment of meaning to virtually any signal."[11] In other words, participants don't even have to agree on what the meaning of some signal is—spoken, gestured, or even written. For example, people in the course of everyday conversations acquiesce to one another's new uses of words just as a way of staying or participating in the conversation. Such acquiescence is situational, because accepting someone else's term or definition in one context does not mean accepting it in all contexts. This arbitrary assignment of meaning implies that languages can evolve quite freely, giving them unlimited extensibility. One reason this can happen is that enforcement need not impose any cost when the signals are honest. In those cases where the signals are dishonest, then there have to be very high social costs. The reason that Spangler was able to be so successful was that he could manipulate the social signaling system and that there were no strong cheater detection and enforcement practices to deter him from the beginning. Had there been, Spangler's deceit would have detected and he would have received the human equivalent of the treatment visited upon the impostor house sparrow. Bergstrom goes on to make a significant point relevant to the Spangler example about the importance of reputation information to create sufficient costs to discourage deception:

One reason to suspect that language may have initially evolved to use in coincident interest situations is that individual reputations—in which individuals become known as liars or as good sources of information—may provide an important "cost" to deception in human communication. While reputations can emerge even without communal "discussion" of an individual's reliability, language certainly facilitates the spread of reputations by allowing individuals to share information about others' reliability.[12]

The notion that *individual reputations* can become a requisite cost for achieving honest communications also underscores the importance of socially-constructed means for defining and enforcing long-lasting individual identities. Reputations by themselves have no significance unless there are socially sanctioned ways for achieving honest and precise signaling. Bergstrom's insight that there would not have to be any "communal discussion" or top-down mechanism to govern any such reputation, once again, brings to mind Adam Smith's "invisible hand" as the underlying governance principle. Rather than making markets in goods, the "invisible hand" is making markets in *social* currencies based upon reputation.

Status signals and social signals are not confined to individual and social relationships. They also play a major role in markets. Markets are not freestanding entities; they are derived from social emotions and relationships. Nor are firms the blind, rational, profit-maximization engines that many economists have purported them to be. Indeed, the same dynamics that affect the cost and credibility of the social signaling of peacocks and sparrows also apply to firms and markets.

Over thirty years ago, Michael Spence, the 2001 winner of the Nobel Prize in Economics, developed a theory of market signals that introduced the notion of social signals into market behavior. Like the notion of the handicap principle in evolutionary biology, Spence's notion of market signals treats the marginal cost of a signal as inversely related to the actor's quality level. In other words, market signals are quality markers that are only credible if they are expensive to produce. Subsequently, sociologists using social network models began to introduce into economics the notion of "status" as a kind of quality indicator for predicting not only market and firm behavior but industry structure as well.

From an evolutionary perspective, status is a socially constructed and enforced signal that mitigates the risks of social exchange. The fact that a social status signal is hard or costly to obtain makes it a credible signal. Hence, the value or credibility of the signal depends upon establishing exclusivity. In his book *Status Signals*, Joel Polodny, dean of the Yale School of Management, shows how status signals affect competition and costs in a wide variety of industries: investment banking, venture capital, wine, luxury goods, technology, and commercial debt. Polodny argued that reputation signals, unlike status signals, are based upon performance, and the expectations of future behaviors are based upon past behavior. Status signals, on the other hand, are based upon an individual's or group's standing in a hierarchy. Whereas an individual's or a group's "reputation" is contingent upon their performance, their status need not be. Indeed, in many societies, the gentry, or those in positional or inherited authority, are exempt from an expectation of particular competence. Those of lower status simply must defer to those of higher status, regardless of competence.

In his study, Podolny has also described a series of quantitative analyses on the role of status signals across multiple industries. He found that in those cases where it is difficult to determine quality, status signals take on particular importance as a kind of socially trusted proxy for quality. Those firms with higher status also have lower production costs than low-status firms because they can charge more for their goods and services and therefore outbid their lower-status competitors for resources. Podolny also found that status "leaks through exchange and deference relations,"[13] meaning individuals and firms lose status by dealing or socializing with low-status groups. Not surprisingly, high-status firms tend to "do deals" together. This is especially true for venture capital investing, in which it is very difficult to assess the risk of a management team executing its plan or the market risk of a new product or service. Under these conditions, status affiliation becomes especially strong, in fact so strong that "first-tier" firms refuse to do deals with "second-tier" firms. Top-tier venture firms, as would be predicted, pay less for their investments than do lower-tier firms. As in the case of investment banking, there tends to be a "herd mentality" in making investments, and investments are made as much to secure status relationships as to achieve financial returns. This produces a kind of self-fulfilling prophecy, whereby high-status players tend to get higher returns than lower-status players simply by the fact that they are high status, and therefore more likely to be believed and accepted—often in blatant disregard of the merits of their technology or expertise.

This condition is known in the sociological and economics literature as the Matthew effect, based on a passage in the Book of Matthew in the New Testament: "For unto everyone that hath shall be given, and he shall have abundance; but from him that hath not shall be taken away even what he hath" (Matthew 25:14–30). It does not characterize a particularly laudable social policy, but rather describes a harsh fact of human exchange: Those that have, get more, and those that have not, get less. Yet as we have seen in the earlier discussions of the Scottish Enlightenment and Renaissance Florence, the Matthew effect can be overcome by changing the rules of the game. New reputation signals and metrics can "invade" a stagnant social order and open up new social and economic possibilities. With the adoption of market economics throughout the world over the last hundred years, both the disruptive and innovative effects of market capitalism are being felt. It is what the economist Joseph Schumpeter somewhat paradoxically called "creative destruction."[14]

Due to the accelerating rate of technological change, cycles of creative destruction are a permanent fixture in financial markets. One of the recent innovators to unseat social hierarchy in financial markets was Michael Milliken. Milliken virtually invented the "junk bond" market by correctly observing that the status oligopolies of top-tier corporate lenders, such as Morgan Stanley, overestimated the actual financial risks of lending to firms with less than stellar Moody credit ratings. By lending to supposedly high-risk firms and charging commensurate interest rates, he and his firm, Drexel Burnham Lambert, generated capital and liquidity for "low-status" companies, and in the process broke the grip of the old boy, "white shoe," network on corporate debt markets:

> If one wants even further qualitative evidence that the issuers of "junk" debt were regarded as low-status, one would only need to look at Morgan Stanley's press announcement when it decided to enter the market for non-investment grade debt. Like other high status banks,

Morgan Stanley was reluctant to enter this market despite the huge profits that the market pioneer, Drexel Burnham Lambert, was earning . . . [W]hen Morgan Stanley finally decided to enter the market, it decided that it would "gentrify" the market through its entry.[15]

These status struggles recall the struggles of innovative and low-status Florentine bankers such as Francesco Datini, with their introduction of double-entry bookkeeping and the business partnership model. In Milliken's case, he was convicted of a felony and went to jail. Yet despite those hits to his reputation, Milliken's innovations in finance were so far-reaching and democratizing that he has achieved his own kind of special status among the financial elite of Wall Street. As "ungentlemanly" and even criminal as his practices were, Milliken, nonetheless, was among the first to break down old status hierarchies in Wall Street and democratize capital for the low-status player and the little man—the *popolino* of the twentieth century. From the democratization of credit cards, once the province of the high-status buyer, to the merchandizing of mutual funds for the "everyman" to the advent of "micro-finance" for even the poorest of the poor in developing countries, there is an irreversible trend to displace pure status relationships with market relationships based upon reputation—that is, with credit scores. This is a sea change in social and economic relationships around the globe. Rather than status hierarchies being the dominant social mechanisms for maintaining credible signaling costs, more open and independent metrics of reputation and risk are being adopted throughout the world to mitigate social and economic risks. From the reputation scores of eBay to publicly available Fica scores for American consumers to the availability of micro-credits in Bangladesh, performance-based metrics are replacing status signals as a means of mitigating risk.

Evolutionary biology provided the insight into how important it was to have a persistent identity where reputation could be verified through costly signals. But because signals are socially constructed and therefore potentially easy to fake, how can high social costs be constructed that make identity and reputation signals credible and trustworthy? The answer lies in having a good story about who you are.

Chapter Eleven

The Power of
Identity Narratives

IT WAS NOT UNTIL 1755, WITH THE PUBLICATION OF DR. SAMUEL
Johnson's *A Dictionary of the English Language* that there was an authoritative, written dictionary of word meanings. Written languages had existed
for thousands of years before, but it wasn't until the eighteenth century
that their definitions were codified and written down. This fact is an extraordinary testimonial to the innate powers of people to learn new terms
and grammar without the need for a written instruction. It also testified
to Johnson's great ability. It was less his encyclopedic grasp of English literature and usage that mattered than his ability to express some of the
rules by which people naturally make sense of words and expressions. In
short, he recounted the story of language in a way that allowed its speakers to recognize their own experience. They validated his work.

Johnson recognized that language, unlike a printed dictionary, would
change. New words would be created, new uses invented. The human
capacity for language provides powerful and naturally grounded conventions for creating socially constructed and trusted identities. Languages
authoritatively add and define new terms while at same preserving the
continuity of established meanings and expressions. Languages don't
change every time a new word or expression is added, and yet they are

capable of adding an infinite number of new terms and expressions. One of the reasons language is so powerful is that as a construct, it is so broadly beneficial; everyone benefits from being able to participate in it. In that sense it is both a metaphor for and a literal example of a network tool that is uniquely human and intimately responsible for our ability to assert and validate identity. The way language works can be instructive in understanding how identity is amassed.

According to one school of modern lexicographers, among them James Pustejovsky,[1] all languages have four relatively simple but universal rules by which new terms are defined and related to one another. Pustejovsky calls them "qualia" (universals) in deference to Aristotle. Only after these conditions are satisfied and the appropriate definitional linkages have been established are new terms authoritatively added to a language's lexicon. So when someone asks, "What do you mean by that?" or "Could you define or explain that to me?" the universal human response is to offer answers that provide four types of information: the authoritative "dictionary" or accepted definition, called the *formal* meaning; an explanation in terms of purpose, that is, how something can be used or what its purpose is, called the *telic* meaning; the *agentive* definition, specifying where something came from; and finally, the *constitutive* definition, which explains what something is a part of. For example, take the definition of the word *hammer*. For the full definition, it is described in four different ways: in terms of its formal definition (dictionary), it is "an instrument for beating, breaking, driving nails, etc."; in terms of its telic definition (purpose), it is "an instrument for striking objects"; in terms of its agentive definition (origin), "it derives from the term "kamen" the Slavic word for "stone," suggesting that the word originally meant "stone weapon"; and finally, in terms of its constitutive definition (what it is part of), it is "an instrument with a solid head, usually of metal, set transversely to the handle." In order to make sense of something new, human beings have to understand it in terms of these criteria; something becomes explained, indeed known, only when its purpose, origin, and relationship to other known things can be established. If something meets this test, then it is defined and is incorporated into not only the lexicon of a culture but also its repertoire of what John Searle has called institutional facts and rules. We saw in Chapter 5 that language has the ability to define new kinds of institutional facts—things that don't exist in nature but are necessary components of organized social life, such as citizenship, kinship roles, religious and civic observances. These institutional facts are also a part of social identity, and as signaling theory tells us, if they are not to be compromised, they too have to be falsifiable only at great cost.

One of the ways societies seem to do this is to use the same processes that all languages use in adding and authenticating new terms. In order for an individual's or a group's identity to be culturally and authoritatively secured, it must be described and explained in terms of the same four criteria of the qualia. Virtually all origin and identity narratives satisfy these criteria. They provide simple stories about where a people came from, the events and actions that created them, for instance, birth from gods, animals, or supernatural forces; who or what they are related to, for example, animal totems, kinship groups, gods, heroes; and finally, the purpose of their group, such as being a chosen people of God, exercising dominion over the earth, or finding divine enlightenment. The goal of such narratives is to assert the boundaries of identity by retaining those distinctions and definitions that preserve necessary, trusted social relationships. In other words, new experiences, terms, roles, technologies, and challenges are labeled in such a way that they are shown to be consistent with the primal origin narrative.

Among the most influential myths or narratives are those that evoke the return of ancestors or a new millennium in which the wrongs and the sufferings of the present will be vindicated and a new and just millennium or social order will be restored. Such millennial movements or myths are common in all the cultures of the world and are triggered by events or circumstances that undermine the viability and eventually the identity of an entire culture or people. The three decades 1860–1890 were such a period for the Sioux Indians of the United States. Their buffalo had been decimated and they had been forced into confining and dispiriting reservations. A series of Ghost Dances originated in the visions of Wovoka in 1889, during which Sioux warriors and women began to undertake nonstop dancing in order to evoke the return of their ancestors (ghosts) to eradicate the powers of the white man and restore their world to its original, natural state. Through the powers of their ancestors, the dancers came to believe that they were impervious to bullets. On December 29, 1890, the United States Cavalry become alarmed and massacred some 300 men, women, and children at Wounded Knee. Similar kinds of millennial movements happened in Europe in the fifteenth century with the Adamite Movement, which was captured so vividly in the triptychs of Hieronymus Bosch, especially the *Garden of Earthly Delights,* which depicts a confusion of identities. These boundary definitions are reinforced and sustained through a variety of social signaling conventions—dialects, grammar, mode of dress, rituals, and behavior. Even television sitcom and soap opera narratives act to reinforce varieties of these fundamental social identities and roles. In the 1950s and 1960s, the TV program *Father Knows Best* reinforced a traditional narrative of patriarchy by having weekly episodes in which the father demonstrated his superiority in handling tricky family problems. Forty and fifty years later, TV sitcom narratives such as *All in the Family, Everybody Loves Raymond, King of Queens, Two and a Half Men,* and *According to Jim* are openly skeptical of patriarchy and offer a more egalitarian and gender-neutral narrative for resolving familial conflicts that challenges the narrative of "traditional family" values.

One of the reasons that Mark Spangler's invented personal history was so plausible was that he was able to meet the narrative identity test. It was clear where he came from, an old Boston family, that he had lived in Weston, that he had attended all the "right" schools and hence was a member of a trusted class that had the requisite credentials— handicapped costs—to be trusted with other people's money. In other words, he seemed to have something to lose if he were deceptive. He met all the authoritative tests: the origin test (the explanation of his success and competences), the constitutive test (his membership in clubs and a social circle), and the telic test (he was a registered money manager). There was also great resistance to challenging any of his claims, as to do so would be to challenge not only his integrity but the integrity of those who had vouched for him.

We are reluctant to meddle with identity narratives. In traditional societies, narratives that define identity are considered sacred and are, therefore, beyond challenge. Indeed, to question sacred narratives is the definition of blasphemy. Until the Enlightenment in Europe, blasphemy offenses were often capital crimes, as eighteen-year-old Thomas Aikenhead discovered in Scotland in 1692. Perhaps we protect identity narratives so fiercely because so much flows from them: without some form of foundational narrative for social identity, even in secular societies there can be no way of securing and enforcing honest reputations, and consequently, no credible means for allocating social rights, duties, and privileges. Hence, identity narratives explaining how a people or cultural hero came into being are necessary for creating costly, credible signals. The severity of the sanctions against blasphemy and dishonor in nonsecular cultures is indicative of the extent to which social cohesion and trust is dependent upon keeping origin narratives intact.

In secular states, the origin narrative is grounded in the constitution. Yet even under this model, there is a tension between keeping the original narrative intact or amending and reinterpreting it to prevent contradiction and incoherence over the passage of time. In the United States, there is fundamental struggle over constitutional identity. Advocates on all sides of the political spectrum are trying to distinguish the principles that are essential for constitutional integrity from those that are circumstantial and contingent. The debates have a flavor that is similar to arguments over the "proper" use of language and "cultural values." Such similarities are more than coincidental, as language is the vehicle by which these issues are being framed and fought.

On the one hand, there are constitutional and cultural conservatives such as William Bennett, Justice Antonin Scalia, William Buckley, and William Safire, who protest the corruption of contemporary American language, the relativism of cultural values, and judicial overreach, and on the other, there are "liberals" such as the ACLU, Supreme Court Justice Stephen Breyer, and former Vice President Albert Gore, who see the Constitution as a "living," evolving document and embrace a plurality of social identities and authorities. The social conservatives regard both social identity and authority as fixed and closed. Definitional boundaries for what is right and what is wrong are fixed and monolithic in their minds. Effective social control demands a credible authority, one that is literal and not subject to the wanderings of interpretation. So, there is consistency among social conservatives on a wide spectrum of issues—from patriarchal child-rearing practices to limitations on emigration to special powers for national security, unitary executive theory, limits to civil liberties, and a moralistic, honor-bound foreign policy. The liberals, on the other hand, see a need to "interpret" the Constitution to address the challenges of the twenty-first century that were unanticipated by the framers of the Constitution.

One of the most effective spokesmen for the conservative position is Supreme Court Justice Antonin Scalia. He argues for an "originalist" and "textual" interpretation of the Constitution, seeing the Constitution as having an "anti-evolutionary purpose." Underlying his view of the Constitution is a Hobbesian skepticism about progressive arguments in general, which leads conservatives to see in societies a proclivity to "rot" rather than "mature."[2] They show further skepticism about governments being likely to act in the interests of citizens.

In sum, social conservatives seem willing to embrace interpretations that allow for the expansion of powers that buttress authority and executive powers at the expense of civil liberties and social justice issues. By contrast, liberals seem willing to render interpretations that expand judicial and legislative powers in order to secure civil liberties and social justice. Whereas the liberal view sees social identity and constitutional authority as evolving, and trusts the government to play a positive role in that evolution, conservatives have no such trust and resist any such evolution as an unconstitutional expansion of powers. Ironically, American conservatives want to limit the powers of the state in matters of property, regulation, and taxation, and yet in a matters of morality, authority, and national security, they are willing to dramatically expand state powers and concede to the executive branch, especially as concerns the role of the commander in chief, those very essential powers of checks and balance, transparency, and accountability that make a democracy tenable.

In this respect, the views of the "originalist" and "strict constructivists" represent a very traditional, even pre-Enlightenment, perspective on how trust and authority are to be achieved socially and governmentally. If contemporary democracies are not to recede into a new form of authoritarianism as the Roman republic did at the time of Cicero, the challenge will be to understand the "social syntax" that makes possible an infinite variety of "grammatical" social and political identities and expressions. With all due respect to Justice Scalia, societies—like all living things—rot and die when they *fail* to evolve. This is especially true in a time of unprecedented technological change. Such arguments for an evolution-resistant constitution have a whiff of the logic of the Ghost Dance discussed earlier, with the potential for similar outcomes. There will always be a tension between the competing needs for liberty and security, and such contests will always test the mettle of a people. Benjamin Franklin put it more succinctly, "He who sacrifices freedom for security deserves neither."

From this perspective, it is easy to appreciate why personal honor—reputation—is so essential and so proudly defended in both secular and nonsecular societies. If people give their word but cannot be trusted or if their honor is readily compromised, so too are their life prospects. From this vantage point, duels and honor killings of siblings and spouses within traditional societies are more comprehensible, however deplorable. Without independent institutions for verifying reputation and identity in both secular and nonsecular societies, traditional enforcement mechanisms will persist as long as they are integral to preserving trust. Even to this day, the transition to secular and civic institutions is incomplete and controversial within the West. In the United States, fundamental tensions persist over the separation of church and state, and it is not clear what direction the country will move on this fundamental question. This is not surprising, given that less than 300 years ago, the governance of social identity within Western societies was grounded in sacred narratives and honor-bound reputation systems. On a global basis, humankind's transition from such identity narratives and reputation enforcement practices is still in its infancy.

In traditional societies throughout the world, the failure of identity narratives to adapt to modern realities is one of the major drivers of international conflict. According to research being at conducted at the Center for Contemporary Conflict at the Naval Postgraduate School,[3] contemporary terrorism, and especially Islamic terrorism, is grounded in the failure of foundation narratives to provide viable, alternative social identities. The fact that many Islamic terrorists are relatively affluent and educated young men who have lived or are living in the West should not be surprising. They and many other Islamic youths have been psychically dislocated by having to straddle different cultures. They are martyring themselves not for material goods or incremental political or economic gains, but for something more fundamental, a sense of identity in the world that is congruent with their origin narratives. They are trying to reenact heroic acts that ritualistically repeat the sacred narratives of Muhammad and thereby place themselves in a kind of mythic, sacred timelessness. The following passage from research from the Center for Contemporary Conflict at the Naval Research Postgraduate School makes this point:

> According to Vlahos, the foundational mythic figure for Islam is (of course) Muhammad. Bin Laden, then, taps into this theme when he portrays himself as following in the footsteps of Muhammad; he too is making a heroic journey, struggling against great odds, in a way that makes him almost as mythic in stature (and hence all the posters and stickers praising him in places like Pakistan or Afghanistan). Part of the reason why he is mythic is because of the second element: bin Laden argues that he is part of a grand struggle against Western imperialism and decadence. His actions are part of a *story* that is linked to the very fabric of Muslim history (and given the fact that this history was in actual fact laced with Orientalism and colonialism, it's not surprising that charges of *neo*-Orientalism and *neo*-colonialism stick so easily). The third aspect of the story is important: it is only by struggling against these dark forces that one can be *renewed*. To fail to struggle is to *fail* to play your part in a narrative that ends with Islam triumphing over the infidel West. Finally, owing to the fourth element, the story contains built in "insulation" from temporary tactical successes on the part of occupying forces: the mystical element of the narrative (especially its otherworldly component involving things like rewards in the afterlife's paradise) means that temporal success won't necessarily "defuse" the logic of the story. . . . [R]esistance can and should continue even if the security situation improves in the short term (although brute facts about human psychology may undermine the effectiveness of that story in the long run in the face of improvements in the procurement of basic needs).[4]

Suicide bombers are fighting the very existence of a secular, questioning, open, and mutable social order; and they are fighting this identity with an all-consuming religious zeal and devotion. Western identity narratives are blasphemous to them. To this group, change is desecration.

As implausible as the appeal by strict Islamists to restore the caliphate of the ninth century may seem to Westerners, there is an equivalent drive among some Christian evangelicals and Orthodox Jews to restore the boundaries and conditions that underlie their own foundation narratives. One of the reasons they are so difficult to comprehend by secular, "realpolitik" policymakers is that their motivations are neither individualistic nor materialistic. As such, their motivations are simply outside the origin narratives of individualistic capitalism and secularism.

Fairness is the balance point of society. A fair society confers legitimacy. When fairness is absent, social pressures can topple the existing social contract and redefine it. A new narrative replaces the old, but the adjustment can be dramatic, even bloody. The new narrative usually provides a rationale for why the old social order failed, is no longer fair, and how and why a new one can and should take its place. Typically, it begins with the assertion that one or another group has not been treated fairly, that a competing group has unfairly appropriated the benefits and powers that society has to offer. To create a new social identity, one that is entitled to the spoils of a new social contract, a negative or scapegoat social identity is needed against which a counter, or in-group identity can be asserted. Historical examples abound: Nazis and Jews, Serbs and Bosnians, Russians and Chechens, Jews and Palestinians, Catholics and Protestants, Turks and Armenians, Turks and Kurds, Hindus and Muslims, Tutsis and Hutus, Sunnis and Shiites, peasants and elite, and so forth. The habit is as old as humanity. Archetypal narratives are invented that pit the "Good" against the "Evil," the believer against the infidel, "Us" against "Them." A new origin narrative is imagined. In the case of secular societies, the criteria for exclusion and vilification are around differences in perceived fairness. In nonsecular societies, the impetus for exclusion, and in many cases, eradication, centers on issues of blasphemy and belief.

The formation of a new social identity, one that legitimizes a favored group or groups, solves only one part of the problem in building a new social order. To overturn an existing social order, as happened periodically throughout Renaissance Italy, also entails introducing new ways of valuing and measuring fairness and competence, exposing the incompetence of entrenched interests, and creating opportunities for social status. In those cases, where equality becomes the primary benchmark for legitimacy, such as in the French and the Russian revolutions, the Great Leap Forward, and the purges of elites by the Khmer Rouge, new identities and reputations are built on metrics of equality. Those that appear more than equal—the elites—are punished. The yardstick of fairness in these contexts entails a leveling, bringing outliers into conformity with a "mean" of preferred social identities and reputations. This metric of fairness differs dramatically from the criteria established during the Italian Renaissance, when public genius came to be rewarded, and a diversity of social identities also came to be rewarded and institutionalized.

Questions about fairness and equality are especially difficult to address in hierarchical, nonsecular societies, in which identities, reputations, roles, and privileges have been set by a narrative of an incontrovertible, divine mandate or revelation. Any change in the social order is a challenge to a sacred belief, and by definition, must be blasphemous. Consequently, there cannot be independent—that is, secular—reputation or performance-based metrics of fairness to hold leaders accountable, because their legitimacy comes not from their actions but from their position in a fixed and sacred social order. The divine right of kings did not guarantee good monarchs, merely that they would be anointed by God. But if the king was a lunatic wastrel, who could argue with God about it? This is an enormous challenge, whose difficulty shows clearly, for example, in attempts to modernize Islamic law, called the Sharia, as so many of the prescriptions are grounded in the Qur'an. In most interpretations of Islam, altering certain practices such as acceptance of homosexuality, marriage to a nonbeliever, conversion to another religion, or adultery is considered an apostasy and is punishable by death.

Nowhere is the premise of fairness more tightly coupled to independent identity and reputation than in the U.S. Declaration of Independence. It is a frontal attack on the principle of status hierarchy and lays the foundation for a new kind of identity narrative that is open, continuous, and self-defining:

We hold these Truths to be self-evident: That all Men are created equal.

Clearly, not all men and women are biological equals. That is not what is meant by this passage. What this declaration of rights does state is a maxim about what is required to have an open, mobile, and regenerative society, where there are no fixed, inherent, or heredity rights. By virtue of equal citizenship, *all* people are free to form organizations, enterprises, and institutions of their own making without being impaired by the legacies of the entitled. The idea of "the citizen" was a profound rebuke to the social order of old Europe. That concept places reputation and merit above status and social standing. It supposes an open and inclusive society. Equal citizenship seems at first to be an assertion of the primacy of individual rights, but its philosophical origins and ethical logic in fact lie elsewhere. It is a group right rather than an individual right. It bears less in common with the Adam Smith of *The Wealth of Nations* than its does with the Adam Smith of *Moral Sentiments,* where sympathy, fairness, and "common stock" are seen as the necessary underpinnings of a prosperous social and economic order. In this respect, the declaration that all men are created equal, as a group of peers, is the antidote to the Matthew effect—"For unto everyone that hath shall be given, and he shall have abundance; but from him that hath not shall be taken away even what he hath"—because, through the assertion of a single social axiom, the governance of peers, it destroys any legitimacy for a privileged social and economic hierarchy.

There is another, later passage from Matthew (25:40), which may have been the inspiration for the declaration of equality: "Whatever you do unto the least of these, you do unto me." For believers, as were many of the signers of the Declaration of Independence, this passage may have been that sacred narrative for legitimizing the principle of equality. A significant number of the narratives in the New Testament depict Jesus as transgressing "status" boundaries, engaging and helping the prostitute, the leper, the pariahs, and the dispossessed, and thereby challenging the social and theocratic hierarchies of the time. This insistence on equality was one of the reasons that early Christianity was stigmatized as a "slave's religion" by the Romans at the time, and similarly, was why many in the European gentry feared and disparaged the principles of the American Revolution.

Just as many biblical and religious narratives and observances reflect the instituting of sound health practices, so they also offer anecdotal wisdom about the "social physics" of groups. For example, the Matthew effect may also operate in status-based social networks, such as privileged hierarchies, where it can be seen as the inevitable product of "power laws."[5] A power law effect occurs when a small number of people come to dominate a social network by becoming a central hub. They are the result of a "snowball effect" of "preferential attachments," meaning that over time, a small number of individuals become preferred over others and come to dominate the network. Essentially, an 80–20 rule kicks in, whereby a majority of people get locked out, not necessarily by intent, but by the invisible culling of unwanted or unknown alternatives. On the Net, this has happened with the search portal market, which has become concentrated into an increasingly small number of very dominant players.[6] Like status networks, power law networks can become highly stable and resistant to change.

Power law networks, like the Matthew effect, will take over unless there is a counternarrative. This is where the "equality principle of the Declaration of Independence" takes over. Digital technologies can be especially powerful engines of equality. By virtue of their ability to blindly interconnect parties around the world, they are redefining the boundaries upon which nations, markets, ethnicity, and identities depend. However, in those quarters where the old hierarchies and boundaries are being challenged and redrawn, there is mounting resistance. From this vantage point, all the old rules that used to work are broken. From the blunt affront of graphic pornography to terrorist beheadings to fraudulent e-mail offers, and a proliferation of unauthorized opinions, and blogs, there is a longing for a return to simple and trusted rules.

With these fears has come a reflex to do something, to demonize, to strike back at the visible cause, "the Net," and thereby bring it into account. Clean up the neighborhood and make it safe for "normal people." The ensuring struggle is between two models of control, one that attempts to arrest change by having closed worlds with rigid boundaries, fixed identities, strong legal sanctions, what some in the Internet call "walled gardens," and the other, an approach that embraces change and encourages unfettered exchange, multiple identities, and a minimum of legal sanctions. Whereas it may be tempting to contrast these competing approaches in terms of "top-down" versus "bottom-up," such a distinction can be misleading. In the transformation of Renaissance Florence, for example, new social networks came from the middle and then over time evolved and stabilized into hierarchies. New metrics for reputation building were introduced, and with it a new social and economic dynamism was unleashed.

During such periods of social redefinition, considerations of social fairness become pivotal to determining what the new social order should be. Is one group trying to be a free rider, trying to use its particular advantages to achieve lock-ins and disproportionate advantages? As we have seen in earlier chapters, when members of a group feel they are being cheated, they tend to become "free riders" and defectors themselves, thereby accelerating social deterioration. Hence, a sense of fairness is essential to keeping social and economic networks viable. That is when the equality principle needs to sets in, to break down dysfunctional social and economic barriers by enabling new social reputation signals to invade and challenge the old status systems. The goal should be to encourage foundation narratives that keep the networks open and prevent them from atrophying from the effects of power laws.

As networks become more interconnected and complex, they simply cannot be centrally controlled. Complex self-organizing networks, such as the immune system and the Net, are not centrally controlled. In both cases, a centralized control point represents a vulnerability, and both systems have evolved to the point where they can be both open and controlled. In the case of the Net, it is designed to grow arbitrarily large and diverse because all the different components are not dependent upon one another. Every new user or new device does not have to have the permission of other devices to be added to the network. In this sense, all components are treated equally in the full sense of equality as expressed in the Declaration of Independence, for they have the right in their identity to be there. They may differ in size and eventual influence, but they have the right to be connected on an equal footing with other components. That is what is meant by "having the intelligence at the edge of the Net." Unlike status hierarchies, there are no prior, privileged players; all devices are created equal. And likewise, for the adaptive immune system. Both are what biologists call "strategically robust,"[7] precisely because there are no components that have privileged powers. They are thus more secure, because they cannot be targeted by a single pathogen and destroyed. Hence, security and robustness are not the result of omnipotent or omniscient components or players, but rather depend upon the persistence and authenticity of the identities of the key members, especially the seven types of leaders discussed in Chapter 9. Security derives from the extent to which people, known and unknown to one another, are willing to trust and cooperate around common goals. And that depends upon their having authentic, reputable identities.

Control of such systems is tricky, at best. Efforts to achieve controls by imposing impersonal formal and economic sanctions can actually undermine people's natural inclination toward altruism and cooperation. Experimental and survey research by biologists, anthropologists, and economists on trust and personal and interpersonal exchange has found that the introduction of formal payments and contracts into personalized forms of exchange actually undermines trust and destabilizes the exchange relationship. Ernst Fehr, a leading institutional and behavioral economist, has conducted a number of experiments on the effect of sanctions on human altruism and has concluded that

> [f]airness-based altruism is a powerful source of human cooperation . . . and that the prevailing self-interest approach has serious shortcomings because it overlooks negative effects of sanctions on human altruism. Sanctions revealing selfish or greedy intentions destroy altruistic cooperation almost completely, whereas sanctions perceived as fair leave altruism intact.[8]

Therefore, a more realistic path to global security is to avoid reliance on coercion and control, and sanctions and rebukes, and instead to establish those conditions under which fairness and transparency can evolve through humankind's innate propensity for trust and cooperation. If the conditions for cooperation cannot be achieved through contracts and sanctions, and if control cannot be imposed top-down, then what are the levers, the intervention points for achieving the qualities of interaction that can achieve sustainable high levels of trusted exchange?

Again, we come back to the central question: How do you create the conditions for socially constructed and enforced honest signaling? How can reputation signals be credibly communicated and authenticated? All variants of the answer entail, in one form or another, having persistent identities—as individuals, groups, and institutions that are accountable to their reputations. Yet even before we can discuss what these identities might be, and how they might be secured, there is the prior question, how can new identities be defined and grounded on a global scale? But this raises a still more basic question: What are the credible origin narratives for a modern, global, diverse community? There must be new origin narratives that can credibly anchor individual and institutional identities to sacrosanct axioms about who and what were are as humans, recognizing that there is no such thing as the "individual" independent of the group. We are a crowd of one. There are no sharp dichotomies between species and environment, between one species and another, nor between one race or one religion and another. Humanity cannot become locked in a zero-sum game with itself. What is required is a new way of framing human identity in an open but precise manner, one that is free of "holistic obscurism" and yet resonates with our natures. Vernon Smith, the Nobel Laureate economist, advocates the need to get beyond notions of narrow self-interest and to embrace a new kind of rationality, what he calls "Ecological Rationality."[9] This notion of reality takes into account the interdependence of individuals and group, all of whom receive joint payoff as members of an entire ecosystem. An ecological perspective has no "externalities," and it is in the interest of all its members to direct the forces of the invisible hand to fully internalize and reduce actual ecological costs.

Chapter Twelve

The Open We—Building
Digital Institutions

AROUND 1968, THE DIGITAL WORLD WAS BORN. NOT FROM A BIG
Bang, but through the agency of a very male, very powerful, and very hierarchical American institution: The U.S. Department of Defense, more
specifically, the Advanced Research Project Administration. The digital
world was then called the ARPANET, soon to become the DARPANET,
and now today, the Internet. It was inhabited by a unique and elite population of computer programmers and engineers, later to become known
as "geeks" and "hackers." For twenty-five years, the ARPANET was a
veritable Eden for geeks. Under the watchful but benign eye of DARPA,
it had an abundance of resources and long-term funding, and its resi-
dents were free to do pretty much what they wanted. Anyone could assume any identity; you could browse not only your fellow hacker's e-mail
and calendar but also those of the director of MIT's Artificial Intelligence Laboratory, and even those of generals in the Pentagon. That soon
changed. It was a world in which you didn't need any money. Everything
was done on a "gift exchange" basis, and it seemed that everyone knew
and trusted one another. It was also a highly creative place; people
posted, shared, and commented on papers and code, and socialized late
into the night. Within this world, some of the first online games sprang

to life (Dungeons and Dragons, Doom), as well as the beginning of the
open source and free software movements. There really were no "bad
guys," no appeals to greed and commercialism. It was an innocent and
idyllic global village, with its own eccentrics and misfits, nothing very
serious, where trust and reciprocity were the currencies of the realm.

Then came the Fall. The Net grew up and became commercial. Soon
the fact that you didn't know with whom you were dealing became a Big
Problem. Not just problems of minors visiting and being solicited by
pornography sites, not just the spamming by sleazy merchants (estimated
by some to amount to 80 percent of all e-mail traffic), but targeted use by
child molesters, identity thieves, fraudulent merchants and buyers, money
launderers, and those threatening national security. Soon, who you *really*
were became very important to anyone you wanted to do business or even
socialize with. It has also become *very* important to some governments;
they felt that they needed to know everything about you in order to protect you. What government didn't know about you from monitoring of
telephone, e-mail, and Web traffic, Google would know by its capture and
indexing of all your Google searches and G-mail accounts. By 2002, media companies in collusion with hardware companies felt it necessary to
put in a "trust chip" (Oh, the Orwellian choice of words: It was really a
"distrust chip") to monitor your personal computer and cell phone to
make sure that you did not violate their copyrights. Sony went so far as
to have some DVDs contain spyware, which unbeknownst to the buyer
monitored the hard drive and reported back what it found to Sony. The
customer outrage forced them to withdraw it, but very likely in the future
someone will bring it back in an even more discreet version. The Net is
moving from an open world of reciprocity and trust to a progressively en-
closed, fearful, punitive, and monitored world of legal and economic sanctions to enforce the interests of influential oligopolies.

Many of those living in the fallen Net now recognize the need for a
new "layer," an "identity layer" that would potentially be part of all operating systems and browsers for not just computers but mobile phones and
other devices as well. This is the first big step in which technical standards move from building communications and information networks to
human, social networks. There are no national governments or international bodies that have ordained or sanctioned the creation of the new

identity layer. But a wide variety of commercial interests that rely upon the Net have come to recognize the need for it. Several years ago, Microsoft tried to impose its own solution, ominously called Passport. Under this plan, Microsoft would be the trusted agent for all personal information and collect and store it on the consumer's behalf. Not surprisingly, few people trusted Microsoft to be the keeper of their personal information, nor did they seem willing to confer upon Microsoft the power to issue their "passport" for traveling the Net. Since then, Microsoft, IBM, AMD, Intel, Oracle, GE, and other companies have come to appreciate the magnitude of the change in the rules for global technology markets. Simply, they came to recognize that they could not control it all—not their customers, suppliers, competitors, not even their technologies. For Microsoft and IBM, this represented a 180° change from their previous business strategies. Both were known as take-no-prisoners competitors, and both had their fights with the Department of Justice. Yet IBM, especially, has become a prominent and vocal proponent of the open source movement. IBM now supports the open licensing of much of its software. Although Microsoft fought the open source movement tooth and nail, just as it did the Internet when it first became commercial, the company has made a significant course correction and has begun to support some open source initiatives. This possible change in business strategy was not the result of any newfound altruism, but rather was a recognition of a new kind of ecological capitalism, wherein corporate interests are intertwined with the interests of customers, suppliers, and even competitors. Microsoft came to recognize that it could not control everything in its world and that it was a part of an ecology of players with whom it was interdependent. Competition is no longer a multiplayer zero-sum game, but a much more complex, cooperative exchange where mutually advantageous outcomes depend on a new kind of ecological rationality.

One of the results of this more open business strategy has been the development of open source software for the new identity layer of the Internet. This is not to say that IBM, Microsoft, Oracle, HP, Sun, Novell, and smaller open source organizations like Mozilla will not be competitors, but that they all recognize that none of them can do it alone, and if a new identity infrastructure is to be accepted by consumers, banks, merchants, and governments, it will have to be open and interoperable in order to be trusted. Even more remarkable, the model for what is called the "open identity network" is that it be "user-centric," that is, it places the controls in the hands of people—not the government, not the corporation. Also, the identity layer is designed so that the storage of information can be fully distributed and supported by a variety of different, and potentially competing companies or organizations. An improbable intellectual and technical advocate of this effort is a Canadian named Kim Cameron, who works for Microsoft as their "identity architect." Kim, as he is known on his blog, openly engages any and all identity advocates and developers who are concerned with making an identity system that is more open. He has identified "seven laws of identity," which act as a kind of seven commandments for those collaborating in building identity systems. These "laws" have been highly influential in setting a new direction for how identity should be treated online, and coming from Microsoft, they carry an enormous amount of clout. Cameron's laws, in an abbreviated and annotated form (for a more technical and comprehensive account, consult his blog),[1] state:

1. **User Control and Consent:** "Identity systems must only reveal information identifying a user with the user's consent."
2. **Minimal Disclosure for a Constrained Use:** "The solution that discloses the least amount of identifying information and best limits its use is the most stable long-term solution."
3. **Justifiable Parties:** "Digital identity systems must be designed so the disclosure of identifying information is limited to parties having a necessary and justifiable place in a given identity relationship." This simply means that only those people who you want to get your information and who need to get your information should be given the minimum identifying information. For example, the fact that you bought a particular book on dieting for $35.00 is something that need only be shared between you and the merchant from whom you bought the book.
4. **Directed Identity:** "A universal identity system must support both 'omni-directional' identifiers for use by public entities and 'unidirectional' identifiers for use by private entities, thus facilitating

discovery while preventing unnecessary release of correlation handles." This law is phrased in rather technical terms. It states that it should not be possible for some unlawful or unauthorized third party to discover your identity from your many interactions on the web. In our travels or interactions on the web we leave links or traces of where we have been, which if correlated, can let a third party piece together who we are. This can be a big problem, but fortunately there are new technologies that make it very difficult for third parties to do this.

5. **Pluralism of Operators and Technologies:** "A universal identity system must channel and enable the inter-working of multiple identity technologies run by multiple identity providers. It is important that people can choose between multiple identity systems, and that the different systems can interoperate with one another."

6. **Human Integration:** "The universal identity metasystem must define the human user to be a component of the distributed system integrated through unambiguous human-machine communication mechanisms offering protection against identity attacks." This is an important design concern in creating an identity system, which is to make it simple and transparent so that people intuitively know what is happening and so that they can rely upon their everyday intuitions to protect themselves.

7. **Consistent Experience Across Contexts:** "The unifying identity metasystem must guarantee its users a simple, consistent experience while enabling separation of contexts through multiple operators and technologies." This is another design goal for the quality of the experience of people using an identity system, arguing that everyone's experience should be the same across different vendors. In other words, there should be consistent conventions of use regardless of the vendor of a particular identity system.

The first of these laws gives the right of control to the user, and it is from this first commandment that all others follow. According to Cameron's definition of identity, a definition that many others accept, anyone can have multiple identities, ranging from complete anonymity to an authenticated identity card for government and defense contractors. In

other words, one can choose how rigorously one's identity is to be protected and how readily and thoroughly personal information is shared. In
the case of government-certified identities, the requirements for authentication can be quite stringent, requiring two factor biometrics such as pictures, fingerprints, or even retinal scans. People naturally have multiple
identities depending on the roles they play—for instance, as parent, professional, citizen, Rotary Club member, Gold Card member, health-care
consumer—and each of these roles is associated with specific kinds of information and permissions. By filling out a virtual "i-card" with your relevant personal information, you don't have to do again. The card is
"smart," in that it know what information to present to a Web site. The
i-card provides a "single sign-on." Few of the identity software developers
expect that most people will want to manage their own identities, so the
assumption is that an industry of "i-card brokers" will emerge that will
compete to provide a rich choice of identity and privacy protection services. This new identity layer will eventually support a myriad of commercial and noncommercial services, where the authentication of certain
aspects of one's identity will be important—you are an over-fifty-five-year-
old world traveler, qualified member of a health-care network, Gold Card
member—as will the conditions under which personal information can be
shared. Such shared services might include dating, travel, music, sports,
charitable investing, health care, and civic, religious, cultural, and political activities.

The new identity layer will also provide the foundation for people to
invent and discover new methods for social signaling, that is, new ways
to express themselves and their preferences, to make recommendations,
build affinities, to protect their privacy, and at the same time to be se-
lectively discoverable to those they want to connect with. One of the
reasons the social networking site MySpace, with over 100 million members, has been so successful is that it enables its young members to deco-
rate their personal spaces much like their bedrooms, with advertisements
of themselves using music, pictures, video, and blogs. The principal
mechanism for enhancing social networking will be meta-data tags.
These are similar to keywords or phrases that people and machines can
add to label content, people, things, events, or whatever. A tag can be
used to find people and information, and to make recommendations. In

this way, reputation systems will naturally emerge for not only people but all forms of digital content, companies, organizations—virtually anything that can be rated. These tags can be used in conjunction with the now popular and free RSSS (Really Simple Syndication Services) to create new distribution channels for all types of digital media based upon subject matter and the recommendations of trusted peers. For example, you could set up your own video channel of sports games, teams, and commentary based upon the ratings and tags of your friends. As the open identity architecture now stands, it supports the free formation of affinity groups based upon any criteria and principles of governance imaginable. Open identity is grounded on the principle of equality, so that there are no special, privileged walled gardens, and therefore, anyone can create his or her own social networks, tagging systems, reputation systems, and even identity authentication systems.

One of the challenges of any identity system is how to "authenticate" someone's identity in a trusted way so that "relying parties," such as merchants, will know that you can pay your bills, or that you are over eighteen, or that you do have the rights and privileges that you say you do. The heart of any secure identity comes down to a question of whom I can trust and who will trust me. One approach is that of coerced disclosure and authentication: having a government issue national identity cards, Social Security cards, passports, or driver's licenses with required biometric authentication such as fingerprints, facial recognition, or retinal scans. These devices could make it relatively hard for the public, but not for dedicated hackers to break into. Hackers have broken through nearly every wall so far erected on the Net; it would be naive to think they couldn't eventually leap over this one. On the dark side, a uniform national identity card would lead to an unprecedented and unchecked concentration of power— whether in the hands of a government or corporations. Unchecked, such power would corrupt governments and corporations alike. And were this type of centralized identity architecture adopted, it could be the equivalent of turning a national government into an autocracy or oligarchy with Orwellian surveillance powers. Yet as extreme and improbable as this approach may seem, it is similar to ones being considered by some European and Asian governments that have already instituted national identity cards.[2] One can only wonder what China, with its human rights record, is envisioning. In the United States, given the broad use of the War Powers Act, the Patriot Act, the violation of the 1978 National Security Act, the abrogation of *habeas corpus* for aliens and citizens in the Detainees Treatment Act of 2005, individual freedoms are less secure than at any other time in American history. The Real ID Act, a national program costing up to an estimated $11 billion that would require secure and authenticated driver's license for citizens, could be the Trojan horse for a national ID card.

The alternative approach is reflected in the design of an open identity system. Architecturally, it would support the principles of equality of individual rights and provide for a highly decentralized and open governance model. If all seven of Kim Cameron's laws of identity were observed in building next-generation identity systems, they would go a long way toward avoiding the nightmare of a digital Panopticon. If Microsoft, IBM, Novell, and others are successful in releasing their versions of the open identity system sometime in the 2007–2009 time frame, it could be available on 300–400 million computers. Moreover, if the open identity system were to be adopted by the next generation of broadband wireless phones, then it could be available on over 1 billion devices. Then, it or its equivalent would set the rules by which a new generation of global identities, social signals, organizations, and eventually institutions would be framed. Given the enormity of the political, economic, and cultural stakes involved, it is unlikely this will occur without a titanic struggle. Rather than governments or even enterprises being the sole drivers of innovation in this reformulation of human identity, innovations will also come from civic society, educational communities, the open source communities, and from the "hackivist" community.

One likely battleground is going to be the issue of anonymity. How can I protect my identity from unwanted surveillance by governments, corporations, or any other party? In China and other societies with governmental control over the media and the Net, this can be a matter of life and death. It will not be sufficient for hackers to carve out a "darknet," where they and their kind can live in anonymity as digital survivalists. Rather, it would be a real benefit to engage the hackivist community to create new types of social, security, and identity technologies that can be used by the mainstream. The real test will be to have *authenticated* anonymity, meaning that a trusted community network authenticates only that amount of information required to complete a transaction or participate in an organization. Rather than having to disclose who you are, as in Kim's Law Number Two, it should be sufficient to disclose the minimum information for a transaction. Google as well as eBay, and many social networking companies such as Facebook and Linkedin, are very vulnerable on this point, because regardless of their stated intention to "do no evil," they currently violate Cameron's seven laws of identity. Moreover, they are wedded to a business model that requires controlling and selling people's data. The danger with divulging more information than necessary is that it can be aggregated by third parties and governments without a consumer's or citizen's knowledge or real consent and potentially be used against that person.

As the stakes in controlling the identity layer become more apparent, governments of all stripes will want to become involved, assert their claims, and extract their tax. Many government officials are now advocating that the Net needs to be brought under some sort of government control. The United Nations, through its International Telecommunications Union (ITU) and the World Trade Organization (WTO), is trying to "govern" the Net. This would be a disaster. It recalls earlier efforts of the ITU and the Posts Telegraph Telecommunications (PTT) mobile network services of Europe to regulate telecommunications and to find some way to charge for e-mail.

Instead of depending on government regulators, it would be preferable, where practical, to have governance principles incorporated into the technology itself so that exchanges could be transparently audited and policies enforced technologically, and disputes electronically resolved. This is all perfectly plausible. Software is being developed at MIT that is "policy aware," so that it audits itself by providing an audit trail of how information is being distributed, stored, and used. By establishing such processes through the appropriate legal and technological frameworks, it is possible to deploy digital institutions that offer a potentially more effective means for resolving some of the problems that have plagued physical institutions—fraud, corruption, lack of transparency and accountability, inflexibility, high coordination costs, lack of responsiveness, and bureaucratic inertia.

Legislators trying to regulate the Net cannot keep up with the technology. In many cases, they simply lack the expertise and resources to
keep up to date with the fastest developing field in modern science, irrespective of their willingness or capacity to act in a broader public interest. This is a harsh truth of contemporary democracies, which have been
in denial of this reality for the last three decades. The remedy is not for
governments to abdicate their public responsibilities and capitulate to
the chimera of "free markets" and "self-regulation," but rather for them
to accept the fact and draft legal frameworks that use and guide technology toward achieving public policy goals. Struggles over fundamental
civil-liberties issues, such as warrantless searches and National Security
Agency surveillance in the United States and governmental control
over personal information in the European Union, will not go away. Yet
such concerns are potentially resolvable with the right mix of legal
frameworks and new anonymizing technologies. Neither the surveillance nor the privacy technologies were available less than a decade ago,
hence the inevitable inadequacy of policies and procedures based upon
dated technologies. Civil liberties and security protections need to be
reinterpreted in the context of more and more human activities becoming embedded in a digital world. Many activities, such as banking and
government services, purchasing a mortgage or health care, organizing
after-school programs, finding a job, or finding a mate, are becoming digital activities. Given that transactions and relationships are becoming
digital, it is only sensible that there be digital institutions to govern and
enable them.

It takes a technology to fix a technology. As technological innovations
on the Net become more and more social and affect how people affiliate,
socialize, work, and govern themselves, the roles of legislatures and policymakers will have to change fundamentally. If properly conceived and
nurtured, a new identity layer can create the social and market incentives
for a starburst of innovations in social, civic, political, and civic institutions. Given the ability of digital institutions to securely and dynamically
update rules and policies, they should be able to enforce sanctions to ensure transparency and impartiality. In this respect, digital institutions
should be invented and adopted by the "end-users" and the citizens themselves, and not imposed by government regulations. This is not to say

that governments should not have a role—a vital role—in framing the parameters and criteria for digital institutions, but that it should be up to networks of communities to invent and test methods for reputation scoring, identity management, dispute resolution, privacy protection, contracting, firm formation, and enforcement. If this approach is taken, then the resulting new social technologies will be the product of those who are subject to them, and as a consequence, they will be more legitimate and effective. In time, they will be as essential to civic and commercial governance as transactions and trading systems were to the formation of the financial services industry decades ago.

It is a cornerstone belief of "free market" capitalism that prices and rational self-interest create markets and market efficiencies. Impersonal self-interested exchange is held to be not only the most effective way to create wealth and innovation but also the underpinning of individual freedom and liberty in a democratic society. The United States, more than any other country in the world, has espoused and proselytized about these principles. The free market advocates who frequent the opinion pages of the *Wall Street Journal* and Fox News feel that markets need to be "free" to perform their magic. Left to their own devices, prices will find the most efficient equilibrium point. Markets act fairly because the hand of the market is not only invisible, it is blind; it does not play favorites. But we know it is hardly blind. Only under the most constrained of circumstances—for instance, in trading commodities—are pricing mechanisms alone fully efficient. Markets are not the product of inanimate, impersonal forces, but rather the social constructions of people, embodying all their quirks and interests.

The new sciences have shown that price is only one of many highly malleable social signals for governing behavior, expressing preferences, and allocating resources. Yet as pricing mechanisms are now used, they are but a crude proxy for many other signals of social preference. Price is inherently "a-contextual," that is, it allows for the comparison of things that are normally not always comparable. For example, should the price of a lifesaving operation really be interchangeable with or comparable to the purchase of a Porsche? Price is not everything. To collapse all luxury goods onto the same dimension as basic needs is to lose critical information and blur social contexts that are absolutely essential to civilized and ethical living. In short, prices can have the effect of extreme reduction-ism: What is the price for a baby, an organ, a species, a mountain, a life, a genome?

In fact, even markets depend upon types of signals other than price, sta-tus, quality, and group preferences. This is something that Adam Smith appreciated, but the concept has become lost through the recent cartoon characterizations of his analysis of the invisible hand. The blind embrace of this cartoon has legitimated a culture of personal and societal greed and excess; the accumulation and protection of wealth is seen as a natural right sustained and legitimated by the astounding paradoxical axiom that somehow the pursuit of self-interest is a public good. Greed may indeed feel good, but not for long and not for many. In Florence, commerce was influenced by neighborhoods, associations, and families, in situations where the parties knew one another, where they could appreciate different dimensions of preference and exchange above and beyond price. Theirs was not the one-dimensional world of a uniform market, but a highly con-textual world in which a plurality of social networks and contexts, and shared understanding, made possible the accumulation of social capital and social currencies for trusted exchange.

By having tightly knit, multiple, and social networks throughout the Mediterranean and Europe, the Florentines arguably were among the first to discover the power of what Chris Anderson of *Wired* magazine has called "long-tail markets."[3] Long-tail markets, unlike conventional mar-kets, are not shaped like bell curves, which is how most economists have characterized markets. Rather, long-tail markets are shaped like a ski slope, with the head of the slope representing those customers who share common preferences, such as low price, and the tail of the slope, that is, the run out as it were, all the different preferences for specialized goods or services. It is noteworthy that the notion of long-tail markets was not ap-preciated until e-commerce became prevalent through the successes of eBay and Amazon. Not until Amazon listed with a minimum of cost a huge number of books, CDs, and electronics did it become economically viable to discover and serve the fine-grained preferences of customers in long-tail markets. Ebay went even further in its discovery of the viral power of social commerce, what has been called "community commerce." By enabling all customers to define, create, and essentially govern through reputation scores their communities of commerce, eBay facilitated the making and the servicing of long-tail markets. Moreover, it was well understood by both the founder, Pierre Omidyar, and the CEO, Meg Whitman, that eBay's success was not due to efficient price and transaction, as was the case with auction sites, which many financial analysts thought eBay was. Rather, eBay's remarkable achievement was about securing the trust of the customer and the community. In effect, eBay made it possible to create new markets around the social preferences of its customers. It made capitalism contextual and social, by allowing for the expression of new dimensions of personal preference, other than price, and by building contexts in which members of the community could trust and interact with one another.

This is just the beginning of a major global disruption on the Net, what some analysts in the industry call the "Big Bang," the transition from enterprise to people-centric services and business models. One of the giant enablers of this will be the adoption by the digital services industry of the customer-centric model of identity and information rights, not only for online computer services but for mobile phone services as well. But even though this model has the backing of the major software and Web services companies, its success is not guaranteed by any means. It will be resisted by incumbent interests—economic and political—that lack the imagination and incentive to change.

Nonetheless, the economic and social promise is enormous. This new form of social capitalism will enable the formation of myriads of long-tail markets to reflect the values and preferences of individual consumers. For the first time, and potentially on a global scale, anyone anywhere will be able to let their purchasing decisions reflect their value preferences. They will be able to form their own commercial communities to direct dollars and resources into those communities, practices, enterprises, institutions, and projects that they deem important. They will be able to do what classical economics has not: provide market-based approaches for incorporating economic externalities, such as environmental degradation and social inequities, into the purchasing choices of consumers. By providing tags that reflect social preferences, the market forces of supply and demand can be used to stimulate the growth of new value-based industries, such as clean energy, affordable health care, education, and sustainable agriculture.

Instead of depleting trust and social capital to offset the costs of economic externalities, social market forces can be used to create social capital and trust as a public good.

By giving individuals control over their own information, including reputations and purchasing preferences and profiles, people will be able to discover and construct their own social and commercial networks. They will be able to import their identities, relationships, and personal information from other networks and into their own "meta-networks." To properly govern such networks, people will be able to "cut and paste" governance code from an open source Web site,[4] and then modify it to reflect their own community governance and information-sharing and privacy policies. Hence, all those social components that enable pluralistic and trusted self-governance, reputations, profiles, membership, and sanctioning rules should be highly portable and extensible.

These capabilities have been developed by an open source initiative called Higgins (after a Tasmanian long-tailed mouse),[5] supported by the Berkman Center for Internet and Society at the Harvard Law School and by IBM, Novell, and Best Buy. This open source framework provides for open interoperability among different identity systems, including Microsoft's forthcoming CardSpace for its Vista operating system. By using a digital identity card, called the i-card, it will be possible to make markets for virtually anything—buyers and sellers of antiques, collectibles, housing, cars, food, sports equipment, video games, and CDs. The resulting social and commercial networks will likely learn and borrow from one another to progressively innovate to improve trust, curb free riding, and create more compelling experiences. What is now an impersonal experience on the Web will increasingly become a more personal and contextual experience. People will know who you are, trade stories, recipes, tips, and photographs and conduct business through the equivalent of a handshake.

Capitalism itself has evolved, from a form of brute force capitalism by "Big Men," dominated by social and political coercion, to a second-generation form of capitalism characterized by market power, mercantile banks, and robber baronism, to third-generation capitalism (3G capitalism), in which government interventions and regulations are applied to make capitalism less chaotic and more equitable, trustworthy, and efficient. A new form of capitalism is emerging called 4G capitalism. It is more autonomous and self-governing than its predecessors and is primarily digital. It uses social preference signals and digital institutions to create markets to internalize economic, social, and political externalities to resolve deep-seated social and ecological issues.

The alternative to open source identity is a "closed" identity system which, when it fails, does so catastrophically. One sign of a failing security system is the "last-ditch" effort to build an "impenetrable" wall to en-circle something or someone you want to protect. This is as true for digital security as it is for physical security. The Great Wall of China did not protect China from invaders, nor did the Maginot Line stop the Nazis' Blitzkrieg, nor will trenches encircling Baghdad secure it against insurgents. As we saw in Chapter 2, when weapons get progressively smaller, cheaper, more deadly, and more accessible, there are no failsafe deterrents. Systems fail and people fail. For every defensive measure, there is a countermeasure. Security, whether it be digital or physical, is a continuous, innovative process within which flexibility, alertness, and responsiveness are critical.

Terrorism doesn't signify a contest between good and evil, a clash of civilizations, or a resurrection of the Nazis in Islamic dress, but rather a contest of identities, a competition for social niches, compounded by ar-chaic reflexes. Such responses have been part of the human condition for millennia. It is different now because of the globally destabilizing consequences of these behaviors, their potential for irreversible damage on a global scale. On the other hand, it is promising that we are begin-ning to understand our natures in much the same way we have under-stood our bodies, and by virtue of that new scientific knowledge, we may begin to make interventions that are actually effective and corrective.

The profiles of the alleged terrorists captured in the United Kingdom for plotting to blow up as many as ten America-bound airplanes are a case in point. All of them are British citizens, many of them second gen-eration, and for the better part of their lives were not especially obser-vant Muslims. They were young men who lived most of their lives without a respected identity in a country where they had little standing. As we saw in Chapter 6, young men are wired for combat, and, like sol-diers, regardless of their religion, culture and nationality, they don't fight and die for abstract ideas, but in order to gain the respect and affection of their peers and mentors. The neurological evidence shows that young men under conditions of stress are virtually incapable of calculating the long-term ramifications of their acts—on themselves and others. That part of their brain simply isn't active.[6] So, when the media show them the people they identify with—men, women, children, the elderly—being humiliated, in distress, and dying, they react with an instinctual need to protect and avenge. These are ancient triggers that respond independent of religion or ideology. They are impervious to logic. The levers of foreign policy and presumptive warfare, torture, and belittling propaganda—especially in the case of the domestically grown terrorist—have absolutely no deterrent effect. More often, it is quite the opposite. The more absolute and singular the response to terrorism is, the more absolute and singular the response of the terrorist.

Engagement, not isolation, is the road to security through the recognition of mutual interests, based on Adam Smith's recognition of the inherently human penchant for "barter and exchange" as a means to evolve common commercial interests and mutual empathy and to build "common stock." His intuitions have been vindicated by contemporary neuroscience: People cooperate with those they identify with; through their mirror neurons, they see others as themselves. Hence, new forms of security will only come with the embrace of shared global identities.

Human beings have great difficulty understanding third- and fourth-order effects. For instance, when someone crashes into the back of your car or insults you, there is a flash of anger and you focus on the immediate cause—and an immediate corrective response. Strike back! In the heat of the moment, people typically don't try to understand the possible chain of events that led up to the accident or the affront. The immediate or first-order cause is uppermost in our minds. But people and nature are much more complex than that. We struggle to keep many different independent strings of causation in our heads. We need to keep it simple, especially if that entails the building of a consensus and communicating with lots of other people. So, finding explanations that go beyond simple first-order causes, such as "he wants to do evil" or "he hates Americans," and asking why is he is so motivated or how his hatred came into being is seen as evasive. Social conservatives are especially resistant to anything more than first-order "agency" explanations because they hold individual agency, and hence personal accountability, in especially high regard—except when it applies to them. Social conservatives also see conflict challenges as requiring a tough, honor-bound response, a kind of symmetry of response in which one's own special brand of manhood dominates. From all this comes the reaction "Bring it on."

The failure to see beyond first-order effects was made apparent to me in a wholly different context: farming. I had been trying to cultivate high-quality hay fields, rich in clover and timothy hay. I had a problem in that my hay fields had been neglected for years and had a high content of goldenrod, milkweed, and hardhack, all very undesirable. I concluded I had to completely plow, cultivate, seed, and fertilize my fields in order to get the hay crop I wanted. This was an expensive undertaking in equipment, gas, seed, fertilizer, and man-hours. For the next two years the yields were good and weed free, but soon after, the weeds began to return. Then a local farmer approached me and asked me why I went to all the trouble and expense of plowing, harrowing, raking, and reseeding my land. "All's you need is some wood ash and some lime and the weeds will go away. Just sweeten the soil a bit and you won't have to fight all those weeds."

He was right. I was so focused on eradicating the weeds, the first-order effects, that I didn't think about why there were weeds in the first place—the soil quality. I felt that the more brute force I used in getting rid of them, visually and immediately, somehow the more successful I would be.

Terrorism will only be ended by looking beyond first-order causes, as some in the U.S. military have realized. They have started to look at terrorism in a larger context. They are capable of asking the many whys, and then seeking out solutions that match the problem. This new initiative is called Strong Angel. Much of the thinking behind it came from members of the Highlands Forum. Strong Angel is the brainchild of Dr. Eric Rasmussen, the surgeon for the Third Fleet in the U.S. Navy, a veteran in many humanitarian operations in Bosnia, Africa, Indonesia, Kashmir, and New Orleans. The goal of Strong Angel is to build a rapid and secure humanitarian response capability within the DOD. It is an experiment in how multi-party coalitions composed of U.S. military, nongovernmental organizations, companies, universities, and local groups can set up their own command and control centers and logistics to provide both security and humanitarian aid. Linton Wells, the deputy assistant Secretary of Defense for Networks and Information Integration, is both an active supporter of the Highlands Forum and the Strong Angel program. A senior military strategist, Lin sees the mission of Strong Angel as "military and civilian activities conducted across the spectrum from peace to conflict to establish or maintain order . . . We want to be able to create a space outside of the Pentagon's network firewalls to offer assistance." Even with his senior position within the Pentagon, it was not easy for Lin Wells to get Strong Angel launched, and it took 300 e-mails to get Dr. Rasmussen and two colleagues assigned to disaster relief in Banda Aceh, Indonesia.

Another active member of the Strong Angel team is Dr. Dave Warner, former military officer, M.D., Ph.D. in neuroscience, computer scientist, and regular at the annual Burning Man event in the Nevada desert. Like Rasmussen, Dave has been involved in many high-risk humanitarian efforts, from Afghanistan to New Orleans. He is an expert on setting up wireless "mesh networks" to support telemedicine and command and control centers for humanitarian relief. He is refreshingly candid in his assessments of the directions of U.S. policy, noting in a briefing about Banda Aceh that he was especially pleased to be involved in "cleaning up a mess that we (meaning the United States) had not made." He is a proponent of the military changing its mission from waging to war to waging peace. Although such a perspective is by no means a part of the mainstream military, it is significant that at least one branch of the DOD not only tolerates such candor but actually values it.

This new thinking on how to counter terrorism is not without successful precedent. The British learned in countering terrorist forces in Oman, Malaysia, and Singapore that force alone was not an effective deterrent, that they had to deploy highly trained special forces who were not only accomplished in the indigenous languages and customs but who could help the people set up schools, hospitals, roads, and other infrastructure. These countries today illustrate what a thoughtful counterterrorism policy might achieve.

For much of this book, I have argued that origin narratives are critical to forming and anchoring group and individual identities. Origin narratives are a kind of "necessary fiction," which even if implausible, keep humans anchored in time and certain of their destiny. These narratives and their associated traditions and rituals are the glue that keep a people connected; they provide sacrosanct axioms for defining a "common stock" and engendering a sense of shared identities and interests that builds trust and empathy.

Since the human diaspora out of Africa 60,000 years ago, thousands of origin myths have sprung up, all sharing the same themes, but each differing in their details, histories, and actors. But the human diaspora is over. All the earth's habitable niches have been filled, and people of all ethnic origins are communicating, traveling, and intermarrying. As never before in human history, rather than asserting our differences, we are having to discover our similarities. With this change comes the opportunity to write a new global origin narrative, one that takes the human genome as its "text." In our genome is not only the history of our species but the histories of the millions of species with which we have coevolved—from microbes to mammoths. Through the interpretation of our DNA records, we can begin to understand the enormous struggles that all peoples went through and appreciate the reasons we are the way we are.

A National Geographic project called the Genographic Project, funded by IBM and the Watt Family Institute, is attempting to do just that. By collecting DNA samples from around the world, it is documenting the human diaspora over the last 200,000 years. In a very creative and entrepreneurial way, the project is also making kits available for a price to anyone who wants to learn their DNA heritage. By swabbing your inner cheek and sending in the sample, you can trace your genetic origin.

This research has the potential to scientifically reframe our origin narratives, not as the exclusive enclave of a particular lineage, tribe, tradition, race, or religion but as a kind of "global narrative" that includes the journeys of all the earth's people. A remarkable feature of this scientific narrative is that it is thematically similar to the many origin myths.[7] There is an Eve—called the Mitochondrial Eve—from whom all humankind is descended, roughly 140,000 years ago. There is also an Adam—from whom all humanity is descended 60,000 years ago. What then is the story of this Adam and this Eve? According to the book of genome, we are all descended from Africa. The people with the oldest genetic heritage in the world today are the San Bushmen. In their faces one can see the traces of the different peoples of the world—the cheekbones of the Inuit, the epicanthic fold of Asians, and the hair of the Bantu.

Just 60,000 years ago, the first modern human beings migrated out of Africa. At that time, as now, the climate began to change and drought became more prevalent. As drought destroyed the grasslands, humans and massive animal herds migrated north. Thus began a journey out of Africa by a small band of humans, estimated to be no more that 200 individuals. Soon after, there was a second migration. This group traveled up through the Middle East, traveling along the Sinai Peninsula up to the coast of the Mediterranean. They were then followed by yet another group that traveled into Eurasia and the plains of Central Asia, following huge herds of bison, antelope, horses, and deer. Given the change in the climate and the need to wear clothes, the pigment of their skins began to lighten to capture vitamin D from the sunlight.

After these people spent roughly 30,000 years in the grasslands of Central Asia, another series of migrations took place: One group traveled out of the plains into northern and then southern India. Another group went into what is now northern China and Korea, forming the largest ethnic group on the earth. The third group migrated north into Central Asia and eventually went into Europe, following the herds of bovines. Their skins lightened even further, due to the need to be clothed and the reduced sunlight.

The genetic texts tell the remarkable story of how the ancestors of the Inuit, the Chukchi, migrated from Central Asia into Siberia, where the temperatures dropped to −100°F. They stayed in this region until the height of the Ice Age, when the Bering Strait froze over, roughly 15,000 years ago. They had been reduced to no more than 20–40 members, but they made their way across the Bering Strait into North America. In a mere 800 years, this tiny band of people populated the entire continents of North and South America, all the way down to Tierra del Fuego.

In just 45,000 years, all the major ethnic and cultural groups of the planet had been established and all major regions of the world had been inhabited by the descendants of a small band of San Bushmen from Africa. Their migrations and subsequent physical and cultural adaptations spanned temperatures of 120°F to –100°F, from deserts to tropics, from mountains to steppes, northern forests, and tropical islands. This is an origin narrative of stunning breadth and drama, describing the heroism and resourcefulness of eight major lineages over 60,000 years.

What is especially compelling about this narrative and its importance for building a global identity is that it shows how interconnected all peoples are and offers a factually heroic narrative that dignifies and explains human differences. It is a scientifically grounded narrative that is inclusive and breaks down any rationale for divisive "we-they" narratives that have been at the center of so many unnecessary human conflicts and sufferings. The challenge is for the peoples of the world to capture and express their different traditions and narratives, to discover themselves in others. The globalization and interconnectivity of digital technologies, even inexpensive technologies for the developing world, make it possible for everyone to express, share, and combine their own global identities. Only then will the curse of the Hobbesian traps be lifted.

Early in my life, I was intrigued by life. What made things alive? Why were they the way they were? The theory of evolution, as I understood it then, bothered and intimidated me. It seemed so mechanical, ruthless, impersonal, especially concerning the many living things that I found so fascinating, wonderful, and irreducible. In my teens, I read Pierre Teilhard de Chardin's book *The Phenomenon of Man*, which had an enormous impact on me. Teilhard de Chardin, a heretic Jesuit paleontologist, argued that there was a purpose in evolution, and that mankind was proceeding on a path toward higher forms of complexity and perfection, what he called the "Omega point." There were three separate spheres: the Geosphere, basically, the geological evolution of the planet; the Biosphere, the evolution of all biological life; and then, the Noosphere, the evolution of knowledge and wisdom.

Even then I knew that teleological arguments of this sort were not valid scientific arguments and that random variation and mutation were the scientifically sanctioned model for evolution. Nonetheless, I was motivated to look at scientifically valid examples of goal-directed behavior, for example, in the field of cybernetics, founded by Norbert Weiner. I was also intrigued by the work of John von Neumann, W. Ross Ashby, and Heinz von Forester on self-organizing systems. It seemed possible to create systems, eventually "artificially intelligent" software programs, and eventually, simplified forms of "artificial life" that seemed to be purposeful, even slightly intelligent. In recent years, these arguments have reappeared through the fields of complex adaptive systems (CAS) and self-organizing networks. According to the research of the physicist Stephen Wolfram and the inventor of genetic algorithms, John Holland, among others, complex forms of life inevitably "emerge" and evolve from relatively simple principles. Computer simulations of genetic evolution and artificial life have demonstrated how over "many generations," things that were inanimate eventually became "self-organizing," capable of defining, protecting, and replicating an unique "identity." The world of "artificial life" made it possible to design hundreds of thousands of autonomous agents, each of which would compete, adapt, reproduce, and even solve complex problems. All these things could happen without having to posit the hand of an intelligent designer. Nature seems to strive not for the perfect but the possible.

The fact that similar evolutionary stable strategies emerge from species with genetically distinct histories has always fascinated me. The fact that insects, birds, mammals, and primates have evolved similar strategies for cooperation suggests that survival is not random, that not all strategies are equally valid, but that there are kinds of inevitable, emergent strategies for social organization.

In playing the survival game, the winning strategy would be to understand how the process of evolution itself worked, and then to use that understanding to build the ultimate survival strategy by creating a "meta-representation" of the process of evolution. As long as you are immersed in a process, you are reacting to it and have no way of controlling it. Hence, you need to get above it in order to control it. As Kurt Godel, Alonzo Church, and Alan Turing have formally proven in the areas of computation and logic, you need a "meta-system" or high-level logic to understand or control a lower-level system.[8] Nothing can be shown to be "complete" or computable in terms of itself, only in reference to a higher level or meta-system. By understanding the higher-level principles that govern the "survival game," then, and only then, is it possible to evolve higher-level strategies that can compete with the forces of natural selection. Such a strategy would always be evolving and incomplete, for as in the scientific method, virtually everything—including evolution and quantum mechanics—is but a "theory," and to be proven correct, all theories must progress satisfactorily through attempts to prove them wrong.

Like identity, truth is incomplete and can only be asserted in the negative—by stating what it is not. Nonetheless, there can be a rational, that is, a demonstrable and replicable basis for moral choices and a "just" social order, but—and that is a big and uncomfortable but for many people—all such rationales will always be incomplete and open so that they can continuously evolve. This position is 180° away from Justice Scalia's advocacy for an evolution-resistant moral order and Constitution.

Every age finds trusted metaphors to explain how the world came into being and how it works. For the Enlightenment, it was Cartesian logic, Newtonian physics, and elegant workings of the watch. Enlightenment thinkers separated mind and matter, emotion and thought, and they equated human and animal actions to those of mechanical automata. The universe was knowable, mechanical, and reducible to the sum of its parts. Legitimate scientific knowledge required objectivity, independent observations, and replicable results. In Richard Dawkin's apt phrase, "God is the Blind Watch Maker." According to this line of thinking, there is no need for teleological explanation at all; evolution is random and directionless. There is neither design nor intent. To quote the prolific Darwinian philosopher Daniel Dennett, teleological arguments are guilty of a fatal "attribution error"—attributing intent where there is none, such as saying that a thermostat tries to keep the room warm; intent and purpose are simply superimpositions of the observer.

But these views, despite their currency today in popular culture and even in the scientific community, are no longer sustainable. Emotions and reason are not separate. We do not derive our identity from simple cognition, and complex processes cannot be reduced to the sum of their parts. Neither animals nor humans are reducible to mechanical automata.

And increasingly, biological evolution and development cannot be explained by random variation. And finally in the area of quantum physics, common-sense notions of causality and the role of the observer and the observed have been fractured beyond recognition. The Newtonian world of the Enlightenment was highly tangible, with concepts of mass, force, and acceleration predominating. But in the world of self-organizing networks and biology and evolution, it is the intangibles—information, rules, grammars, codes, sequences, transcription, and recombination— that increasingly shape our understanding of the world and ourselves. When theories about these intangibles result in concrete technologies, such as the digital computer and software, the Internet, genetic engineering, regenerative medicine, and most recently, quantum computers, they become huge, organizing metaphors.

There are many contending explanatory metaphors for the post-Enlightenment world, some of which have been discussed in this book. Quantum computing, for instance, has not been discussed because it is so new, controversial, and still in the speculative phases of development. Indeed, many prominent physicists doubt the possibility of any form of quantum computing in the foreseeable future. Yet the application of quantum principles to the design of tangible technologies—whether it be in new materials, computing, or communications devices—will invariably alter conventional notions of reality. According to its advocates, quantum computers have the potential to solve complex problems, such as cracking many of the encryption codes in use today, modeling the behaviors of molecules, and solving classes of problems that are intractable for the best of today's supercomputers. The promise of quantum computing depends upon a scientific model of reality that is more accurate and powerful than any computational mechanisms derived from the binary logic of the digital computer. Quantum computing uses Qubits, quantum bits, to make its calculations. Qubits are sub-atomic particles—quanta—that are in a state of superimposition. They are simultaneously waves and particles, and only resolve themselves, that is, yield an answer in computing terms, through the act of measurement.

These are mind boggling notions, defying common sense, and are an affront to many widely held convictions about the nature of reality. It will be a long time before they become a part of the vernacular of everyday life and institutions. Yet, just as the ideals and the science of the Enlightenment dismantled the science and authority of Feudalism, so, too, will the findings of these new sciences replace Enlightenment ideals and institutions with their own. In the future, evolutionary biological derived identity and origin narratives may well provide the basis for new identity narratives, potentially shattering the Hobbesian traps that have locked humanity in cycles of divisive violence for millennia. Yet even today, what the perspective of the new sciences make clear is that it is futile to separate the part from the whole, the observer from the observed, the individual from the group. We are, indivisibly, a crowd of one. Our survival depends upon it.

Appendix

Figure 2. Divergent projected climate changes (2000 to 2100)

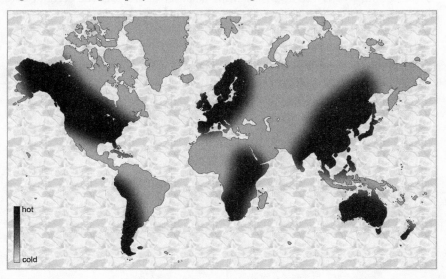

hot

cold

Global Warming (2000 to 2100): rising temperatures cause migrations, extinctions, storms, and wild fires; disease-carrying insects increase in numbers; glaciers melt.

see: "Global Warming Early Warning Signs." Environmental Defense et al. 1999. www.climatehotmap.org (2004)

continues

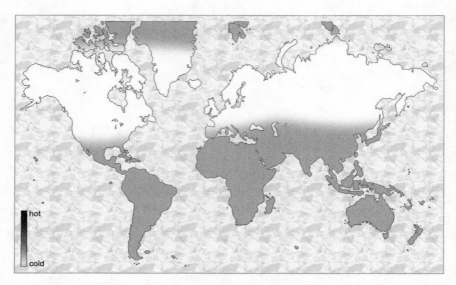

Global Cooling (2010 to 2020): melting polar ice desalinates the ocean, causing currents to cool and slow; heavy rains and droughts decrease food supplies; some regions become uninhabitable.

see: "An Abrupt Climate Change Scenario." Schwartz and Randall. 2003.
www.ems.org/climate/pentagon_climate_change.pdf (2004)

Notes

Prologue

1. See http://www.dod.mil/nii/NCW/.

2. There is an initiative in the Pentagon, partially an outcome of Highlands Forums meetings, called Strong Angel, in which the intent is to use the logistical, medical, and security capabilities of the military to provide humanitarian support in areas of extreme duress, whether from natural forces or military conflict. It is a new model of what the DOD can do to become "peacemakers" rather than "warfighters." It has attracted an exceptional number of committed and talented military personnel. See http://www.strongangel.org.

Chapter One

1. Thomas Hobbes, Leviathan, XIII.13, 1660, http://oregonstate.edu/instruct/phl302/texts/hobbes.

2. Charles Krauthammer, "Democratic Realism: An American Foreign Policy for a Unipolar World," February 12, 2004, http://www.aei.org/publications/pubID.19912,filter.all/pub_detail.asp.

Chapter Two

1. Daniel P. Schrag, talk at Santa Fe Institute, Business Network Meeting, October 2002. See Daniel P. Schrag and James McCarthy, "The Sea," chap. 15 in Allan Robinson et al., eds., *Biological-Physical Interactions and Global Climate Change: Some Lessons from History* (New York: John Wiley, 2002).

2. Jared Diamond, *Collapse: How Societies Choose to Fail or Succeed* (New York: Penguin, 2005).

3. Raymond Kurzweil, collected writings. See http://www.kurzweilai.net/meme/frame.html?m=10 (February 2004).

4. Hans Moravec, articles and papers. See http://www.frc.ri.cmu.edu/~hpm/hpm.pubs.html (February 2004).

5. Victor Vinge, "Technological Singularity," *Whole Earth Review*, December 10, 1993.

6. Raymond Kurzweil, *The Age of Spiritual Machines* (New York: Viking, 1999).

Chapter Three

1. Richard Landes, ed., *Encyclopedia of Millennialism and Millennial Movements* (New York: Routledge, 2000).

2. Philip Jenkins, "The Next Christianity," *Atlantic Monthly* (October 2002), pp. 53–74.

3. Ibid.

4. Ibid., p. 4.

5. Rick Brennan and R. Evan Ellis, "Information Warfare in Multilateral Peace Operations: A Case Study of Somalia," in David S. Alberts and Daniel S. Papp, *Information Age Anthology: The Information Age Military*, vol. 3 (Washington, D.C.: CCRP Publications Series, March 2001), p. 608.

6. ABC News, "Somalia: Who's Who." See http://www.abcnews.go.com/sections/world/DailyNews/somalia_who.html (February 2004).

7. Brennan and Ellis, "Information Warfare," p. 606.

8. Ibid., p. 615.

9. Ibid., p. 621.

10. Ibid., p. 622.

11. Ibid., p. 629.

12. Also see Brent R. Norquist, "Somalia: Origins of Conflict and Unintended Consequences," Marine Corps Command and Staff College, Quantico, Virginia, 2002.

13. Marlise Smith, "Trial Centers on Role of Press During Rwanda Massacre," *New York Times*, March 3, 2002.

14. Philip Gourevitch, "We Wish to Inform You That Tomorrow We Will Be Killed with Our Families," in *Stories from Rwanda* (New York: Piccador Press, 1999).

Chapter Four

1. See Defense Information Systems Agency, http://www.disa.mil.

2. Carl von Clausewitz, *On War*, ed. and trans. Michael Howard and Peter Paret (Princeton: Princeton University Press, 1976, rev. 1984).

3. Ibid.

4. Sun Tzu, *The Art of War* (New York: Dover, 2002).

5. Adam Smith, *The Wealth of Nations* (New York: Random House, Modern Library, 2000), p. 485.

6. Adam Smith, *The Theory of Moral Sentiments* (Edinburgh 1759), see Adam Smith Institute, http://www.adamsmith.org, Part I, *Of the Propriety of Actions . . .* , Chap. 1, *Of Sympathy.*

7. Ibid., Part III, *Of the Foundation of Our Judgments . . .* , para. III.I.86.

8. Ibid., para. VI.II.16.

9. Dr. Eamonn Butler, director of the Adam Smith Institute, *The Theory of Moral Sentiments* (London: 2001), http://www.adamsmith.org.

10. Antonio Damasio, *Descartes' Error: Emotion, Reason, and the Human Brain* (New York: Avon Books, 1994).

Chapter Five

1. See Ernst Fehr and Bettina Rockenbach, "Detrimental Effects of Sanctions on Human Altruism," *Trends in Ecology and Evolution* (2005), http://www.iew.unizh.ch/home/chairs/fehr.

2. Gaulin and McBurney, "Social Behavior," in *Psychology: An Evolutionary Approach* (Upper Saddle River, NJ: Prentice Hall, 2000).

3. "An ESS, or evolutionarily stable strategy, is a strategy such that, if all the members of a population adopt it, no mutant strategy can invade." See John Maynard Smith, *Evolution and the Theory of Games* (New York: Cambridge University Press, 1982). In other words, ESS is a strategy such that when all the members of a population—or species—adopt it, there is no rational reason to adopt any other strategy.

4. See Elliott Sober and David Sloan Wilson, *Unto Others: The Evolution and Psychology of Unselfish Behavior* (Cambridge: Harvard University Press, 1998); Robin Dunbar, *Grooming, Gossip, and the Evolution of Language* (Cambridge: Harvard University Press, 1996), p. 66.

5. Ibid., p. 66.

6. Ibid., p. 72.

7. Antonio Damasio, *Looking for Spinoza: Joy, Sorrow and the Feeling Brain* (Orlando, FL: Harcourt, 2003), p. 160.

8. Ibid.

9. Ibid.

10. "Humans evolved cheat detection as a separate mental component," says evolutionary psychologist John Tooby of the University of California, Santa Barbara. "Our brains have specialized programs like computer programs, specific for various applications," he says. Kendall Powell, "Brains Sniff Out Scam Artists: Evolution Might Have Programmed Us to Compute Fairness," *Nature*, August 13,

2002, http://www.nature.com/nsu/020812/020812–1.html (June 2004). Also see Emma Young, "Brain's 'Cheat Detector' Is Revealed," *New Scientist*, August 12, 2002, http://www.newscientist.com/news/news.jsp?id=ns99992663 (June 2004).

11. Robin Dunbar, Chris Knight, and Camilla Power, *The Evolution of Culture* (New Brunswick, NJ: Rutgers University Press, 1999).

12. Leda Cosmides and John Tooby, "Evolutionary Psychology: A Primer," Center for Evolutionary Psychology, Santa Barbara, University of California, 2002.

13. The issue of the modularity of the brain is a complex and highly contested topic, whose arguments are beyond the technical scope of this book.

14. Lawrence Sugiyama, John Tooby, and Leda Cosmides, "Cross-Cultural Evidence of Cognitive Adaptations for Social Exchange Among the Shiwiar of Ecuadorian Amazonia," *Proceedings of the National Academy of Sciences*, no. 3529, August 2002, vol. 99, issue 17, pp. 11537–11542.

15. Dunbar, *Grooming*, p. 61.

16. Giacomo Rizzolatti et al., "Premotor Cortex and the Recognition of Motor Actions," *Cognitive Brain Research* 3 (1996): 131–141; G. Rizzolatti and L. Craighero, "The Mirror-Neuron System," *Annual Review of Neuroscience* 27 (2004): 169–192.

17. Personal correspondence from George Lakoff, 2003.

18. There is debate between those who espouse the "selfish gene" model of Richard Dawkins (*The Selfish Gene* [New York: Oxford University Press, 1976]) and those who take the cooperative or altruistic view of evolution (Sober and Wilson, *Unto Others*).

19. Damasio, *Looking for Spinoza*, p. 161.

20. John H. Clippinger, *Biology of Business: Decoding Natural Laws of Enterprise* (San Francisco: Jossey Bass, 1999).

21. Terrence Deacon, *The Symbolic Species: The Co-Evolution of Language and the Brain* (New York: Norton, 1997).

22. Steven Pinker, *The Language Instinct: How the Mind Creates Language* (New York: HarperCollins, 1994).

23. Noam Chomsky, *New Horizons in the Study of Language and the Mind* (Cambridge, U.K.: Cambridge University Press, 2000).

24. Dunbar, *Grooming*, p. 78.

25. John Searle, *Mind, Language, and Society: Philosophy in the Real World* (New York: Basic Books, 1998), p. 121.

26. Carl T. Bergstrom et al., "The Peacock, the Sparrow, and the Evolution of Language," Santa Fe Institute, May 2001, p. 25; M. Lachmann, Sz. Szamado, and C. T. Bergstrom, "Cost and Conflict in Animal Signals and Human Language," *Proceedings of the National Academy of Sciences USA* 98: 13189–13194.

27. Tao Gong and John H. Holland et al., "A Computational Model of the Co-Evolution of Lexicon and Syntax," Department of Electronic Engineering, City University of Hong Kong, 2005, unpublished manuscript.

28. See John Holland, *Hidden Order: How Adaptation Builds Complexity* (New York: Addison-Wesley, 1995); Stuart Kauffman, *The Origins of Order: Self-Organization and Selection in Evolution* (New York: Oxford University Press, 1993); and Stephan Wolfram, *A New Kind of Science* (Champaign, IL: Wolfram Media, 2003).

29. Searle, *Mind, Language, and Society*, p. 124.

30. See M. T. Clanchy, *From Memory to Written Record: England, 1066–1307* (Cambridge: Harvard University Press, 1979).

31. Searle, *Mind, Language, and Society*, p. 130.

32. Ibid., p. 129.

33. Ibid., p. 159.

34. Deacon, *The Symbolic Species*, p. 343.

35. Robin Dunbar, *The Human Story: A History of Mankind's Evolution* (New York: Faber and Faber, 2004).

36. Ibid., p. 46.

37. Ibid., p. 161.

38. George Miller, "The Magical Number Seven, Plus or Minus Two: Some Limits on Our Capacity for Processing Information," *Psychological Review* 63 (1956): 81–97.

39. Ibid., p. 51.

40. Geoffrey Hughes, *A History of English Words* (London: Blackwell Publishers, 2000).

41. Ibid., p. 4.

42. Steven Mithen, *The Singing Neanderthals: The Origin of Music, Language, Mind, and Body* (Weidenfeld and Nicholson, 2005); Alison Wray, *Formulaic Language and the Lexicon* (New York: Cambridge University Press, 2002).

43. Sober and Wilson, *Unto Others*.

44. See J. Flack and F. B. M. de Waal, "Any Animal Whatever: Darwinian Building Blocks of Morality in Monkeys and Apes," *Journal of Consciousness Studies* 7 (1–2) (2000): 1–29; F. B. M. DeWaal, "The Chimpanzee's Service Economy: Food for Grooming, Evolution, and Human Behavior," *Elsevier Science* (November 6, 1997): 375–386.

45. See Eric Beinhocker, *The Origin of Wealth: Evolution, Complexity, and the Radical Remaking of Economics* (Cambridge: Harvard Business School Press, 2006), p. 435.

Chapter Six

1. Spenser Wells, *The Journey of Man: A Generic Odyssey* (New York: Random House, 2004).

2. Michael Shermer, *The Science of Good and Evil* (New York: Owl Books, 2004).

3. James Buchan, *Crowded with Genius: The Scottish Enlightenment, Edinburgh's Movement of the Mind* (New York: HarperCollins, 2003), p. 12.

4. Ibid.

5. Richard Nisbett and Dov Cohen, *Culture of Honor: The Psychology of Violence in the South* (New York: Perseus Books, 1996).

6. Adam Smith, *The Wealth of Nations* (New York: Random House, Modern Library, 2000), p. 18.

7. Andy Clark, *Being There: Putting Brain, Body, and World Together Again* (Cambridge: MIT Press, 1998).

8. Ibid.

9. Sarah Brosnan and Franz B. M. de Waal, "Variations on Tit-for-Tat: Proximate Mechanisms of Cooperation and Reciprocity," *Human Nature* 13 (1) (2002): 129–152.

10. Kevin McCabe, "Reciprocity and Social Order: What Do Experiments Tell Us About Econimic Growth?" Mercatus Center, George Mason University, 2003.

11. John Maynard Smith, *Evolution and the Theory of Games* (Cambridge, U.K.: Cambridge University Press, 1982).

12. McCabe, "Reciprocity and Social Order."

13. V. E. Stone et al., "Selective Impairments of Reasoning About Social Exchange in a Patient with Bilateral Limbic System Damage," *Proceedings of the National Academy of Sciences* 99 (17) (2002): 11531–11536.

14. Hillard Kaplan and Michael Guruen, "The Natural History of Human Food Sharing and Cooperation: A Review of a New Multi-Individual Approach to the Negotiation of Norms," in Herbert Gintis, Samuel Bowles, and Ernst Fehr, *Moral Sentiments and Material Interests* (Cambridge: MIT Press, 2005), pp. 75–113.

15. Ibid.

16. Richard Dawkins, *The Selfish Gene* (Oxford: Oxford University Press, 1989).

17. Dan M. Kahan, "The Logic of Reciprocity: Trust, Collective Action, and Law," Yale Law School, Public Law Research Paper no. 31; Gintis, Bowles, and Fehr, *Moral Sentiments and Material Interests*, p. 366.

18. Gintis, Bowles, and Fehr, *Moral Sentiments and Material Interests*.

19. Antonio Damasio, *Descartes' Error: Emotion, Reason, and the Human Brain* (New York: Avon Books, 1994).

20. Steven Pinker, *The Blank Slate: The Modern Denial of Human Nature* (New York: Viking, 2002).

21. Rizzolatti and Craighero, "The Mirror-Neuron System."

22. John Holland, *Hidden Order: How Adaptation Builds Complexity* (Reading, MA: Addison Wesley, 1996).

23. Smith, *Wealth of Nations*, p. 14.

24. David McCullough, *John Adams* (New York: Simon and Schuster, 2002), p. 222.

Chapter Seven

1. John F. Padgett with Paul McLean, "Was Florence a Perfectly Competitive Market? Transactional Evidence from the Rennaissance," *Journal Theory and Society*, 26: 209–244, 1997.

2. John F. Padgett with Paul McLean, "Economic Credit and Elite Transformation in Rennaissance Florence," forthcoming *American Journal of Sociology*, p. 3, http://home.uchicago.edu/~jpadgett/papers/published/credit.pdf.

3. John F. Padgett and Paul McLean, "Economic and Social Exchange in Rennaissance Florence," (July 2, 2002), unpublished manuscript, p. 2.

4. Personal communication from Paul McLean, December 2007.

5. Ibid.

6. Ibid.

7. Ibid.

8. John F. Padgett, "Organizational Genesis, Identity, and Control: The Transformation of Banking in Rennaissance Italy," in *Networks and Markets*, edited by James E. Rauch and Alessandra Casella (New York: Russell Sage, 2001), pp. 211–257.

9. Iris Origo, ibid.

10. Padgett and McLean, "Elite Transformation and the Rise of Commercial Credit in Renaissance Florence, 2003," forthcoming *American Journal of Sociology*, 2006, p. 14.

11. Ron Burt, *Structural Holes* (Cambridge: Harvard University Press, 1995). According to Burt, economic power resulted from those who brokered between networks, in spaces he called structural holes.

12. John F. Padgett, Christopher K. Ansell, "Robust Action and the Rise of the Medici, 1400–1434," *American Journal of Sociology*, 98: 1259–1319, 1993.

13. Ibid., p. 53.

14. Luca Fantacci, "The Monetary Regime of the Rennaissance; Complementary Currencies for Domestic and Foreign Exchange," International Economic History Congress, Helsinki, Session 61 2006, p. 16.

15. Ibid., p. 17.

16. Bernard Lietaer, *The Future of Money, Creating New Wealth, Work, and a Wiser World* (Random House: London, 2001).

Chapter Eight

1. Command and Control, U.S. Marine Corps manual, PCN 142 0000100, p. 114.

2. Magnolia Series Number Four, *No Greater Love: Roy Wheat in Vietnam*, 1992. For more information, visit the U.S. Marine Corps Library: http://www.lib.usm.edu/libraryfocus/spring00/rmwheat.html (Feb. 2004).

3. Ibid.

4. Dunbar, *Grooming,* p. 72.

5. Ibid.

6. Adam Cohen, *The Perfect Store: Inside eBay* (Boston: Little, Brown, 2002). This is also the view of Muhammad Yunus, recipient of the Nobel Peace Prize in 2006, and inventor of microfinance.

7. "eBay (A) The Customer Marketplace," Harvard Business School Case Study 9-602-071, p. 3, http://www.ebay.com.

8. Ibid., p. 3.

9. "2001 Annual Report," eBay Investor Relations, p. 1, http://investor.ebay .com/annual.cfm (February 2004).

10. Ibid., p. 10.

11. "eBay, Inc.," Harvard Business School Case Study 9-700-007, p. 10.

12. See http://www.eclipse.org; http://www.globus.org; http://www.apache.org; and http://www.bugzilla.org.

13. Stephen Weber, *The Success of Open Source* (Cambridge: Harvard University Press, 2004).

14. Steven Withers, "An Overview of Distributed Grid Computing," *Technology and Business Magazine,* GRID Today, November 4, 2002. See http:// www.gridtoday.com/02/1104/100635.html (February 2004).

15. For example, see Kelly and Ranger, "Whitehall Vows to End Proprietary Lock-In," July 25, 2002, http://www.vnunet.com/News/1133883 (February 2004).

16. Command and Control, U.S. Marine Corps manual, p. 114. See also Paul Zak, "Trust," Capco Institute, *Journal of Financial Transformation* 7 (April 2003): 17–23.

17. Robin Dunbar, "Culture Honesty and the Free Rider Problem," in Robin Dunbar, Chris Knight, and Camilla Power, *The Evolution of Culture* (New Brunswick, NJ: Rutgers University Press, 1999), pp. 194–213.

Chapter Nine

1. Joseph Ellis, *Founding Brothers: The Revolutionary Generation* (New York: Vintage Books, 2000), p. 47.

2. Ibid., p. 42.

3. Ibid., p. 124.

4. Jerome Barkow, Leda Cosmides, and John Tooby, *The Adapted Mind: Evolutionary Psychology and the Generation of Culture* (Cambridge: Oxford University Press, 1992).

5. Ernst Fehr and Bettina Rockenhack, "Detrimental Effects of Sanctions on Human Altruism," *Nature* (March 2003).

6. Alfred Lord Tennyson, "Ode on the Death of the Duke of Wellington," November 18, 1852.

7. Ibid.

Chapter Ten

1. Bruce Butterfield, "The Rise and Fall of Mark Spangler," *Boston Globe,* June 24, 1986.

2. Desiree French, "A Cautious Investor Asked the First Questions," *Boston Globe,* April 26, 1986.

3. Ibid., April 26, 1986.

4. See www.feralchildren.com.

5. Richard Lewontin, *The Triple Helix* (Cambridge: Harvard University Press, 2002), p. 48.

6. F. Esponda et al., "On-Line Negative Databases," Third International Conference on Artificial Immune Systems (ICARIS 2004) Proceedings, September 2004, pp. 175–188.

7. A. Zahavi, "Mate Selection—Selection for a Handicap," *Journal of Theoretical Biology* 53 (1975): 204–215.

8. Bergstrom et al., "The Peacock, the Sparrow and the Evolution of Language," *Santa Fe Institute* (May 2001), p. 15.

9. Ibid.

10. Ibid.

11. Ibid., p. 19.

12. Ibid., p. 25.

13. Joel Podolny, *Status Signals: A Sociological Study of Market Competition* (Princeton: Princeton University Press, 2005).

14. Joseph Schumpeter, *Capitalism, Socialism, and Democracy* (New York: Harper, 1975, originally published 1942).

15. Podolny, *Status Signals*, p. 86.

Chapter Eleven

1. James Pustejovsky, *Generative Lexicon: Language, Speech, and Communication* (Boston: MIT Press, 1998).

2. Ibid.

3. William D. Casebeer and James A. Russell, "Storytelling and Terrorism: Towards a Comprehensive 'Counter-Narrative Strategy,'" *Strategic Insights* 4 (3) (March 2005).

4. Ibid., p. 8.

5. R. Albert, H. Jeong, and A-L. Barabasi, "Diameter of the World-Wide Web," *Nature* 401 (1999): 130.

6. Albert-Laszlo Barabasi, *Linked: The New Science of Networks* (New York: Perseus, 2002).

7. C. R. Allen, "Ecosystems and Immune Systems: Hierarchical Response Provides Resilience Against Invasions," *Conservation Ecology* 5 (1): 15.

8. Ernst Fehr and Bettina Rockenbach, "Detrimental Effects of Sanctions on Human Altruism," *Nature* 422, March 13, 2003.

9. Vernon Smith, "Constructivist and Ecological Rationality in Economics," Nobel Prize Lecture, Stockholm, 2002.

Chapter Twelve

1. See http://www.identityblog.com.

2. London School of Economics and Political Science and Politics, The Identity Project, research status report, January 2006.

3. Chris Anderson, *The Long Tail: Why the Future of Business Is Selling Less of More* (New York: Hyperion, 2006).

4. See http://www.ning.com for how software can be "cloned."

5. See http://www.socialphysics.org for more information on Higgins.

6. See http://www.socialphysics.org.

7. According to the structural anthropologist Claude Levi-Strauss, a "structural equivalence" in myths means that they have equivalent meanings. See Claude Levi-Strauss, *Structural Analysis of Myths* (New York: Basic Books, 1972).

8. Kurt Godel, "On Formally Undecidable Propositions of Principia Mathematica and Related Systems, II," trans. Martin Hirzel, November 27, 2000; A. Church, "An Unsolvable Problem of Elementary Number Theory," *American Journal of Mathematics* 58 (1936): 345–363; A. M. Turing, "On Computable Numbers, with an Application to the Entscheidungsproblem," *Proceedings of the London Mathematical Society*, ser. 2, 42 (1936–1937): 230–265.

Index

PublicAffairs is a publishing house founded in 1997. It is a tribute to the standards, values, and flair of three persons who have served as mentors to countless reporters, writers, editors, and book people of all kinds, including me.

I.F. Stone, proprietor of *I. F. Stone's Weekly*, combined a commitment to the First Amendment with entrepreneurial zeal and reporting skill and became one of the great independent journalists in American history. At the age of eighty, Izzy published *The Trial of Socrates*, which was a national bestseller. He wrote the book after he taught himself ancient Greek.

Benjamin C. Bradlee was for nearly thirty years the charismatic editorial leader of *The Washington Post*. It was Ben who gave the *Post* the range and courage to pursue such historic issues as Watergate. He supported his reporters with a tenacity that made them fearless and it is no accident that so many became authors of influential, best-selling books.

Robert L. Bernstein, the chief executive of Random House for more than a quarter century, guided one of the nation's premier publishing houses. Bob was personally responsible for many books of political dissent and argument that challenged tyranny around the globe. He is also the founder and longtime chair of Human Rights Watch, one of the most respected human rights organizations in the world.

For fifty years, the banner of Public Affairs Press was carried by its owner Morris B. Schnapper, who published Gandhi, Nasser, Toynbee, Truman, and about 1,500 other authors. In 1983, Schnapper was described by *The Washington Post* as "a redoubtable gadfly." His legacy will endure in the books to come.

Peter Osnos, *Founder and Editor-at-Large*